Canada

ENGLISH CANADA PROVINCE

Teachers *of a* Nation

Teachers
of a Nation

A HISTORY OF JESUITS IN ENGLISH CANADA
1842–2013

VOLUME 1
IN THE JESUIT HISTORY SERIES

Joseph B. Gavin, S.J.

NOVALIS

© 2015 Novalis Publishing Inc.

Cover design: Martin Gould
Photographs and illustrations provided by the Jesuits in English Canada, The
Archive of the Jesuits in Canada, and other sources. Copyright and attribution
provided where the photographs or illustrations appear.
Map on endpapers: © Archives of the Jesuits in Canada
Layout: Audrey Wells

Published by Novalis

Publishing Office
10 Lower Spadina Avenue, Suite 400
Toronto, Ontario, Canada
M5V 2Z2

Head Office
4475 Frontenac Street
Montréal, Québec, Canada
H2H 2S2

www.novalis.ca

Library and Archives Canada Cataloguing in Publication

A history of Jesuits in English Canada, 1842-2013.

(Jesuit history series)
Includes bibliographical references and indexes.
Contents: Volume 1. Teachers of a nation / Joseph B. Gavin, S.J.
-- Volume 2. Builders of a nation / Jacques Monet, s.j., executive editor.

Issued in print and electronic formats.
ISBN 978-2-89688-124-6 (v. 1 : bound).--ISBN 978-2-89688-128-4 (v. 2 :
bound).-- ISBN 978-2-89688-125-3 (v. 1 : mobi).--ISBN 978-2-89688-126-0
(v. 1 : epub).-- ISBN 978-2-89688-127-7 (v.1 : pdf).--ISBN 978-2-89688-129-1
(v. 2 : mobi).-- ISBN 978-2-89688-130-7 (v. 2 : epub).--ISBN 978-2-89688-131-4
(v. 2 : pdf).

1. Jesuits--Canada--History.

BX3711.A1H58 2015   271'.53071   C2015-900018-1

Printed in Canada.

We acknowledge the financial support of the Government of Canada through the
Canada Book Fund for business development activities.

5   4   3   2   1   19   18   17   16   15

Editorial Committee

Jacques Monet, s.j.
Executive Editor

Joseph B. Gavin, S.J.
Editor

John D. Meehan, S.J.
Assistant Editor

This book is dedicated to the memory of all the Jesuits who worked in higher education in English-speaking Canada.

CONTENTS

ACKNOWLEDGEMENTS

The Jesuit History Series has been initiated and supported by the Canadian Institute of Jesuit Studies.

I owe a great debt to several people. A number of the Jesuits among these I knew and know personally; many of them were and are professors and administrators in Canadian institutions of higher education, and are mentioned throughout this study. To all of them I am grateful for their insights and recollections.

Very special words of gratitude are also owing to the staff of the Archive of the Jesuits in Canada, Montreal, especially to Céline Widmer, Bruce Henry, Theresa Rowat, and Jacques Monet, s.j., for their unfailing assistance; to the Provincial Superiors of the Canadian English-speaking Jesuits for their ongoing financial and moral encouragement; to members of the Loyola Jesuit Community, Montreal, and of the Ottawa Jesuit Community for their patience and forbearance in listening to my never-ending accounts of the "doings of Ours"; to Professor Samira McCarthy for her helpful suggestions concerning part of this work; and to Prescy Alumaga and Mahal Yu-Daquiado for their invaluable secretarial assistance. For Anne M. Delicaet, who died before this book went to the printer, I reserve a very special thanks for her generous help and support. To Anne Louise Mahoney, who for Novalis Publishing copy edited and proofread this volume, goes my sincerest appreciation. An ever-vigilant and probing editor, her never-failing patience and good humour, her tactful suggestions and incisive queries, have made this book much better and, in the end, more readable than it otherwise would have been. I owe her considerable thanks.

Any omissions, misinterpretations, or errors are mine alone.

Joseph B. Gavin, S.J.

ABBREVIATIONS

AJC	Archive of the Jesuits in Canada
AUCC	Association of Universities and Colleges of Canada
CAUT	Canadian Association of University Teachers
CCA	Campion College Archives, Regina
CCHA	Canadian Catholic Historical Association
Desjardins	Paul Desjardins, s.j., *Le Collège Sainte-Marie de Montréal* (Montréal: Collège Sainte-Marie, 1940), vol. 1
DCB	*Dictionary of Canadian Biography*
DJB	*Dictionary of Jesuit Biography: Ministry to English Canada, 1842–1987* (Toronto: Canadian Institute of Jesuit Studies, 1991), vol. 1; *Dictionary of Jesuit Biography: Ministry to English Canada, 1988–2006* (Toronto: Canadian Institute of Jesuit Studies, 2007), vol. 2
Friesen and Lebrun	Gerald Friesen and Richard Lebrun, eds., *St. Paul's College, University of Manitoba: Memories and Histories* (Winnipeg: St. Paul's College, 1999)
Lecompte	Édouard Lecompte, *Les Jésuites du Canada au XIX siècle* (Montréal: Imprimerie du Messager, 1920)
LCM	*Loyola College, Montreal, 1906–1914* (Montréal: Imprimerie du Messager, 1914–1915), vol. 1; *Loyola College, Montreal, 1914–1921* (Montréal: Imprimerie du Messager, 1915–1921), vol. 2

GLOSSARY OF JESUIT TERMS

A s do many institutions, the Society of Jesus has developed its own terminology and vocabulary. Some of these were taken from the traditional language of the Church and of other Religious Orders; some were based on the writings of the Jesuits' founder, Ignatius Loyola, on the Constitutions of the Society of Jesus and their "complementary norms," or on the decrees of the Jesuits' General Congregations. Others were improvised in Canada. A glossary of Jesuit terms used in this book therefore might be useful.

Assistant A senior Jesuit administrator in Rome who advises and assists the Superior General in the governance of the Society of Jesus, either Regional (e.g., Assistant for India) or General (one of four who assists the Superior General in the governance of the Society of Jesus). See also below, "Minister" and "Socius."

Biretta Originally, a head-piece for monks and priests to protect their heads from the elements; a stiff, square unadorned black cap with three ridges across the crown, once worn by Jesuits after first vows. The biretta disappeared from use between the late 1950s and early 1960s.

Brother A man who has taken the three vows of religion and is a member within a Religious Congregation or Order but who is not in Holy Orders; traditionally, in the Society of Jesus, referred to as a Coadjutor Brother, although this terminology has gradually gone out of use since the 1960s.

Bursar The treasurer of a Jesuit Province, Community, school, or college.

Cassock A long black robe worn by Jesuits, without buttons and secured at the waist with a woollen cincture. In

Canada, the term "Blackrobe" was used to refer to a Jesuit during the seventeenth century; it went out of use during the late 1960s to early 1970s.

Community   An ecclesiastically approved house for members of a Religious Order; a group of Jesuits living together under the authority of a designated Rector or Superior; sometimes referred to as "local Community." According to Canon (Church) Law, there had to be three or more Jesuits living together to form a Religious Community, although more recently only two Jesuits can be declared to form a Community.

Consultors   Jesuits appointed in each Community by the Provincial Superior, at the suggestion of the Superior or Rector, to advise him; Jesuits appointed by the Superior General from the Province to advise a Provincial Superior. The number of Consultors in local Communities varies according to the Community's size; the number of Consultors for a Provincial Superior is set at four.

Cura Personalis   Latin meaning "care for the individual person"; a significant responsibility of a Provincial Superior towards the individual members in the Province, and of a Rector or Superior towards the members of his Community.

Curia   A Latin term originating in ancient Rome, now used to describe the central administrative office in the universal Society of Jesus (Rome) or in a Jesuit Province; hence the term "curial."

Dean of Studies   One responsible for an academic programme of an educational institution; in modern North American Jesuit high schools, this is the principal. For a time, the term designated the one appointed by the Provincial Superior to assist in the educational formation of Jesuits.

Formation	The period beginning with the Novitiate for the training and educating of Jesuits, and ending with Final Vows. See below, "Vows."
General Congregation	The supreme legislative body of the Society of Jesus that elects the Superior General; an official meeting of delegates of the whole Society of Jesus; the Jesuit equivalent of a monastic General Chapter; there have been thirty-five General Congregations since 1558.
Instructor of Tertians	The Jesuit priest who directs Jesuit priests and Brothers in their final year of formation; sometimes referred to as Tertian Master or Master of Tertians. See below, "Tertianship."
Jesuit	As a noun, a member of the Society of Jesus; as an adjective, pertaining to the Society of Jesus; adapted from the Latin word *Jesuita* (a follower of Jesus), and in common use today, even officially.
Junior	The term formerly used for a Jesuit Scholastic and Brother in the period of formation known as the Juniorate. See below, "Juniorate."
Juniorate	The term formerly used for the house and for the period of classical and humanistic studies, usually for a two-year period for Jesuit Scholastics immediately following the Novitiate; also used for Brothers in their technical training after the Novitiate.
Master of Novices	The Jesuit priest who directs Jesuit novices in their first two years of formation; also referred to as "director" of novices. See below, "Novitiate."
Minister	A term for the assistant to a Rector or Superior; one who is responsible for the practical and material needs of a Jesuit Community; also, traditionally, the one who assigns pastoral ministry for members of a Community.

Ministry	The term used by Jesuits to refer to their works by which they render aid and service to others; often referred to as "apostolate."
Mission	Usually an area or centre where the Gospel is preached, often in foreign lands, hence the term "missionary"; may also be referred to as a regional administrative unit of Jesuits. The term is often applied to an assigned task, and is sometimes used for popular preaching in a parish.
Novice	The term used for someone in the first period of spiritual formation in religious life, usually referred to as the Novitiate. For the Jesuits, the term refers to the individual during the first two years of Jesuit formation in the Novitiate.
Novitiate	A house for novices, and a place for their spiritual discernment, training, and testing, which includes the Spiritual Exercises of Ignatius Loyola; the first two years in the course of Jesuit formation. At the end of this period, the first vows in the Society of Jesus are pronounced; also known as the Second Probation. See below, "Vows."
Ordination	The conferring of the holy orders of sub-deaconate, deaconate, and priesthood; traditionally, and unlike other Religious or diocesan candidates to the priesthood, Jesuits received the sub-deaconate and deaconate during their third year of theological studies and the priesthood followed shortly afterwards that same year. Since the 1980s, the sub-deaconate has been abolished while the deaconate is conferred at the end of the third year of theological studies, followed a year later by the ordination to the priesthood.
Philosophy	Usually a three-year period for the pursuit of philosophical studies and related disciplines; hence terms such as "philosopher" (for the student who studies philosophy) and "philosophate." Traditionally, for

the Jesuit, this period followed four years after his Novitiate years and two years after finishing his Juniorate studies. In more recent years, the taking of a Jesuit's philosophical studies depends on his previous studies and with what graduate degrees he entered the Novitiate.

Prefect   The traditional term for certain administrative officers in a Jesuit institution (e.g., prefect of studies, prefect of discipline).

Province   The common division of the Society of Jesus for administrative and jurisdictional purposes. There can be more than one Jesuit Province in a country: for example, in Canada, the Province of French Canada and the Province of Upper Canada. The use of the word dates back to Roman times and to the beginnings of the Society of Jesus in the sixteenth century; hence the terms Provincial Superior and Provincialate.

Provincial Superior   The major Superior in charge of a Jesuit Province, appointed by the Superior General for three years, and usually renewed once only.

Ratio Studiorum   A Latin term meaning "plan of studies"; the document outlining the programme of studies for all Jesuit educational institutions; basis of the Jesuits' classical college system of education (classical course). First published in 1599, it has been modified several times since.

Rector   The Superior of a Jesuit Community or institution, such as a college, university, or school, appointed by the Superior General for a three-year term (renewable usually only once); hence the term "rectorship."

Refectory   A traditional term signifying the dining room of a monastery or university college and used since the sixteenth century for the dining room of a Jesuit

Community; hence a refectorian would be the one in charge of the refectory. It is rarely used today except in very large Jesuit houses.

Regency A term used to refer traditionally to the teaching years of a Jesuit Scholastic between his studies of philosophy and of theology; hence the term "Regent"; more recently, the term is used for the years of a Jesuit Scholastic between his studies of philosophy and of theology, whether he is teaching or not.

Religious An ecclesiastical term used for a man or woman in a Religious Order or Congregation under vows. See below, "Religious Order" and "Vows."

Religious Order Ecclesiastical term to denote a community of men or women bound by common customs and rules of life, and who pronounce the three vows of religion. Orders are distinguished from Congregations by their solemn as opposed to simple vows; Jesuits alone pronounce perpetual vows after the Novitiate. See below, "Vows."

Retreat The term referring to a specific period of spiritual exercises and prayer such as three days, eight days, or thirty days; retreats may be directed, preached, or made privately. See below, "The Spiritual Exercises."

Retreat House A place or centre for lay retreats (see "The Spiritual Exercises"), reflection, and spiritual renewal programmes.

Scholastic The traditional term used to designate a Jesuit student during his formation between the Novitiate and final vows; it is used to distinguish Jesuit students from Jesuit Brothers in formation: a Scholastic was formerly addressed as "Mister" until ordination.

Scholasticate The term used for Jesuit houses of formation following the Novitiate.

Society of Jesus   From the Latin *Societas Jesu*; the official title of the Jesuits as a Religious Order, abbreviated as S.J. (English language) or s.j. or S.I. (most other languages); equivalent to the term "Jesuit Order" or to the "Jesuits." In most languages, except English, the Latin term has usually been translated as "Company of Jesus."

Socius   A Latin word meaning "ally" or "companion"; used formally in the Society of Jesus to designate the assistant to the Provincial Superior, who is appointed by the Superior General; also used for the assistant to the Master of Novices; an alter ego of the Provincial Superior.

Sodality of Our Lady   An association founded by the Jesuits in 1563 at their Collegio Romano, Rome, to foster a devout Christian life of prayer and social action for lay people, under the patronage of Mary, the Mother of God.

The Spiritual Exercises   A manual composed by Ignatius Loyola, the founder of the Society of Jesus, reflecting his spiritual conversion, and based on his methods of prayer and personal decision making; used during Jesuit retreats (see above, "Retreat"), either personal or those retreats given to others. See above, "Retreat House."

Superior   The one designated to administer a Jesuit Community, and appointed by the Provincial Superior with the approval of the Superior General.

Superior General   The major Superior of the Society of Jesus, usually referred to by Jesuits as "the General" or "Father General"; chosen for life by a General Congregation to direct the Jesuits between Congregations; sometimes referred to as "The Black Pope."

Tertian   The term for a Jesuit priest or Brother in the final year of spiritual formation.

Tertianship   The final year of Jesuit formation, also known as the Third Probation: the First being postulancy and the Second being the Novitiate. It is a synthesis of spiritual, intellectual or technical, and pastoral formation and is sometimes referred to as "spiritual theology."

Theology   The period set aside for the study of Church doctrine, scripture, Church history, liturgy, and pastoral practices; usually of a four-year duration; hence, terms such as "theologian" (for the student who studies theology) and "theologate" (for the house where these studies take place).

Upper Canada Province   The name given to the English-speaking Canadian Jesuits in 1924 when the Province of Canada was divided into the English-speaking Vice Province of Upper Canada (in 1939, the Province of Upper Canada) and the French-speaking Province of Lower Canada; in theory, the area served for each Province was set according to the two national language groups; in 2006, the name for the "Province of Upper Canada" became "The Jesuits in English Canada."

Vicar General   A Jesuit empowered to act as the Superior General of the Order during the grave illness or death of the Superior General, or when the Superior General is especially occupied.

Vice Province   An administrative unit of the Society of Jesus that, due to its insufficient number of members and finances, has not yet attained the status of a Province (see above, "Province" and "Upper Canada Province"); rarely used today for distinguishing local Jesuit administrative units.

Vice Rector   The Superior of a Jesuit Community or institution, such as a college, university, or school, appointed by the Provincial Superior with the approval of the Superior General for a three-year term (renewable usually only once).

Visitor   A Jesuit appointed by the Superior General to visit a Province on his behalf; usually designated to investigate the governance, finances, and state of religious life in a Province, sometimes with the full authority of the Superior General, and at other times with limited authority. The office was abolished in the 1960s.

Vows   The three vows of religion—poverty, chastity, and obedience—are common to all Religious Orders and Congregations. These are perpetual in the Society of Jesus: that is, the Jesuits' first vows are simple and perpetual, and are pronounced at the end of their Novitiate of two years. After a specified time of formation ultimately determined by the Superior General, and after the Jesuits' Tertianship, the Jesuit priests and Brothers are approved by the Superior General to pronounce their final vows. A Jesuit must ask the Provincial Superior in writing to pronounce his final vows; traditionally, some pronounced simple vows (Spiritual and Temporal Coadjutors), while others pronounced solemn vows (Solemnly Professed), which included their special fourth vow of obedience to the Sovereign Pontiff with regard to missions. Since the 1960s, most Jesuit priests are invited to pronounce the four vows.

Introduction

The Jesuit Framework and Context

Montreal. Winter 1838. Bishop Jean-Jacques Lartigue and his new coadjutor, Bishop Ignace Bourget, are reflecting on the dark mood of the diocese, so depressed and divided in the wake of the cruel repression that followed the violent rebellions of the last two years. On a suggestion by a young Sulpician priest, John Larkin, they eagerly agree to invite the celebrated French Jesuit preacher Pierre Chazelle to come to Montreal and direct a retreat to the eighty-three priests of the diocese.

A native of Co. Durham, England, Larkin had entered the Séminaire Saint-Sulpice near Paris in 1823. After making the Spiritual Exercises of St. Ignatius Loyola under Chazelle's guidance, he was ordained in 1827 and sent to Montreal. There he joined the faculty of the Collège de Montréal, where he taught the classics and, in 1831, very firmly refused an appointment as coadjutor to Bishop Alexander Macdonell of Kingston. Later, in 1847, on the sudden death of Bishop Michael Power of Toronto, Larkin was sent the Papal bulls of appointment to that see. One he tore up; the other he sent back by return mail.

Meanwhile, Pierre Chazelle had become, in the summer of 1833, the president of St. Mary's Seminary (later, in 1837, College) near Bardstown, Kentucky. He was delighted to receive the invitation to preach in Montreal. Arrangements were made for August 1839.

Both Bishop Bourget and John Larkin had ulterior motives. Bishop Bourget was hoping to found a Jesuit college in Montreal. Larkin was in the process of deciding to enter the Society of Jesus. He did so in October 1840, and later served in Toronto, Montreal, Fordham, London (England), and New York, where he died in 1858. Chazelle, for his part, became the first Jesuit of the restored Society of Jesus to set foot in the old colony of New France.

The ten-day retreat to the diocesan priests of Montreal, 7-17 August 1839, was a remarkable success. Chazelle was a spell-binding charmer. His visits to the memorable sites of Jesuit missions and his recalling the perseverance of the first settlers, the courage of the explorers, and the holiness of the martyrs all brought forth emotional pleas from Bishop Bourget, his clergy, and the laity for Chazelle and other Jesuits to return.

Bishop Bourget, who had succeed Lartigue on 18 April 1840, decided to travel to plead in person with Jan Roothaan, who had been elected General Superior of the Jesuits in 1829. Chazelle would join the bishop there. Bishop Bourget's famous manifesto *Appel aux Jésuites*, signed in Rome on 2 July 1841, reminded the General Superior of the epic of the Jesuits in New France and of the serious needs of both the native people and the educational institutions of Canada East. Roothaan was truly moved by the references to the heritage of New France. He immediately communicated with Clément Boulanger, the new (February 1842) Provincial Superior of the Province of France, ordering the return of the Jesuits to the area and appointing Chazelle as Superior of the Mission.

So it was that a group of eight French Jesuits who were preparing for a mission to Madagascar were astonished to find themselves asked instead to "return" to Montreal. "Returning" was, in fact, what they were doing, and not being "restored", as they were by Pope Pius VII in the "universal Church" in 1814, or in Naples and other parts of the Catholic world before and after that. In Canada, the Order has never been suppressed.

In 1773, when Pope Clement XIV suppressed the Order, the Jesuits of New France survived intact thanks to legal skulduggery on the part of Bishop Briand and Lieutenant Governor Theophilus Cramahé of Quebec, as well as Governor General Sir Guy Carleton. Forbidden to recruit, however, the Jesuits gradually died out, the last in 1800, although through their considerable estates they continued as a corporate personality in trust to the Crown. In the 1840s, the Jesuits asked to have their properties back, but other claimants having arisen, their request was not settled until all parties eventually agreed to the terms of an arbitration by Pope Leo XIII in 1888.

On 21 April 1842, the returning nine Jesuits left Le Havre, France, for New York, where they arrived on 25 May, and then on 31 May at Laprairie. In addition to Chazelle, that travelling Jesuit Community included Félix Martin from Paris, who would become the architect of a new church in Kahnawake, play a major role in the building of St. Patrick's in Montreal, design the Jesuit Novitiate in Sault-au-Récollet, and found St. Mary's College in 1848. He would also become the first, in 1858, to publish the whole set of the historic *Jesuit Relations*. After the death of Chazelle in 1845, Martin would be appointed Superior of the Canadian Jesuit Community.

In contrast, Dominique du Ranquet left directly to minister among the native people, along with Brother Joseph Jennessaux. They went first to Walpole Island, Canada West, in Lake St. Clair, then in 1844 to Wikwemikong and Fort William, Canada West, for a total of fifty-six years for du Ranquet and forty for Jennesseaux. They became the leading figures among the Jesuits of Canada West, being the first to return to the native people in Canada since the death in 1781 of the ground-breaking lexicographer Pierre Potier, who was the last Jesuit Missionary of the old Society of Jesus. Among the others, Paul Luiset went on in 1843 to open the first Canadian Novitiate at Laprairie, where the nine Jesuits had first arrived, and then, a year later, in Montreal. It was there, on 9 September 1843, that Augustin Régnier became the first Canadian-born novice. Rémi-Joseph Tellier and Brothers Pierre Tupin and Emmanuel Brenans remained in Laprairie: the first as pastor of the parish until 1849, the others as cook and factotum for the Jesuit Community.

The parish of Our Lady of The Nativity in Laprairie had lost its pastor when Michael Power was ordained as first bishop of Toronto on 8 May 1842, three weeks before the Jesuits arrived. Not unfittingly, Bishop Bourget passed the parish on to them. The *seigneurie* was part of the Jesuit Estates (and the common would be awarded to them in the papal arbitration of 1888). Literally, the Jesuits had returned.

Thus it was with the second group of Jesuits that arrived in Toronto via New York on 24 July 1843 and went on to Sandwich (Windsor) in time to celebrate St. Ignatius Day, 31 July, in Pierre Potier's church: Pierre Point and Jean-Pierre Choné. Point would serve there for fifteen years, while Choné would move on in 1844 to the unceded reserve at Wikwemikong, Canada West, where the Jesuits have served uninterruptedly ever since.

New York–Canada Mission
1846–1879

By 1846 there were forty-six Jesuits in Canada and thirty in Kentucky, but in both places there seemed to be nothing but problems. In Kentucky, the results of their efforts to develop St. Mary's College in the face of the open unfriendliness of Bishop Benedict Flaget of Louisville was very discouraging. Also disappointing were the delays in opening Félix Martin's Collège Sainte-Marie in Montreal. Then there was the pressing and persistent determination of Bishop John Hughes of New York to have the Jesuits take over his floundering St. John's College in Fordham.

In Paris, Clément Boulanger decided to come to North America. Abbreviating his term as Provincial Superior, he obtained from the General Superior sweeping discretionary powers as Visitor. He exercised them shortly after his arrival in New York by deciding to withdraw the Jesuits from the Kentucky mission and assign them to Fordham. By 1846, he had concluded the negotiations with Bishop Hughes to transfer St. John's College to Jesuit administration and ownership.

He then further decided to bring together the Canadian and New York Jesuits into one New York–Canada Mission, with its headquarters in New York, and himself as the Superior with a term extending to 1855. The new mission was to continue to be dependent on the Province of France for personnel, and for its funding on Pauline Jaricot's *Œuvres de la Propagation de la foi*.

By 1869, the number of Jesuits in the Mission had risen to 121, the Northern Ontario Missions were expanding, and so were the number of Jesuit parishes and churches, such as in Guelph, Chatham, and Montreal. The mission became "independent," though France would continue to send personnel. By the late 1870s, however, various priorities among the Jesuits in the United States made it important that New York separate from Canada and join with the Maryland Province.

In 1879, another Visitor with full discretionary powers, Edward I. Purbrick, S.J., a fluently bilingual Englishman, moved to "repatriate" most of the Canadian Jesuits working in the United States. Realizing that the Canadian Mission could not afford independent status, he recommended that it be incorporated into the English Province, which was what happened. On his return to London, Purbrick was appointed Provincial Superior of the English Province of the Society of Jesus.

The English Province 1879–1887

Between 1879 and 1887, the English province paid the expenses of all Canadian Jesuits in formation, some £10,000 a year. In return, Canadian Scholastics in training taught in English schools and colleges. The number of Jesuits rose from 182 to 214 and, during the eighties, for the first time the majority were Canadian-born. The College of the Immaculate Conception in Montreal was readied to receive Scholastics for studies in philosophy and in theology. As well, between August 1886 and November 1887, another Visitor, John Baptist Lessman, a German Jesuit from Westphalia, reported that Canada was ready to become an Independent Mission. In 1887, Pierre Hamel, born in Sainte-Claire, Lower Canada, in 1832, was appointed Superior, the first Canadian-born Major Superior in the history of Jesuits in Canada.

The Canada Mission
1887–1907

The times of the Independent Mission were prosperous with settlements, consolidations, and new beginnings. The claims and opinions on the Jesuits' Estates, in dispute for over three quarters of a century, were finally reconciled by papal arbitration, with the Jesuits receiving the largest portion, including the Common at Laprairie. Also by papal intervention, in the Apostolic Constitution *Iamdudum*, the privileges granted by the Holy See to the distinct Jesuit academic programme, the *Ratio Studiorum*, were recognized at Collège Sainte-Marie and later at Loyola College, Montreal, making them autonomous in the granting of degrees; the building at the Immaculée-Conception college, begun in 1882 in Montreal, was now fully ready to receive Jesuit Scholastics for their studies in philosophy and theology.

The Immaculée's chapel became Montreal's largest church, serving some three thousand parishioners when it opened officially in 1887. In Guelph, the large church, Our Lady Immaculate—begun in 1877 and crowning the top of "Catholic Hill," the land a gift from the city's founder, John Galt—was completed and consecrated in 1888, but for the towers. Other foundations were Sainte-Anne-des-Pins parish in Sudbury along with fifteen other parishes in Sault-Ste-Marie diocese, as well as half a dozen more at the Lakehead, notably with the founding by Ludger Arpin, s.j., in 1895 of St. Patrick's Parish, now the Cathedral of the diocese of Thunder Bay.

By 1907 the numbers of Jesuits had risen from 214 in 1887 to 329; they had programmes and institutions to ensure the whole of a priest's or Brother's formation in Canada. The Mission was ready to become a Province. On 15 August, Édouard Lecompte, the Superior of the Mission, and by then Provincial Superior, travelled with his staff to Huronia, to the new parish at Waubaushene, then thought to be the site of the death of the "Canadian Martyrs." They went on pilgrimage to render thanks for the Canadian Jesuits' coming of age.

The Province of Canada
1907–1924

If growth in the numbers of yearly entrants into the Novitiate and the quality of works taken up are both true indicators, the Canadian Jesuits' years as a united self-governing Province were blessed and prosperous. Yearly entries into the Novitiate at Sault-au-Récollet went from thirty-two in 1907 to thirty-seven in 1913; then, after an English-speaking Novitiate was opened in Guelph, Ontario, the combined figures went from twenty-seven in 1914 to thirty-six in 1917 and forty-eight in 1924. New parishes were opened in Winnipeg, Steelton, Montreal, and Vancouver, just as new colleges were chartered in Sudbury, Edmonton, Regina, and, after a disastrous fire, a new one in St. Boniface, and a moved one in Spanish, Ontario.

Jesuit itinerant preachers began to make their mark. Edward J. Devine, already a well-known popular writer of novels, became famous among the railway workers along the Canadian Pacific Railway line. "His parish," he once wrote, was "586 miles long by four feet ten inches wide." He bragged that he had "slept on every kitchen table from Chapleau to Fort William." In 1902, he was preaching very successfully in St. John's when he was asked to go to the Catholics on the gold rush along the Klondike. He set out immediately for Nome, Alaska, across the continent at its widest points, writing all the way a diary he later published in New York as *Across Widest America* and in Paris as *À Travers l'Amérique*.... He must be one of the rare Canadians to have had a best-selling page-turner in both languages on sale simultaneously in two world cities. At the time of his death in 1927, he was said to be the best-known English-speaking preacher in Canada. Another highly recognized Jesuit writer at the time was the geologist and astronomer Isidore Kavanagh, who had trained in Manchester, England, and was elected a member of both the British Association for the Advancement of Science and the Royal Astronomical Society of Canada. He was a leading member of the Canadian Government Expedition to Labrador that observed and photographed the famous eclipse of August 1905.

As a Jesuit Province, Canada was asked to take responsibility for a "foreign Mission." Between 1907 and 1912, it accordingly sent men to Alaska, whence in 1897 William Judge, S.J., known as "the Saint of Dawson," had followed his parishioners to the Klondike. Some two dozen Canadians served, especially in Nome, Kokerine, and Fairbanks, until 1912, when the Mission was transferred to the California Province of the Society of Jesus. Later, in 1918, Édouard Goulet became the first of some seventy-five French-Canadian Jesuits to go where Bishop Philippe Côté—the first of only two Canadian Jesuits ever to be made Bishop—"founded" the diocese of Suchow, China, in 1946.

Meanwhile, at the Sault-au-Récollet, both the growing numbers of postulants and the availability of land in Guelph on the large estate of a prominent Catholic family, the Bedfords, led to the establishment of a Novitiate for the English-speaking novices. Accordingly, on 6 September 1913, seventeen novices moved to St. Patrick's Hill, as it was then called, near Guelph, the forerunners of hundreds who would eventually constitute the English-speaking Province. By 1924, the average number of English-speaking entrants had steadily held at a dozen or so. Meanwhile, in Montreal, a new Loyola College was being built in the west end, the first multi-building Catholic college in Canada and sensationally designed in collegiate gothic English style.

The promise of these beginnings in the new Canadian Jesuit Province soon was darkened by the devil of discord. The growth of an intense French-Canadian nationalism, stimulated by quarrels over schools and linguistic rights in Manitoba and Ontario, invaded Jesuit Communities and institutions, especially in Montreal, Sudbury, St. Boniface, and Edmonton. Students and much of the faculty at Collège Sainte-Marie were enthusiasts at the forefront of this nationalist movement. The coming of the Great War in August 1914 made the tension all but unbearable. In Rome, the new Superior General, Wlodimir Ledóchowski, overwhelmed by conflicting reports, decided to send another Visitor, Canada's fourth.

William I. Power, S.J., was an Irishman who spoke and wrote French elegantly and fluently. He had worked and served as the

Mission's Superior in Louisiana. He was in Canada at the height of the French–English tensions over conscription and the Ontario school laws, between 4 April 1917 and 8 July 1918. That did not prevent him from being shocked more by the Province's debt than by the "national" tensions. He did, nonetheless, strongly recommend that within six to eight years the Province be divided along linguistic and geographic lines. To achieve that, he appointed John Milway Filion as Provincial Superior.

Fluently bilingual and decidedly bicultural, Filion served as Provincial Superior of the Province of Canada between 1 July 1918 and 17 June 1924, and then as Provincial Superior of the new Vice Province of Upper Canada until 17 May 1928. His years in office were dominated by two issues: the division of the Province on 27 June 1924, and the beatification of the Canadian Martyrs, which took place on 29 June 1925.

From Vice Province to Province
1924–2013

Growth and Expansion
1924–1965

Within a few weeks of the division of the Province, John M. Filion and his Socius, Henry L. Cormier, moved to set up the administration of the new English-speaking entity. It was the first of nine moves in the next eighty-four years of the Provincial offices, a true contrast to the administration's practice since 1842, when the headquarters of the Mission remained stable at Collège Sainte-Marie for seventy-six years, and to the French Canadian Province, which has moved only twice in the last thirty-five years.

The new Province was on the move. In numbers, certainly; the original 137 English-speaking Jesuits of July 1924 more than doubled to 280 in ten years, then grew steadily to 331 in 1944, to 405 in 1954, and to 473 in 1965. So also in the number of requests from bishops across the country to take on new parishes: by 1980, the Jesuits of Upper Canada had the responsibility for eight major parishes, from St. Pius X in St. John's to Immaculate Conception in Vancouver, with

Halifax, Montreal, Toronto, Thunder Bay, and Winnipeg in between. So again by 1963, the number of high schools grew, spreading from Gonzaga High School in St. John's to Campion High School in Regina, with schools in Halifax, Montreal, Kingston, Toronto, and Winnipeg in between. So also for colleges, again in 1963, established from St. Mary's University in Halifax to Campion College in Regina, with Loyola College, Montreal, and St. Paul's College, Winnipeg, in between. In 1924, "on the move" also meant enabling the new Vice Province of Upper Canada to control its own formation programme. The purchase in 1930 of the old, dilapidated, crumbling, filthy building at 403 Wellington Street West, adjacent to the railway yards in Toronto, allowed the English-speaking Jesuits to house and teach their own Scholastics in philosophy and later, after 1943, in theology.

None of this expansion and growth during a national depression and wartime conditions could have been possible without the unstinting help of the Loretto Sisters and the Sisters of St. Joseph in Toronto, or without the guidance, support, and fundraising of the Jesuit Seminary Association, which was founded in 1949 by Wilfrid T. Harris, S.J. In 1957, the association helped to organize the two-year National Jesuit Fundraising campaign that made possible, within a few years afterwards, the building of a new Novitiate in Guelph and a new seminary of theology in Willowdale: Regis College, designed by the noted architect Peter Dickensen. They opened in 1960 and 1961 respectively.

By that time, the Second Vatican Council had been called, and much of the Catholic and Canadian Jesuit world had begun to change. The framework, however, set in place by the events and people of the previous century, was a solid one to meet the challenge.

Joseph B. Gavin's book on Jesuit colleges and universities goes into fascinating detail about their beginnings and their survival throughout the Great Depression and the war years, and into the more promising post-war times of prosperity. He shines a new and original light on Loyola College's impossible dream of becoming a university and on William H. Hingston's even more startling plan to turn little Regiopolis College in Kingston into the Catholic University of Canada. His plan threw into helpless amazement most of the Jesuits, not to mention the Canadian bishops. Gavin explains the repeated crises at St. Paul's College, Campion College's fragile but steady growth, and the insistence on independence at St. Mary's University. He draws attention to the strength of the intellectual ministry of such Jesuit literary scholars as Gerald F. Lahey and Patrick M. M. Plunkett, the mathematician R. Eric O'Connor, and the astronomer M. Walter Burke-Gaffney. Nor does he forget the pastoral ministry of the colleges' Jesuit faculty, who worked on "weekend supply" for years to help diocesan priests in distant parishes, often from Winnipeg as far as Minnesota, or from Regina as far away as North Dakota.

Renewal and Transformation 1965–2013

For all the Jesuit Colleges, the years of the Second Vatican Council as well as the changes in the Canadian government's policies on funding higher education proved to be a turning point. The story in each one of these became one of critical transition towards association with other religious and secular traditions. By the mid 1970s, after the ups and downs of many negotiations that led to various degrees of federations, mergers, and withdrawals, the Jesuit colleges were full and proud partners in Canada's unique nationwide network of government-funded religious colleges and universities. Those changes in the modalities of the Upper Canada Province's involvement in higher education added to the accompanying steady decline in the numbers of Jesuit university professors and led to a redeployment of the Province's manpower as well as to a new choice of priorities. These latter, especially after the promulgation of the decrees of the Jesuit Order's Thirty-First and Thirty-Second General Congregations in 1965–1966, attended by Angus J. Macdougall and Roderick A. F. Mackenzie, and in 1974–1975, attended by Terence G. Walsh and William F. Ryan, all received new focus after these decrees introduced fundamental reforms in the Jesuits' formation programme, and proclaimed as the "priority of priorities" "the service of faith in which the promotion of justice is an absolute requirement."

These "new" priorities, especially the emphasis on social justice, had a profound effect on the choice of ministries, as the chapter by Dr. Peter Baltutis in Volume 2 shows. Meanwhile, the proportion of Jesuits in the Upper Canada Province involved in higher education was changing dramatically. When the Vice Province was created in 1924, out of a total of 137 Jesuits, only fifty-five had finished their formation. Among these, only eight were in college work, at Loyola in Montreal and at Campion in Regina. Two decades later, in 1949, out of 225 active Jesuits, fifty-six were in higher education. After a further ten years, in 1959, out of 322 active Jesuits, only forty-eight were in higher education. A decade later still, in 1969, the figures were 177 active Jesuits and forty-four in higher education.

The number of Jesuits working with the native people, on the other hand, remained constant. Michael J. Stogre's chapter at the beginning of Volume 2 reflects on this steady presence of the Jesuits alongside the native people. It was, after all, one of the two main motives that had brought the Jesuits back to Canada in 1842, and one that was strongly inspired and strengthened, as Michael L. Knox points out, by devotion to the memory of the Jesuits and the Huron Christians who gave up their lives for their Christian faith.

The evolving 1960s and 1970s were marked by a third priority, decreed by the Thirty-Second General Congregation's emphasis on the necessary involvement of Jesuits in what the Congregation called "The modern means of communication." Ahead of the Congregation's decree, John Egli O'Brien, S.J., enrolled at the University of Southern California to complete doctoral studies in communications. He returned to Loyola College in Montreal in 1965 to found there the first department of communication arts in Canada. He was followed by Marc Gervais, s.j., and David R. Eley, S.J. The first recipient of a doctorate in communications in Canada at McGill University in 1979, Eley went on to found the communications department at the University of Ottawa before moving to Toronto in 1985 to establish the Jesuit Communication Project. He was joined a year later by John J. Pungente, S.J., a graduate in communications from the University of San Francisco. This led, among other initiatives, to Pungente's award-winning ten-year monthly television program, *Scanning the Movies*, and to the two volumes of *Finding God in the Dark*, co-authored with Geoffrey (Monty) Williams, S.J.

The years between the beginning of the Thirty-First General Congregation in May 1965 and the closing of the thirty-third in October 1983 profoundly transformed the Upper Canada Province. The "Faith and Justice" priority inspired the founding in Toronto in 1979 of the Jesuit Centre for Social Faith and Justice by James F. Webb, S.J., who had been working for some time on issues relating to affordable housing in Toronto's South Riverdale neighbourhood. The centre became an important actor on issues relating to Central America, refugees, public health, and social justice issues in general, as did *Compass: A Jesuit Journal*, between 1983 and 1987. It was edited by Mr. Robert Chodos, who recruited such well-known Jesuit writers as Michael F. Czerny, John E. Costello, David R. Eley, Marc Gervais, and Martin J. Royackers.

Also in 1979, the Jesuit ministry among the native people became another high priority when Michael M. Murray, S.J., created the Anishinabe Spiritual Centre in Espanola, Ontario. In cooperation with the Jesuit theological faculty at Regis College in Toronto, the centre sponsored the first programme in Canada for the formation of Aboriginal deacons. In 1984, members of its first graduating class were invested with specially prepared stoles by Pope John Paul II during his historic visit to the grave of Saint Jean de Brébeuf in Midland.

Two years earlier, in 1977, S. Douglas McCarthy, S.J., and William T. Clarke, S.J., organized a farm community on the lands that had served since 1913 as the anglophone Jesuit Novitiate in Guelph. The group was made up of former prisoners, persons with disabilities, and otherwise homeless people. Over the years, under the leadership of James Profit, S.J., the care of the farm evolved into a serious ecology project.

Simultaneously and also in Guelph, the liturgical and prayerful practices of the Jesuit Novitiate attracted outsiders who sought spiritual counsel and direction from John J. C. English, John Veltri, Eric G. Jensen, Geoffrey (Monty) Williams, and others. Their influence and practice, as well as their growing association with the Loyola

Retreat House—which Clifford N. Rushman, S.J., had moved from Oakville in 1964—led to the founding of the Ignatius Jesuit Centre. It was soon internationally acclaimed for its adapting the Spiritual Exercises of Saint Ignatius Loyola to individually directed retreats of meditation and prayer in sessions of three, five, eight, thirty, and even forty days, with each one of these options attracting hundreds of retreatants every year.

Was it merely a coincidence that during the years between 1960 and 1984, the Provincial Superiors, Gordon F. George, Angus J. Macdougall, Edward F. Sheridan, and William F. Ryan, were all men with professional degrees from leading Canadian, American, and European universities? Were they introducing a new paradigm for Jesuits of the twenty-first century? In any event, they certainly changed the Province's priorities, and incidentally also "rehabilitated" the Jesuits' involvement in parish ministry. It had been more or less dormant since 1931, when William H. Hingston, then Provincial Superior, decided to sell to the diocese of Hamilton the historic Church of Our Lady Immaculate in Guelph. Later, in 1969, Angus J. Macdougall took the step of agreeing that the Jesuits would be responsible for the large multi-cultural inner-city parish of Our Lady of Lourdes in Toronto. It was the climax of decisions to open new parish churches in Montreal, Winnipeg, and Halifax. "Rehabilitated," or, as Winston Rye's chapter on parish ministry shows so eloquently, it was "going back" to the first choices taken up by the returning Jesuits of the 1840s in Laprairie (1842), Sandwich (1843), Guelph (1852), and Chatham (1857). Today, dozens of Jesuits also work out of parishes as chaplains in hospitals, schools, drop-in centres, convalescent homes, and other similar institutions.

The Jesuit administrative and decision-making framework set up in 1924 for the newly established Upper Canada Province remains solidly in place today, although the name of the Province was changed to "The Jesuits in English Canada" in 2006. "Upper Canada" had been a sore point with the French-Canadian Jesuits since 1924, when many of them felt affronted at having to become "Lower Canada." In 1969, they unilaterally decided to become "French Canada." Because the Jesuits of the Upper Canada Province, whose origins were Scottish, Irish,

French, and many other national backgrounds, refused to be dubbed "English," the Province had to wait eighty-three years until a consensus emerged around the label "The Jesuits in English Canada," with the word "English" held to mean "English-speaking." Otherwise, nothing administratively in the framework of the Province has changed.

What did change, however, was the mood and spirit of discourse, understanding of relationships between Jesuits, between "ours" and "externs," between Jesuits and others. The "spirit" of the Second Vatican Council, the legacy of the Thirty-First to Thirty-Third General Congregations, the assurance, confidence, and promise of the 1960s, none of these has disappeared.

That, however, is *today*, and is not history. My introductory preface comes to an end. History is what you are looking for.

May I say that over the last five years, the committee of authors thoroughly enjoyed the many sessions of discussions and the many weeks of writing that have led to these books. We hope you enjoy them. Our meetings went on into 2013, when we became even more mindful and appreciative of the hundreds of Jesuits who began their Religious life at St. Stanislaus Novitiate, Guelph, Ontario, which opened over a century ago on 12 September 1913. We still have much more to say. We are also very grateful to our friends at Novalis Publishing, as we are to our Superiors in the Jesuit Order.

Jacques Monet, s.j.

1

Montreal

St. Mary's College, 1842–1896

"Notre collège va bien; il est en vogue dans ce moment"
—Louis Gravoueille, s.j.

Before Pope Pius VII restored the Jesuits as a Religious Order in the Catholic Church on 7 August 1814, there had been efforts to have them and their colleges once again in Canada.[1] In 1805 and later in 1811, Edmund Burke, the vicar general for Nova Scotia, on behalf of his bishop, Joseph-Octave Plessis of Quebec (1806–1825), had unsuccessfully invited English Jesuits to open a college in Halifax.[2] Likewise, the bishop himself, in 1806, in a letter to Pope Pius VII and

---

1 The Jesuits, or the Society of Jesus, as the Jesuits were officially named, were suppressed by the papal brief *Dominus ac Redemptor noster* of Pope Clement XIV on 21 July 1773. Because the brief had to be effected locally by bishops and, in some instances, by rulers, it was not uniformly implemented. In some areas, therefore, the Jesuit Order never died out fully. In Canada, by then under the British Crown, the Jesuits were never formally suppressed. They were forbidden, however, to accept novices. Consequently, they died out by attrition. The last Jesuit, Jean-Joseph Casot, died in Quebec City on 16 March 1800. DCB, vol. IV, 134–135. For a succinct account of the suppression of the Jesuits, cf. Robert E. Scully, S.J., "The Suppression of the Society of Jesus: A Perfect Storm in the Age of Enlightenment," *Studies in the Spirituality of Jesuits*, 45, no. 2 (2013), 1–42.

2 DCB, vol. V, 123–125. Edmund Burke (1753–1820) had been appointed vicar general of Quebec and superior of the Missions of Upper Canada in 1794. Later, in 1801, he moved to Halifax to become vicar general of Halifax, and in 1817 titular bishop of Sion.

to the Jesuits' Superior General, Tadeusz Brzozowski, s.j. (1814–1820), then living in Russia, had requested that Jesuits be sent to work in Halifax and among the native peoples in Upper Canada. Brzozowski had responded positively to him, and four Jesuits were appointed to the mission, two from England and two from Russia. Yet due to the Napoleonic wars in Europe from 1799 to 1815, and the subsequent dangers of travel, nothing came of those invitations: the Jesuits were unable to get passage, and their official return to Canada would have to wait another twenty-seven years.[3]

Pierre Chazelle, s.j., was greatly instrumental in stirring anew the interest in having the Jesuits once again in Canada. While in Rome during the spring of 1841, he met Ignace Bourget, the second bishop of Montreal (1840–1876). It was, in fact, their second meeting. Chazelle had directed a ten-day retreat two years earlier during August 1839 to the eighty-three priests of the diocese of Montreal. He was the first Jesuit to visit there since the restoration of the Society of Jesus in 1814. His presence aroused considerable reminiscences of the Jesuits' presence in New France: their exploits, their courageous lives, and their colleges and missions. Bishop Bourget was captivated. He had a great need for more priests and religious women within his vast diocese. It was, he was convinced, time for the Jesuits to return, and he set out to bring them to his diocese.[4]

To that end, Bishop Bourget had journeyed to Europe from 3 May to 23 September 1841 to seek out priests and Religious women to work in his diocese. In particular, though, he wanted Jesuits in Montreal. They had, he believed, the resources and experience to found missions within his diocese, and most especially to establish colleges and work with native peoples. Indeed, from the beginning of his episcopal appointment, he had recognized the pressing need for establishing educational institutions in Montreal, and had envisaged founding a combined commercial and classical college (*collège classique*). Thus, he composed his third appeal, *Appel aux Jésuites* (2 July 1841), which

---

3   DJB, vol. 1, x.

4   Lecompte, 27–33; DJB, vol. 1, 56–57; Gilles Chausée, s.j., "Les Jésuites et le projet de sociale de Mgr Bouget", *Societé Canadienne d'histoire de l'Église catholique, Session d'étude,* 53 (1986), 41–50.

presented a strong argument to the Jesuits' Superior General, Jan Philippe Roothaan (1829–1853), for allowing their return to Canada.[5] By reclaiming the monies from the "Jesuits' Estates", Bishop Bourget was confident that he could fund the founding of Jesuit colleges. Financial support from that source, however, was never forthcoming during his lifetime.[6]

Bishop Bourget did get his wish to have Jesuits once more in Montreal, or at least across the St. Lawrence River in Laprairie, a small village with an imposing church, La Nativité-de-La-Prairie-de-la-Magdeleine. Roothaan had responded positively to Bishop Bourget's appeal. He appointed Chazelle to re-establish the Jesuits in Canada. After visiting the Provincial Superior of France in Paris, Clément Boulanger, to ask for Jesuits willing to assist him on the new mission, Chazelle, along with five other Jesuit priests and three Brothers, set sail for the Canadian mission, which would be administered by the Province de Paris. With him were Félix Martin, Paul Luiset, Dominique Chardon du Ranquet, Joseph-Urbain Hanipaux, and Rémi-Joseph Tellier, and Brothers Emmanuel Brenan, Joseph Jennesseaux, and Pierre Tupin. They arrived in Montreal on 31 May 1842.[7]

Chazelle had hoped to open a college in Montreal as soon as possible. Yet the Sulpician Fathers, although supportive of the Jesuits' return to Canada, were not overly enthusiastic about Jesuits being on

---

5   Lecompte, 33–34. The *Appel aux Jésuites* is also quoted in full in Gérard Jolicoeur, *Les Jésuites dans la vie manitobaine, 1885–1922* (Saint-Boniface: Centre d'études Franco-Canadiennes de l'Ouest, 1985), 218–219; DCB, vol. XI, 94–105.

6   For an account of the Jesuits' Estates and the controversies surrounding that, cf. James R. Miller, *Equal Rights: The Jesuits' Estates Act Controversy* (Montreal: McGill-Queen's University Press, 1979). "The Jesuits' Estates" refers to the property in Lower Canada that had belonged to the Jesuits prior to the death of the last Jesuit in Canada, Jean-Joseph Casot. With that, all the Jesuits' properties reverted in trust to the British Crown. After the Jesuits' return in 1842, there was a concerted effort either to grant to the Catholic Church in Quebec all or some of the Jesuits' former property or, preferably, its monetary equivalent, and to recompense the Jesuits. After decades of considerable wrangling and negotiating over the dispensing of the monies, eventually the issue was settled in "The Jesuits' Estates Act", passed by the legislature of Quebec in July 1888. The Jesuits were to receive $160,000.00; a further $140,000.00 was to go to Université Laval; $100,000.00 was assigned to selected dioceses; and $60,000.00 was destined for Protestant educational institutions.

7   Lecompte, 36. Cf. also DJB, vol. 1, 55–58; 129; 154–155; 333–334. The original intention had been to appoint the French Jesuits to the mission of Madagascar.

the island of Montreal.[8] At first, Bishop Bourget offered the Jesuits a small *collège classique* at Chambly, on the Richelieu River southeast of Montreal, which the Sulpicians had begun in 1767. To the bishop's disappointment, however, the Jesuits declined that offer. The inhabitants of Laprairie wanted Chazelle to establish a college there, and both he and the bishop were interested. Again the Sulpicians objected.[9] Instead, the Jesuits founded a school there, and because the departure of the curé, Michael Power, to become the first bishop of Toronto (1842–1847) had left the parish without a priest, they assumed responsibility for the parish as well.[10]

Meanwhile, in the autumn of 1842, the coadjutor archbishop of Quebec, Pierre-Flavien Turgeon, pressed Chazelle to open a college in Nicolet, north-east of Montreal. Chazelle turned down that offer for lack of manpower and finances. Yet the hope of founding a Jesuit college did not end there. Even the Jesuit bishop of Boston, Benedict Joseph Fenwick (1846–1866), invited the Jesuits at Laprairie to establish and direct a college in Boston. They declined that request for the same reasons.[11]

Bishop Bourget had not been overly favourable to establishing a college in Laprairie; he preferred having one in Montreal. Even if initially the Jesuits seemed confined to the south bank of the St. Lawrence River, and thus outside Montreal, Bishop Bourget was determined that in time they would found a combined commercial and classical college for young men within the city. He was not one to give up easily. In October 1843, he delegated his vicar general of the diocese, Hyacinthe Hudon, to travel to Kingston in Canada West,

---

8   Lecompte, 36–37. By 1842, Montreal was the largest and richest city in Canada, having more than 45,000 inhabitants, of which there were 30,000 Catholics (23,000 French-speaking and 7,000 English-speaking). In 1844 it became the capital of the United Provinces of Canada, following Kingston's period as capital from 1841 until 1844.

9   DJB, vol. 1, 57; Lecompte, 42–44; 60–65; Desjardins, 19–25.

10 Lecompte, 48–49; DCB, vol. VII, 705–706. Power was appointed the curé of Laprairie and vicar general of the diocese of Montreal in 1839. He was consecrated first bishop of Toronto on 8 May 1842 in his parish church by Rémi Gaulin, the bishop of Kingston (1840–1857). The Jesuits left the parish in 1854. Cf. Murray W. Nicholson, "Michael Power: First Bishop of Toronto," CCHA, *Historical Studies*, 54 (1987), 27–38.

11 DJB, vol. 1, 57; Desjardins, vol. 1, 25; Lecompte, 146–147.

where he was to explain to the members of the legislative assembly of the Province of Canada the bishop's views and desires.[12]

By 1845, there was considerable discussion among Catholics in Montreal about building such a Jesuit college. A sloped site overlooking Montreal known as the Donegani Orchard, which adjoined St. Patrick's church—at the time under construction—was considered a possible location. Nothing immediately came of that idea, however, and another three years would pass before a Jesuit college was established nearby, to the east of St. Patrick's.[13]

In the intervening time, during the early 1830s to the late 1850s, cholera and typhus epidemics ravaged Montreal. The more serious of those were typhus in 1847 and cholera in 1832, 1833, 1834, 1851, 1852, and 1854. During 1847, nine priests and thirteen Religious women fell victim to typhus while working among the ill. The Sulpician Fathers especially had been devastated by the disease, and due to a subsequent shortage of manpower, they found it difficult to continue their ministry. Despite whatever reservations they might have had about the Jesuits ministering in Montreal, they nonetheless asked for English-speaking Jesuits to assume responsibility for St. Patrick's church, which had opened in March 1847 to serve the English-speaking Catholic immigrants. Four Jesuits took up residency in the presbytery during July 1848.[14]

Félix Martin succeeded Chazelle as Jesuit Superior in Canada East in 1844. Well versed in the pedagogical knowledge he had acquired in France and Belgium, he had had in mind for some time to establish a *collège classique* and, from early 1845, with the backing of Bishop Bourget, had been searching for a suitable site, but without much

---

12   Desjardins, vol. 1, 27; 35–39; Lecompte, 146; DCB, vol. VII, 423–424. Hudon was appointed the vicar general of the diocese of Montreal in 1841. He died from typhus, contracted while assisting Irish immigrants in Montreal during the typhus outbreak in 1847. The present-day provinces of Ontario and Quebec were called, respectively, Upper Canada and Lower Canada from 1791 to 1840. Following the Act of Union in 1840 and until 1867, the two colonies were united into the Province of Canada, but designated as Canada West and Canada East. At the time of Confederation, 1 July 1867, Canada West and Canada East became the separate provinces of Ontario and Quebec.

13   Desjardins, vol. 1, 45–48.

14   Lecompte, 119–128; 131–132; Desjardins, vol. 1, 51–57; 212–213; DCB, vol. XI, 587–589. Along with Pierre-Louis Morin, Félix Martin had been one of the architects of St. Patrick's.

success. The Sulpicians had even offered him some property to the west but outside Montreal, which was called Mont Croix-Rouge. Because Martin intended a college for day-students only, he judged that the site would be too far from the city.[15]

Eventually, on 20 August 1846, he settled on the "Donegani Orchard", which was owned by Giovanni Donegani, a wealthy Italian Montrealer. To Martin, it seemed to be an ideal location because, as he noted, "at this height, a building could be seen from every part of the city." Donegani's property was valued at more than £8,000.00; he sold it to Martin for £2,250.00 on the condition that a daily Mass be celebrated for him until the last of his children had died. There, in May 1847, the foundations were laid for the first Jesuit college in Canada since their restoration.[16]

On 20 September 1848, Bishop Bourget finally got his wish. A Jesuit bilingual classical college opened to the east side of St Patrick's church in a temporary but ramshackle wooden building (*"le petit collège de bois"*), which also served as the presbytery for the Jesuits at St. Patrick's. An equally run-down but smaller tenement nearby the Jesuits' presbytery housed the boarders. An announcement in the *Montreal Herald* stated that students would find a "complete Classical and Commercial Course" in English and French. Indeed, as the newspaper noted, "The English and French languages will receive equal attention in each of the Classes." Along with stating which subjects would be required, and what the tuition would be, it also pointed out that "The German and Italian Languages and Drawing are taught, but they will form an extra charge."[17]

---

15   Lecompte, 146–147; Desjardins, vol. 1, 40–42. Mont Croix-Rouge, or Croix-Rouge as it was more familiarly known, was a fine piece of property situated at the present corner of rue Guy and boulevard René-Lévesque (formerly Dorchester Boulevard). In 1861, La Congrégation des Sœurs de la Charité de Montréal, better known as Les Sœurs Grises, purchased it, and thereon built their large Hôpital Général ten years later. In 1879, a magnificent chapel with an elegant tower and spire were added. Twenty-two years later, the Sisters opened their Motherhouse and an orphanage there. Concordia University purchased the property in 2004.

16   Lecompte, 147–148; Desjardins, vol. 1, 45ff; DCB, vol. XI, 588.

17   Desjardins, vol. 1, 55–57; 59–65; Lecompte, 147–148. William Grey founded the *Montreal Herald* on 11 October 1811 as a weekly newspaper. Over time, it became an influential weekly, then a tri-weekly, and finally a daily, except for Sundays, and carried several different names: *Montreal Herald, Montreal Daily Herald, Montreal Herald and Daily Commercial Gazette, The Herald*. Its final edition appeared on 18 October 1957.

Martin was named Rector of Collège Sainte-Marie/St. Mary's College, as the bilingual college was officially named, and began the academic year at *"le petit collège de bois"* with four other Jesuits. Seven French-speaking and six English-speaking male students enrolled, five of whom were boarders. By year's end, there were fifty-seven students. The academic programme or classical course (*Cours classique*) was patterned on the traditional Jesuit educational ideals expressed in their *Ratio Studiorum,* which had been published in 1599 under the direction of the then Superior General, Claudio Aquaviva, s.j. (1581–1615), and defined the educational system for the Jesuits in their colleges.[18]

Over time, *Ratio Studiorum* had become the abbreviated title for *Ratio atque Institutio Studiorum Societatis Jesu.* From 1584 to 1599, the document had gone through several stages of trials and committees by Jesuits in their colleges in various parts of Europe and elsewhere. Simultaneously, it was also directly influenced by an international group of Jesuits at their Collegio Romano in Rome. As a result, the *Ratio Studiorum* was a compilation both of the educational methods and best practices of Jesuits in their colleges and of the prevalent classical and humanist educational ideals in European universities throughout the Renaissance period. As well as containing rules for governance for Jesuit officials and teachers, the *Ratio Studiorum* emphasized the natural sciences along with the Latin and Greek classics, philosophy and theology, and faith and morals. It insisted that subjects be taught thoroughly through compositions, discussions, disputations, repetitions, and contests. Physical exercise and benign discipline combined with the course of studies aimed to produce a well-rounded, articulate graduate.[19]

By the end of its first three years, the college's quarters and the students' residence were still temporary, and had been judged to be inadequate. The new and much grander building, designed in the fashionable neo-classical manner of the day by Martin, was finally

---

18   Lecompte, 148–149. Cf. also Jean Cinque-Marc, *Histoire du Collège Sainte-Marie de Montréal, 1848–1969* (Montréal: Editions Hurtibise, HMH, 1998).

19   The *Ratio Studiorum* has remained an enduring and much-admired document whose importance and influence have been proven over the centuries. The title has been shortened further by Jesuits to the *"Ratio".*

finished in 1851 on nearby rue de Bleury. His original model for the college, however, had been noticeably modified because of financial restraints. A Protestant journalist of the day referred to the new college building as "La Bastille des Jésuites", while elsewhere it was described as "solid but naïve" in design. A year later, in November, Martin obtained the incorporation of a bilingual college from the parliament of the United Provinces of Canada.[20]

The college moved to its new building during the late summer of 1851. Its enrolment had reached nearly 150 students, while the Jesuits' faculty and staff numbered twenty, and after that increased yearly to the point that within two decades after the college's foundation, there were anywhere from thirty-five to over fifty Jesuit priests, Scholastics, and Brothers there, and close to 300 boarders and day-students. By 1859, the college's Prefect of Studies, Louis Gravoueille, s.j., could boast to a Jesuit friend in Paris that "notre collège est l'image la plus exacte des collèges de France.... Notre Collège va très bien; il est en vogue dans ce moment. On compte sur trois cents élèves pour l'année prochaine. Les études marchent bien. Elles sont à peu près sur le pied du *Ratio Studiorum*."[21]

From the time of the college's transferral to 1180 rue de Bleury, Martin had struggled, with imagination and determination, but with little money and few resources, to build a strong academic institution, yet one that also emphasized the arts, especially theatre. Arthur E. Jones, S.J., himself a renowned scholar and archivist of a later generation at St. Mary's College, described Martin as an "antiquary, historiographer, architect and educationalist." Jones might well have added "archivist and librarian", since Martin had established not only a sound academic institution, but also what would become the famed archive and library of St. Mary's College, which contained not only valuable documents relating to the history of the college itself, but also maps, letters, papers, and other material pertaining to the history of the Jesuits in Canada. When the college closed in 1969, the archival materials were transferred to the archive of the Province of French Canada, then housed at Saint-Jérôme, Quebec, and, after 2009, became

---

20   Desjardins, vol. 1, 94; 101–106. Martin's original model is on display in AJC.
21   Ibid., vol. 2, 26.

part of the combined archive in Montreal of the two Jesuit Provinces in Canada, English-speaking and French-speaking.[22]

The college drew students from Montreal and nearby, and from the United States, as well as from every social level, English-speaking and French-speaking alike. They followed the traditional Jesuit classical course in history, Latin and Greek classics, English and French literatures, grammar, mathematics, philosophy, religion, music, chemistry, and physics. Over the years, a variety of non-humanistic courses in both languages was also offered in the natural sciences, astronomy, and commerce (until 1888), and law (from 1851 to 1867). Many graduates went on to achieve considerable fame and influence, in Montreal, in Canada, and around the world, for well over 100 years: in the arts, in politics, in commerce, in law, and in the Church.

The courses in law were established by a layman, François-Maximilien Bibaud, who for some time had been eager to create a law school in Montreal. He formed a nine-member committee of lawyers, which drew up a plan for such a foundation. The committee members then wrote Bishop Bourget and Martin, and adroitly argued that the college ought to set up a chair of law for French-Canadian Catholic students in competition with the one McGill College was organizing for English-Canadian Protestant students. Loath to see young Catholic men studying law in the Protestant McGill College, Martin and the bishop quickly concurred with the committee's plan. The law school opened on 1 September 1851.[23]

Although never hesitant to promote himself or to brag about the quality of his own teaching, Bibaud did aim to have high academic standards. In time, enrolment in the law school increased from eleven in 1851 to fifty-six in 1863. Despite the growing reputations of the law schools at Laval and McGill, his was, Bibaud proudly asserted, "the fashionable programme." When, however, and contrary to all expectations, he announced his retirement on 1 September 1867, his school departed with him, and eventually became part of Université de Laval à Montréal, a branch of Laval in Montreal (later to become the

22   Ibid., vol. 1, 101; DJB, vol. 1, 157–158.

23   DCB, vol. XI, 70–71; Lecompte, 308; Desjardins, vol. 2, 60–62.

Université de Montréal). The law school's demise at St. Mary's College, however, had little to do with Bibaud. It was brought about because of legislation by the Quebec legislature in 1867 that decreed that schools of law had to be attached to a college or university, and because of the growing friction between Bishop Bourget and Université Laval, which had refused to recognize law degrees from St. Mary's College.[24]

Martin had obtained the original incorporation of the college in November 1852 from the united Parliament of the Canadas. When Université Laval founded, with limited academic privileges, its branch in Montreal on 6 January 1878, St. Mary's College received its academic status from there through the papal decree *Iamdudum* on 2 February 1889. Because, as *Iamdudum* noted, the college was "outstanding", old, and revered, and because the new Université Laval à Montréal was to benefit from the settlement of the Jesuit Estates, the college was granted special control over its courses and examinations. It was a privilege unavailable to other classical colleges. In effect, that meant that the college's members could organize the examinations of its students and give to those it found proficient a written certificate stating they were worthy of the degrees that Université Laval conferred on the young men of equal merit in its affiliated colleges. Thus, on the advice of the authorities of the college and qualified under the curriculum and examinations set by the college itself, the graduates, after satisfactory examinations, would receive the same diploma that the Université Laval granted to its own graduates. While there was not full autonomy conferred on the college in its degree-granting status, it was certainly favoured academically relative to other colleges at the time. Only later, on 8 May 1919, by the same papal decree, *Iamdudum*, was the autonomous academic status of the Université de Montréal secured, but with the bishop of Montreal nominated as vice chancellor. In the following year, with all its special privileges remaining intact, the college affiliated with the Université de Montréal, instead of with Université Laval.[25]

Although in the end it is hard to credit any one of Martin's achievements as greater than another, without doubt his vision that

---

24   Desjardins, vol. 2, 65–102; Lecompte, 308.

25   Desjardins, vol. 1, 124ff; Lecompte, 308.

the English and French languages in the college should be on equal footing was certainly among his major accomplishments. The college's bilingual title reflected the reality of Montreal's population at the time. The proportion of English-speaking to French-speaking students in the college during the 1850s was about three English to eight French students, while in the courses in civil and mechanical engineering, the students were mainly English-speaking. Almost two thirds of the boarders spoke only English; among those were several unilingual Americans.

Consequently, during the 1850s and 1860s, Jesuit Superiors of the New York–Canada Mission, Jean-Baptiste Hus (1855–1859), Rémi-Joseph Tellier (1859–1866), and Jacques Perron (1866–1869), had even pondered whether to develop the college as an English-speaking institution only. Their thoughts seemed to be confirmed by statistics. The census of 1871 showed that of Montreal's total population of 115,000, English speakers had a slight majority (58,144 English-speaking to 56,856 French-speaking). Ten years later, however, the census indicated that the francophone population of Montreal had surpassed that of the anglophone. From 1868 onwards, a similar parallel existed in the college; an English classical course was officially established during that summer. As a result, by September 1888, there had developed, in fact, two colleges in one. Significantly, too, in 1890 Lewis H. Drummond, S.J., assumed administration of the college for two years, the first and only English-language Rector ever appointed to St. Mary's College.[26]

LOYOLA COLLEGE, CLASSICAL COURSE, 1896–1921

"Good Christians, good citizens, good scholars"
—Gregory O'Bryan, S.J.

No one was surprised, therefore, at the physical separation of the two language sectors when Loyola College opened on 2 September 1896 as a separate English-language institution.[27] Henceforth, the two

26   DJB, vol. 1, 93–96; DCB, vol. XV, 303–305.

27   Until 2011, only one history of Loyola had been published, that of Timothy P. Slattery, *Loyola and Montreal: A History* (Montreal, 1962). Although the book offers a good overview of the

colleges would thrive in Montreal until well into the twentieth century as two parallel but independent Jesuit educational institutions, the one serving the English-speaking population and the other the French-speaking population in Montreal and beyond. While enrolment at Loyola College rapidly increased during its opening years, and the college had to move from St. Catherine's Street to Drummond Street in 1898, and again in 1916 to a permanent site on Sherbrooke Street West, there at 1180 rue de Bleury, Collège Sainte-Marie remained until 1969, side by side with the splendid collegiate Church of the Gesù.[28]

A four-page prospectus published in 1896 by Gregory O'Bryan, S.J., who had been appointed to organize the new college in the former Sacred Heart Convent on St. Catherine's Street, explained the rationale for establishing such an English-language college. In a General Statement of the prospectus he wrote: "For some years past, side by side, with the French Course, an English Classical Course has been successfully taught and well attended at St. Mary's College. It has now been deemed expedient to separate the two courses, and to have the English Course in a building apart, under exclusively English control and direction."[29]

The prospectus also outlined the intent and practice of the new college: "The aim is to develop the moral and mental faculties of the students, to make good Christians, good citizens, good scholars—men who shall be an ornament to religion and the upholders of Christian society. Monthly reports of behaviour, application and progress are sent to parents and guardians. Insubordination, continued neglect of

---

college, and contains a lot of information, all in all it is more anecdotal in its presentation, is not very well written, has some serious omissions, and is not always accurate.

28   Desjardins, vol. 2, 121ff. The Gesù was designed by Patrick Keely, a prominent architect of the day, and opened on 3 December 1865 as a *chapelle publique*. The Sulpician Fathers donated $2,000.00 to the building fund for the church which, in today's value, would equal about $260,000.00. Later, in 1878, the first "electric candle" (electric light) in Canada was installed in front of it. In the church's basement is housed the oldest extant theatre in Montreal. After the Jesuits withdrew from the college, in 1969, it was absorbed by the new Université du Québec à Montréal (UQAM), and the college's building was eventually demolished. The Gesù was spared. It has been reiterated that the Gesù resembles the Jesuits' Church of the Gesù in Rome, built in the mid to late sixteenth century. In fact, except in name, the Montreal church does not resemble the Roman church whatsoever.

29   Eventually, the prospectus for the years 1906 to 1921 were published as *Loyola College, Montreal, 1906–1914*, vol. 1 (Montréal: Imprimerie du Messager, 1914), and *Loyola College, Montreal, 1914–1921*, vol. 2 (Montréal: Imprimerie du Messager, 1921).

study and bad conduct are ordinary causes of dismissal." As in most other Jesuit schools, too, O'Bryan established Loyola College along traditional lines, with the eight-year programme of a classical college and similar to what had been in use at St. Mary's College since its foundation.

O'Bryan designated two general classifications in his prospectus: the first four years were the "High School Course" and the following four years the "Collegiate Course". Sometimes these were referred to as the "Junior Years" and the "Senior Years" respectively. By including the two general categories, which were in use for the next twenty-five years, his intention was to indicate that the first four years were academically less advanced than the final four years; it did not mean that a student would graduate with a high school diploma after four years. Rather, graduation followed only on completion of the eight-year classical course.[30]

Before beginning at Loyola College, a "Preparatory" year was required for those students judged to have insufficient foundation to start the eight-year programme. The majority of students, however, began the first year of "Rudiments" (sometimes called "Latin Rudiments"). Within that were four divisions of studies, each equally important. First was "English", which emphasized the study of Butler's *Catechism*, Shuster's *Bible History*, English grammar, spelling, and easy literary English classics, Canadian geography, English composition, dictation, writing and reading, and elocution. Second was "Latin", which included Kingdom's *Latin Grammar* and *Latin Exercises I*, *Cicero ad usum Sextanorum*, and Latin composition. Finally, "Arithmetic" and "French", with Macmillan's *Progressive Course I* as the textbook, concluded the third and fourth categories of "Rudiments".

---

30   It should be borne in mind that the students' range in age was quite marked, with the very youngest being around twelve or thirteen years in the "Preparatory" year, to the twenty-one-year-olds, and sometimes older, in the final year of the "classical Course". That is why, in the original architectural plans for the new Loyola College on Sherbrooke Street in 1913–1915, there were to be two distinct buildings flanking each side of the Refectory Building: one to the north-east side, the Junior Building, and one to the south-west side, the Senior Building. The latter, however, was never constructed. Although less used in the latter decades before 1992, the title "Junior Building" remained.

The second, third, and fourth years of the classical course were designated "Third Grammar" (or sometimes "Syntax" or "Special Latin"); "Second Grammar" (or "Method"); and "First Grammar", which was often referred to as "Repetition" because a good deal of time was spent on reviewing and reflecting on the material of the previous years. Progressively, more was demanded each year of a student. Advanced exercises in textual translation and in the writing of themes with special exercises were assigned to test the student's linguistic abilities. Each of the three years was divided into the same categories as "Rudiments", but with "Greek" as an added category and "Arithmetic" changed to "Mathematics". As well, under "English", in "Third Grammar", Canadian history was added; in "Second Grammar", ancient and Roman history; and in "First Grammar", the history of the Middle Ages. Weekly throughout each of the years, *aemulatio* and *repetitio* were also important exercises in every classroom. With these, the first four years were completed.

The fifth and sixth years of Loyola's classical course were termed "Humanities" and "Rhetoric", and were devoted to more advanced studies. Similarly divided into the five categories of the fourth year— "English", "Latin", "Greek", "Mathematics", and "French"—these years consisted of a thorough examination of religion, the great authors of each of the four languages, and, under "Mathematics", the study of algebra, geometry, and trigonometry. Modern history was added in "Humanities", and the history of England in "Rhetoric". Again, *repetitio* and *aemulatio* were weekly exercises.

The final two years of the classical course, "I Philosophy" and "II Philosophy", were considerably different from the previous six years. They were more advanced and thorough. A substantial amount of each week was spent on *repetitio*, that is, reviewing not only recently taught new matter, but also going over, in a general way, all the previous years of studies.

Accordingly, the final year but one, "I Philosophy", had four general categories of studies: "Evidences of Religion" studied Christian religion under revelation, biblical studies, tradition, faith, the Trinity, and "The Four Last Things"; "Philosophy" included logic, ontology, cosmology, psychology, and natural theology; *The History of Philosophy* investigated, among other authors, John Henry Newman's *Idea of a University*; and "Mathematics" and "Sciences" encompassed plane and spherical trigonometry, chemistry, geometry, zoology, geology, mineralogy, and physical geography.

The concluding year, "II Philosophy", had three general categories: "Evidences of Religion", which examined the Christian religion under Christian ethics, Ecumenical Councils of the Church, Pope Pius IX's *Syllabus of Errors*, God as Redeemer and Grace, and the Sacraments; "Philosophy", which studied general ethics, the right of property, domestic society, God's society, international law, the rights of the Church, Pope Leo XIII's social encyclical of 1891, *Rerum Novarum*, and the study of "political economy"; and "Mathematics and Sciences", which offered advanced mechanics, hydrostatics, electricity—in 1896 still a relatively new discovery—magnetism, astronomy, light, and heat. With that completed, the successful student would be eligible to graduate from the classical course with a Bachelor of Arts degree, which was granted through Université Laval up until the founding of the Université de Montréal on 8 May 1919 as an independent university. Following 1896, this same prospectus, including O'Bryan's "General Statement", was used each year until 1921, with only minor adjustments.[31]

The Gazette of Montreal solemnly announced the college's opening: "This step has been taken at the earnest solicitation of the English-speaking clergy and laity of the city; and they have promised every help towards furthering this praiseworthy undertaking." It was situated across from Collège Sainte-Marie, *The Gazette* noted, and the "[Jesuit] Fathers have rented the suitable buildings at the (south-east) corner on [2084] St. Catherine's and Bleury Streets, lately vacated by the Ladies of the Sacred Heart."

Although O'Bryan and F. Wafer Doyle, S.J., took up residence in the new building, officially the Jesuits at Loyola College still remained part of the Jesuit Community of Collège Sainte-Marie, at least until

---

31   LCM, vol. 1, 3; DCB, vol. XIII, 776. No copies of the prospectus survive prior to 1906 in the Jesuit archives; copies after 1906 to 1921 were published in two volumes.

1898, at which time they formed their own Community with O'Bryan as the Superior. Altogether they totalled eight Jesuit priests and two Brothers. O'Bryan also was appointed Prefect of Studies (1896–1900) over the 150 English-speaking students enrolled in the three junior years of the classical course.[32]

Among those first Jesuit professors at Loyola College was Isidore Kavanagh, one of the outstanding astronomers of his day in Canada. He had studied geology and astronomy in England during the 1880s as a young Jesuit, taught the "physical sciences" at St. Mary's College, Montreal, and at St. Boniface College, St. Boniface, before rejoining the faculty at St. Mary's College in 1896 and then becoming part of the small group of Jesuits at the newly founded Loyola College. His principal interest was astronomy, and he devoted all his research and lectures to that discipline. Renowned among his scientific peers, he was elected a member of the Royal Astronomical Society of Canada and was invited to join the Canadian Government Expedition to Labrador to photograph the total solar eclipse on 30 August 1905. For his contribution to scientific research, he was awarded an honorary doctorate from St. Francis Xavier University, Antigonish, Nova Scotia.[33]

From the beginning, the intention of the college's officials had been not to remain long in the small quarters on St. Catherine's Street. Already within the first year of the college's life new quarters had to be rented behind the existing ones. O'Bryan had been hoping to build a larger college building elsewhere, one that would suit the rapidly growing student body. In 1896, he commented that Loyola College would occupy new buildings, more suitable "both as to extent and locality, to the needs of our growing English Catholic population." That hope was fulfilled sooner than he may have expected. Early in the morning of 12 January 1898, a fire all but destroyed the college's buildings, forcing students and faculty to return to Collège Sainte-Marie for shelter. They remained there for a month until Loyola could

---

32   In 1922, *The Loyola College Review* noted that during September 1901, "the first class of Philosophy at Loyola [had begun]. The authorities had not tried to force the growth of the College, but laid a sure foundation by adding, each year, the next higher class. The members of Special Latin of 1897 were thus come [sic] to Philosophy in 1901."

33   DJB, vol. 1, 159.

take over the former Tucker Building at 68 Drummond Street. A new wing was constructed during that summer to house classrooms and a residence for the Jesuits; it opened in October. There Loyola College would remain until its transferral to a new site further to the west at what would later become 7141 Sherbrooke Street West.[34]

Due to his precarious health, O'Bryan was able to remain as Prefect and Superior only until July 1899. He was succeeded by William J. Doherty, S.J., whose health also broke down within a few months; O'Bryan was then named the college's first Vice Rector. Yet because of his continuing poor health, O'Bryan had to resign two years later, and was succeeded by Arthur E. Jones, S.J.

Jones was among the most distinguished scholars in Canada of his day. From 1885 to 1918, he was the archivist of St. Mary's College. Because of his skilful recognition of the handwriting of several seventeenth- and eighteenth-century Jesuits of New France, the authorship of many important archival manuscripts was identified. Over the years, too, he travelled extensively throughout "Old Huronia" searching out the early sites, working from seventeenth-century maps and documents, where the Jesuits had laboured throughout that area. Among his many publications was *Old Huronia*, an account of his travels, which the Ontario government published in 1909 as the "Fifth Annual Report of the Ontario Archives". He was the first Jesuit elected as a fellow of the Royal Society of Canada, and in 1913 was granted an honorary LL.D. from the University of Toronto for his remarkable research, scholarship, and publications.[35]

Because Jones had considerable health problems—he was of massive girth—he stepped down from the office of Rector. On 3 August 1903, Alexander Gagnieur, S.J., formerly the Rector of Collège Sainte-Marie, replaced him. Gagnieur remained as Vice Rector for only two years, however, due to poor health. Again, O'Bryan was appointed on 7 August 1905 to the office, but this time as the college's first Rector. His term was brief, also: he died suddenly on 6 June 1907 of a heart

---

34   Ibid., 261; Slattery, 81; 95ff.

35   DJB, vol. 1, 157–158.

seizure, two days after he had held the second annual meeting of "The Loyola College Old Boys Association".

The "Old Boys" association had been dear to his heart. On 6 October of the previous year, during the founding meeting, John Thomas Hackett had been elected the first president of the association. Two years later, the future renowned military figure and beloved governor general of Canada (1959–1967), Georges-Philéas Vanier, who had entered the college in 1897, became vice president for two years, then in 1910, president for two years, and again president in 1920 for two further years.[36]

During the second annual meeting of the Old Boys, to those in attendance, O'Bryan was clearly a thoroughly exhausted man; several noticed how painful the effort of delivering his address to the alumni had been for him. Indeed, his speech, during which he addressed the future of Loyola College and the need for its graduates to seek out justice and truth, and to stand firm in their faith, was his last public one. Ironically, he himself had commented privately after he had concluded, "I'll have to give up speaking altogether." When he died, he was only forty-nine years of age.[37]

From many perspectives, O'Bryan's untimely death was most unfortunate for the college. Under his guidance, and through his vigorous recruitment of students, especially several from English-speaking Canada and from the eastern parts of the United States, the college had quickly expanded. To meet that growing enrolment, he not only had moved the college to Drummond Street, but also increased the number of Jesuits at the college from nine in 1896 to seventeen by 1907. Their numbers continued to grow to the point that by the 1920s, Loyola College annually had about twenty-two to twenty-five Jesuits.[38]

---

36   Ibid., 88; 120; 295; Slattery, 84–87. Eventually, The Loyola College Old Boys' Association became the Loyola College Alumni Association. Hackett subsequently served as a Member of the House of Commons and a Senator.

37   Slattery, 84–85.

38   By the 1960s, Loyola College was among the largest Jesuit Communities in the Upper Canada Province, with more than forty members; the majority of them worked in either the college or the high school.

Along with more space provided for classrooms, a further advantage of the new site on Drummond Street was the availability of recreational facilities at nearby rinks, tennis courts, lacrosse and football fields, and areas for track and field events, something greatly lacking at the St. Catherine's Street location. The Old Victoria Rink, located between Drummond and Stanley Streets north of Dorchester Boulevard, was rented for the boarders during the winter months. It was during those years on Drummond Street that Loyola's hockey, lacrosse, and football teams began to take shape. Over the following decades, these would become renowned in Montreal and elsewhere.[39]

On 10 March 1899, Loyola College was incorporated by the provincial Parliament. The bill was drafted by the solicitor general of Canada, Sir Charles Fitzpatrick (1896–1902), and the prime minister, Sir Wilfrid Laurier (1896–1911), who was consulted on the matter, agreed to lend his support to the bill's passage. Dr. James J. Guerin, a former member of the provincial cabinet and later mayor of Montreal (1910–1912), whose son, Thomas, was one of the first students at Loyola, sponsored "The Loyola Bill" in the Quebec legislature.[40]

In the original draft of incorporation presented to the legislators, there was a degree-granting clause that in effect gave Loyola College university status: "The College may confer the degrees of bachelor of letters and bachelor of arts, and for that purpose it is authorized to make regulations respecting the course to be followed, and the examinations required for obtaining such degrees." That clause, however, was deleted at the time of the bill's passing in the legislature, the first of many rejections for such a status that would occur over the next seventy years. Instead, after the bill's second reading, an "affiliation clause" was inserted at the prompting of Joseph-Clovis-Kemner Laflamme, rector of Université Laval (1893–1899; 1908–1909), in response to the objections of the archbishop of Montreal, Paul Bruchési (1897–1939); Bruchési was not supportive of a degree-granting charter for Loyola College before he could establish a university in Montreal separate from Université Laval. The privileges of *Iamdudum* were

---

39   The Old Victoria Rink held the first hockey finals for the Stanley Cup in 1893, which was won by the Montreal Hockey Club. The rink closed in 1937.

40   Slattery, 72.

upheld, and affiliation was granted with Université Laval that aimed to give to Loyola College the same academic status as that of Collège Sainte-Marie.[41]

In all ways, from its beginning and during the opening decade of the new century, Loyola College was fulfilling an important educational need for the growing English-speaking Catholic population of the city. That was appreciated. The *True Witness and Catholic Chronicle* captured the mood of many English-speaking Montreal Catholics: "Here then were the two sides of Catholic college life: on the one hand intellectual thoroughness, the striving after the highest culture, the most enlightened methods of instructions; on the other, the inculcation of faith and piety, virtue and true manliness, the setting forth of Catholic ideals in all their excellence."[42] The college conferred its first degree, through Université Laval, on 22 June 1903, and was presided over by the vicar general of the archdiocese, Zotique Racicot, along with Loyola's Vice Rector, Arthur E. Jones, S.J. According to a writer of *The Gazette*, the ceremony was impressive: "Loyola College conferred its first degree last evening when its closing exercises were held in Karn Hall in the presence of a large number of relatives and friends of the students."[43]

Several extra-curricular programmes quickly became part of student life in the college. The first such programme, the Loyola Literary Society, was formed as early as November 1896. In 1910, the Catholic Social Service Guild was founded by four Loyola graduates, and went on throughout the next many decades to serve the Catholic Church in Montreal. Soon, too, theatre, music, sports, debates, public elocution contests, and a Latin *Disputatio* gradually had become regular features of any semester. A visiting priest, D. V. Phelan, editor of *The Casket*, a Catholic newspaper in Antigonish, Nova Scotia, was present in June 1907 at one of the first *Disputatio*, held in the presence of the archbishop of Montreal. The thesis defended during this "Philosophical

---

41   Gregory O'Bryan, letter to Rafael Cardinal Merry del Val, 26 December 1898, AJC, Box C-414; Slattery, 72–76.

42   "Concerning Loyola College", 20 May 1899.

43   Slattery, 104. François-Théophile-Zotique Racicot became vicar general in 1897 and auxiliary bishop of Montreal in 1905. He died in 1915.

tourney," as a reporter from *The Gazette* called it, was "The Church is a Perfect Society." According to Phelan, a young student skilfully defended the thesis "not merely against a fellow-student but against the keen thrusts of His Grace and another visitor.... I had no idea that Loyola was doing such a high class of work."

Wilfrid Laurier visited Loyola College on 22 September 1904. His nephew, Robert Laurier, from Arthabaska, Quebec, was a student there, and while visiting Montreal, the prime minister called upon the college and the Jesuits. He was among the greatest orators of his day. Such an opportunity to hear him speak, for he was greatly popular among English-speaking Canadians, at least in Montreal, was not to be missed. He did not disappoint. With his well-known oratorical flourish, he delivered a superb speech in English, which he spoke flawlessly, and during which he encouraged his audience to love and service of their country.[44]

As early as 1899, it had become obvious in every way that, sooner or later, the college's facilities on Drummond Street would become insufficient. Despite the lack of money in the college, O'Bryan was convinced that, in order to plan for the future, he should begin a search for a larger property. Somewhere in the expanding area between Atwater and Victoria Streets seemed suitable. Several locations were considered. In the end, all proved unsatisfactory for differing reasons. Then O'Bryan made an audacious decision.

On 5 January 1900, with John C. Coffee, S.J., the college's Treasurer, O'Bryan purchased fifty acres of the Decary farm with the hefty sum of $25,297.10, which had been loaned from the Canadian Jesuits' Mission fund. The debt of purchase was finally liquidated twenty-five years later by the then Rector, Erle G. Bartlett, S.J., and that money used to help build Martyrs' Shrine at Midland, Ontario.

The Decary farm was located close to the Canadian Pacific Railway tracks and near the south-eastern limits of what was known as Côteau Saint-Pierre and Montreal Junction. The two places later became part of the prosperous Montreal suburb of Notre-Dame-de-Grace, or "NDG," as it is popularly referred to by English-speaking

---

44   Ibid., 94–95. Years later, Laurier's grandnephew, Laurier C. Harvey, would also be a student at Loyola, and would enter the Jesuit Novitiate at Guelph on 1 February 1955.

Montrealers, and of the wealthy English-speaking independent town of Montreal West.[45]

No roads reached the new property, other than a small dirt path, and there was no promise of any to come. Because of its isolation from Montreal, the purchase was considered by many—including most Jesuits—an act of folly. About all that was said positively about the area was that it "produced the best musk-melons in North America". That was the famed "Montreal melon". Among many English-speaking Montrealers, Loyola's purchase was derisively known as "The Loyola Melon Farm". Eventually, O'Bryan and Coffee were proven right, and were then credited with "foresight", and indeed even with assisting in the development of that western part of Montreal. To meet that demand, the city promised to provide streetcars along what would become Sherbrooke Street West.[46]

By 1913, the college's buildings on the Drummond Street site had become wholly congested and deemed inadequate to meet the demands of a burgeoning college. The newly appointed Rector, Thomas J. MacMahon, S.J. (1913–1917), engaged architects and appointed Coffee as special legal advisor to supervise the planning and constructing of the buildings on the new campus. Equally important, if not more difficult, MacMahon had to persuade sceptical Catholic parents to send their sons to that remote and thinly populated farm area. It was not easy; a lot of doubt still remained about the feasibility of having a college there. Yet failure was not in MacMahon's vocabulary, for himself or for others. He was strongly disciplined and determined to make the new campus a success.[47]

Work began immediately. MacMahon's taste for beautiful ambiances soon became evident. The exterior walls of the college were to

---

45   Coffee had been a prominent Montreal lawyer before becoming a Jesuit, DJB, vol. 1, 62. The sum of $25,297.10 would have the value of over half a million dollars today.

46   Slattery, 123–134. The south side of Sherbrooke Street, which for years remained a melon patch, also served as an orchard. By the 1950s, and despite its agricultural use and rather scruffy appearance, it was referred to as the "South Campus". Eventually, the present-day Loyola High School would be built on part of that property.

47   DJB, vol. 1, 62-63; 203. The small sidestreet that leads to the present-day Loyola High School was named in Coffee's honour in 1930, along with three parallel streets that abut the northwestern side of the college's property, each named respectively in honour of O'Bryan, MacMahon, and William F. Doherty, S.J.

be of light-hued brick faced with a matte surface of Greendale bricks trimmed with Indiana limestone or terracotta, and set upon a base of Montreal limestone. Within, the beautiful solid oak doors of linen-fold design leading to the offices, the chapel, and parlours on the main floor of the Administration Building were a close copy of those at the University Church of St. Mary the Virgin, Oxford, England; the "Sodality Chapel" under a gable at the west end of the Junior Building was designed with a lovely timbered ceiling; the interiors of the students' dormitories were modelled after those in the Naval Academy at Osborne, England; the dining rooms were designed with leaded glass windows, high ceilings, ornamented beams, and red English quarry tile on the floors; and the handsomely carved wooden handrails, along with other finely executed wooden details at the entrance, were altogether beautifully finished, which gave the college's main foyer a distinguished and elegant appearance.[48]

Within two years, in 1915, some students moved into the unfinished buildings. During the summer of the following year, the whole college officially transferred into what became known as the Junior Building, the Refectory Building, and the Administration Building. Coffee, who was visiting from Winnipeg, where he had been appointed parish priest of St. Ignatius Parish in 1909, was invited to celebrate the first Mass in the new college on 5 August 1916. Access to the college was made easy by the completion of the streetcar line along Sherbrooke Street from central Montreal. The Prospectus of 1916–1917 could boast that "the electric cars pass the door making the College of easy access from all parts of the city; while the close proximity of the Canadian Pacific railway station at Montreal West is an immense advantage to outside students."[49]

The administration wing of the college, with its golden-toned brick, its gables and windows of leaded glass, would not be finished for another several years, while more wings and cloisters would eventually complete the campus. Indeed, and however unfinished the college appeared, the Prospectus of 1916–1917 bragged that the campus "deservedly ranks as one of the finest in the country." Built in an age

48   Slattery, 136.
49   LCM, vol. 2, 3; DJB, vol. 1, 62–63.

that greatly admired the gothic past, Loyola College came to be noted for its beauty and site placement. Designed in the "collegiate" neo-gothic style or collegiate gothic, as it was usually called, the college was reminiscent of the mediaeval colleges of Oxford and Cambridge, with a hint of Flemish-style gothic on the gabled upper windows and roof lines. Throughout North America in Jesuit universities and colleges, it was customary to design buildings in that style, and Loyola College became known as an excellent example of it. Indeed, the "General Statement" of the Prospectus approvingly noted that "competent judges have pronounced them the most beautiful college structures in Canada. They are thoroughly fireproof and the ventilating system and sanitary appliances are of the very latest pattern."[50]

Almost at once, however, there was concern that the buildings had not been practically designed and constructed. Because none of the original architectural plans for the land to the west of the property were executed, the Senior Building, intended for the students of the final four years, had not been built, nor had the chapel, which was to be behind the Central Building between the Administration Building and the Refectory. Likewise, the plans for the two buildings that were to flank each side of the Administration Building had not been implemented. When, in 1917, John M. Filion, s.j., was appointed Minister/Bursar of the Jesuit Community of Loyola College, he was not impressed with what he found. Dolefully, he recalled later that there were burst pipes, leaking roofs, and disintegrating terracotta because construction had been abandoned due to lack of funds. "The aesthete," he wrote, "may have been satisfied with the new buildings in those difficult days, but they did not alleviate the headaches of the bursar."[51]

Finances and debts were the major worries of the college's Jesuit officials during the opening two decades of the twentieth century. Hampered by serious debts, mainly arising from the purchase of the property, along with the increasing annual operating costs due to inflation during the war years, at times the future of Loyola College seemed precarious, and by 1917, even bleak. "It was," Filion com-

---

50 Ibid. The neo-gothic English perpendicular style was often favoured in the United States for universities and colleges.

51 Slattery, 184; DJB, vol. I, 111–114.

mented, "Loyola's worst year of penury." Improvements would have to wait for a few more years.[52]

In 1917, because there were no Catholic churches within the immediate area, MacMahon persuaded Archbishop Bruchési to allow local English-speaking Catholics to attend Sunday Mass on campus. On 17 June, Thomas P. Gorman, S.J., became the first priest-in-charge of the newly established St. Ignatius Loyola Parish. Masses were celebrated in the college's makeshift chapel behind the Administration Building. It would take another sixteen years before a fitting chapel, along with an auditorium/theatre beneath, would be opened for the college and the parish, thanks to the inheritance of Francis C. Smith, S.J., the son of a wealthy Montreal family. Before pronouncing his final vows in the Society of Jesus on 2 February 1931, Smith would dispose of his patrimony in favour of the construction of a new chapel and auditorium.[53]

From the beginning of the college, tuition and board remained within the financial range of most middle-class Catholic Montrealers. By 1906, the yearly fees amounted to $250.00; by 1916, they were $400.00. After that, tuition continued to rise according to the cost of living. As well, every effort was made to establish student scholarships; within the first ten years of the college's life, seven were given out. In its syllabus for 1911–1912, the first request for "Perpetual Scholarships" was noted. To found such a scholarship, a sum of money sufficiently large was needed "to yield an annual interest that would cover the yearly tuition fees of one student. For this an endowment of $1,000.00 would be required." By 1919 that requirement had grown to $1,500.00, and afterwards increased yearly according to inflation.[54]

The first perpetual scholarship was "The Margaret Wall Scholarship", donated in 1912; it was awarded that academic year. The number of scholarships grew each year so that by the 1920s, the college was awarding a considerable number annually. In the decades following, Loyola prided itself on a wide range of perpetual and

---

52 Slattery, 184.

53 DJB, vol. 1, 326.

54 LCM, vol. 1, 64. An endowment of $1,000.00 and $1.500.00 would be the equivalent of over $20,000.00 today.

annual scholarships and bursaries, many of which were still awarded decades later.[55]

Only with the appointment of William H. Hingston, S.J., as Rector in 1918 was there any hope of financial relief for Loyola College. He was the son of Sir William Hales Hingston, a famed surgeon, former mayor of Montreal (1875–1877), and a senator who had come to know everyone of importance in Montreal. As well, like his father, Hingston was an optimist and visionary, a man who had more than ordinary courage and a sense of *noblesse oblige*. Nothing ever seemed impossible to him. With considerable enthusiasm, he took on the responsibilities of Rector by identifying four priorities that he would address during his administration: the question of Loyola's annual financial shortfalls; the reorganization of the academic programme of both the college and the high school sectors; student enrolment, which had fallen significantly during the war years; and the attaining of a university charter for the college.[56]

Immediately, he tackled Loyola's major problem, its pressing financial needs, by implementing a fundraising drive. To assist him, he formed an advisory board of prominent Catholic businessmen under the patronage of Thomas G. Shaughnessy, 1st Baron Shaughnessy. The drive began on 22 April 1919 with a banquet in the Ritz-Carlton Hotel on Sherbrooke Street. It ended on 7 May after the extraordinary sum of over $300,000.00 had been raised from 2,500 contributors. Six years later, when he would leave the Rector's office on 31 July, Hingston had raised a considerable amount of monies, enough not only to retire debts and firm up the general financial state of the college, but also, by 1921, to complete the building of two storeys onto the Administration Building and, by 1927, to attach an impressive central tower to it.[57]

Most significantly, Hingston set out to revise Loyola College's academic programme with the assistance of a new Prefect of Studies,

---

55   Ibid., 29.

56   Ibid., 138–141; Slattery, 184. Cf. also DCB, vol. XIII, 474–475, and Alan Hustak, *Sir William Hingston (1829–1907): Montreal Mayor, Surgeon and Banker* (Montreal: Price-Paterson Ltd, 2004). Fluently French-speaking, Sir William Hales Hingston was elected twice to serve one-year terms: 1875 and 1876. Until the twenty-first century, he was the last mayor of Montreal whose mother tongue was English.

57   Slattery, 184–186. The purchasing value of $300,000.00 would be well over $5 million today.

Eduardo de la Peza, s.j. (1920–1923).[58] Beginning in 1918, the prospectus of Loyola College noted a fundamental change in store by referring for the first time to two separate units: high school and college: "The Collegiate Course, which follows upon the High School Course, embraces a period of four years…. It leads to the Degrees of Bachelor of Letters, Bachelor of Science and Bachelor of Arts." It is true, of course, that for many years the prospectus had distinguished the first four years of the classical course by denoting these as "The High School Course" and the last four years as "The Collegiate Course". Yet that distinction was really one of a division between the lower and the upper grades of the classical course. On the other hand, what the reference in 1918 was pointing towards was a major difference: a complete modification away from the classical course educational system to the North American one.

In 1919, a further change became evident. Although the traditional division of classes of the classical course was still being used, in the list of students for the academic year 1919–1920, the first four years were divided into I Year High, II Year High, III Year High, and IV Year High, while the last four years became 1 Year Arts, II Year Arts, III Year Arts, and IV Year Arts. For those majoring in science, the last four years were divided similarly to the Arts programme. A system of course credits, as used in the United States, also was introduced into the college's programme, along with the establishment of options in the second half of the Arts course: Arts (General), Arts (Pre-Medical), and Arts (Pre-Science). As well, and alternately for the college section, the terms Freshman, Sophomore, Junior, and Senior came into use. Such terms, used for the years in the college, but sometimes also in the high school, were based on the American model. Loyola College was one of the few educational institutions in Canada that ever used this American terminology.

---

58   DJB, vol. 1, 281. A Mexican by birth, de la Peza had arrived at Loyola College in 1919 as an exile from Mexico's revolution and subsequent persecution of priests. He remained until 1923 before moving to Melbourne, Australia, and eventually returning to his homeland.

Loyola College/
Concordia University, 1922–2006

"Remember how it all sang with a rhythm we could feel"
—A student, c. mid 1960s

After 1921, Hingston had been able to achieve the complete revision of the academic programme of Loyola College, from the classical college model to one more in accord with North American schools and universities, with a high school curriculum terminating after four years, and a separate four-year collegiate programme concluding with a Bachelor of Arts degree. That, in effect, separated Loyola College into two distinct units: Loyola College and Loyola High School.[59] The prospectus for 1921 treated the studies of the "College Department" entirely apart from that of the "High School Department". That meant that Loyola College had become a separate Loyola College High School, as it was called for the first time, with a four-year programme after which one graduated, and a college with a four-year arts and science programme after which one graduated with a Bachelor of Arts. From that, the term an "Eight-year man" came into use for those students who, having graduated from Loyola College High School, continued in the college for a Bachelor of Arts degree. Additionally, the college year was changed to thirty-six weeks, beginning in the third week of September, while the high school year of thirty-seven weeks opened a week ahead. There were, therefore, two terminal courses, each on its own four-year schedule. By those significant revisions, Hingston and de la Peza wanted that the college's graduates could be admitted without hesitation into every English-language university in North America. After 1921, such admission became possible.[60]

Hingston was assisted considerably in bringing about those changes not only by de la Peza but, after his departure from the college in 1923, by another distinguished Jesuit educator and preacher, Thomas I. Gasson. He had been born in England and had emigrated to the

---

59   For a history of Loyola High School, cf. Joseph B. Gavin, S.J., *From "Le petit collège de bois" to 7272 Sherbrooke Street West: A Brief History of Loyola High School, Montreal* (Montreal: Loyola High School, 2012).

60   Henceforth, the degrees for Loyola graduates would be granted by l'Université de Montréal.

United States as a young boy, converted to Catholicism, and eventually became a Jesuit. In 1895, he was appointed to Boston College to teach philosophy, which he did for the next twelve years, was President of Boston College (1907–1914) and served as dean of the graduate studies programme at Georgetown University, Washington (1914–1922). He arrived in Montreal to give a retreat to the Catholic Laymen's Retreat Association, an organization that had been founded at Loyola College, with Hingston's encouragement, in September 1918.[61] Later, Gasson returned to Montreal to direct retreats and to advise Hingston on academic affairs. In September 1924, he was appointed professor of religion and philosophy in the college, and a year later became Prefect of Studies. He quickly proved himself a worthy successor to de la Peza, and an important presence in the college following Hingston's retirement as Rector that year. His primary responsibility was to maintain what had been established already, and especially to uphold the academic standards of the college. By the time of his death in 1930, his reputation as professor and administrator, along with his geniality, good humour, and elocution skills, had greatly endeared him to students and faculty members alike.[62]

What Hingston was not able to achieve for Loyola College during his years as Rector, despite his singular efforts to do so, was to obtain a university charter. Already independent in its administration, curriculum, and examinations, in 1920 the college had become associated for its degrees with the new Université de Montréal. Rome reconfirmed on 5 January the college's privileges arising from the *Iamdudum* decree; those were written into the university's civil charter of 14 February 1920. Yet in Hingston's mind, and in the minds of many Catholics, Loyola College should grant its own degrees. By 1920, he believed that Loyola's time had come, and began to work assiduously to persuade both ecclesiastical and civil authorities of that fact.

The Jesuit Provincial Superior, John M. Filion (1918–1924), however, was distrustful of Hingston in the matter of the charter, and believed that Hingston acted impulsively and without regard

---

61   Joseph Fallon, S.J., A. Joseph Primeau, s.j., Edward J. Devine, S.J., and John H. Keenan, S.J., all had had a part in the founding of the Catholic Laymen's Retreat Association.

62   DJB, vol. 1, 123–124; Slattery, 257–259.

for the proper procedure between a Rector and a Provincial Superior. Of course, to a large degree, Filion was correct in his concerns, and had good reason not to have confidence in Hingston. Indeed, Filion was especially not pleased at Hingston's haste in pursuing the charter, and at times could be quite sharp in his criticism of Hingston, even once accusing him of not only impetuosity but also of disobedience, a rather serious charge, given the Jesuits' vow of obedience. During the autumn of 1922, when Filion was making his Provincial Visitation in Western Canada, considerable correspondence occurred between the two. Much of that concerned Hingston's hastiness to obtain a charter, and Filion's critical reaction to Hingston's plans.[63]

Nevertheless, at heart Filion was not opposed to Loyola College being granted a university charter. In fact, he was sympathetic to that idea. He believed that the special needs of English-speaking Catholics warranted such, and agreed that negotiations should continue, however cautiously, towards obtaining a charter. Later, during the autumn of 1923, he would actively pursue that matter in Rome. Realizing, though, that opposition from the bishops of Quebec was strong, he agreed that for the time being, the efforts to obtain a charter should be withdrawn.[64]

In the meantime, however, the Premier of Quebec, Louis-Alexandre Taschereau (1920–1936), seemed favourable to Hingston's cause, and in 1922 had promised a grant of $350,000.00 to help establish the new Loyola University. To further that, and to the annoyance of Filion, a prominent Catholic and Loyola graduate, Dr. Bernard

---

63   William H. Hingston, S.J., telegram to John M. Filion, s.j., 30 October 1922; William H. Hingston, S.J., telegram to John M. Filion, s.j., 31 October 1922; William H. Hingston, S.J., letter to John M. Filion, s.j., 1 November 1922; William H. Hingston, S.J., telegram to John M. Filion, s.j., 2 November 1922; William H. Hingston, S.J., letter to John M. Filion, s.j., 2 November 1922; John M. Filion, s.j., letter to William H. Hingston, S.J., 2 November 1922; John M. Filion, s.j., telegram to William H. Hingston, S.J., 2 November 1922; John M. Filion, s.j., letter to William H. Hingston, S.J., 3 November 1922; William H. Hingston, S.J., telegram to John M. Filion, s.j., 3 November 1922; William H. Hingston, S.J., telegram to John M. Filion, s.j., 4 November 1922; William H. Hingston, S.J., letter to John M. Filion, s.j., 6 November 1922; William H. Hingston, S.J., letter to John M. Filion, s.j., 8 November 1922; John M. Filion, s.j., letter to William H. Hingston, S.J., 12 November 1922; William H. Hingston, S.J., letter to John M. Filion, s.j., 21 November 1922, AJC, Box C-414.

64   DJB, vol. 1, 113. Georges Gauthier, letter to William H. Hingston, S.J., 3 November 1922, AJC, Box C-414.

A. Conroy, sponsored a joint "Petition of Loyola College and its Governors" in November of that year in the Quebec Legislature. In the end, though, they withdrew the petition at the request of the suffragan bishops of Montreal, who deemed that it was an inappropriate time for such a request.[65]

Despite that setback, yet still filled with high expectations and spurred on by a supportive letter from Premier Taschereau, Hingston decided to try another approach. In the spring of 1924 he visited Rome—a fact known only to a few Montrealers—to plead his case. Filion had advised Hingston against such a visit, arguing that the time was unsuitable. Hingston persisted. "I could not manage him," Filion later complained. Thus, reluctantly he granted Hingston permission to visit Rome even while sternly warning him that his mission there would fail. Several years later, in a letter to the then Provincial Superior, Thomas J. Mullally, S.J. (1938–1945), Filion gave a slightly different version of the events. He recalled that he had "asked the General [Superior] to call him [Hingston] to Rome and let him fight his case there with Cardinal Bisleti. Well, he lost and badly."[66]

Hingston prepared a meticulous brief for presentation. He met Wlodimir Ledóchowski, the Jesuits' Superior General (1915–1942); Gaetano Cardinal Bisleti, Prefect of the Congregation of Seminaries and Studies (1915–1937); Rafael Cardinal Merry del Val, Special Envoy to Canada (1897–1899), and Secretary to the Congregation of the Holy Office (1914–1930); Donato Cardinal Sbarretti, formerly Apostolic Delegate to Canada (1901–1910); Gaetano Cardinal de Lai, Prefect of the Congregation of the Council (1903–1908); and then had an audience with Pope Pius XI (1922–1939). Although received graciously and sympathetically by everyone he met, and especially by the Pope and by the Superior General, Filion's warning that he would not achieve a charter was correct. Neither the Pope nor the Superior

---

65 Wlodimir Ledóchowski, s.j., letters to John M. Filion, s.j., 10 May 1919; 27 November 1919, ibid. Montreal's suffragan bishops were Joseph-Guillaume-Laurent Forbes, diocese of Joliette (1913–1928) and Joseph-Médard Émard, diocese of Valleyfield (1892–1922). The grant would be worth over $4.5 million in today's dollar value.

66 William H. Hingston, S.J., letter to Joseph Welsby, S.J., 27 February 1924; Premier Louis-Alexandre Taschereau, letter to William H. Hingston, S.J., 26 April 1924; John M. Filion, s.j., letter to Thomas J. Mullally, S.J., 18 October 1938, AJC, Box C-414.

General supported Hingston's request. Even before the audience with Hingston, Pius XI knew that both the Superior General and Cardinal Bisleti were opposed to such a charter for Loyola College, and that Archbishop Bruchési was determined that the college would remain firmly affiliated with the Université de Montréal. Nothing, therefore, came of Hingston's Roman visit, or of his long efforts to achieve university status for the college.[67]

Any further attempt to change Loyola College's academic status would have to wait for another day. Indeed, after he succeeded Filion as Provincial Superior in 1928, Hingston was again working to get a charter for Loyola College through the coadjutor archbishop of Montreal, Georges Gauthier (1923–1939). Yet Gauthier would not support him. In truth, Hingston's dream of a Loyola University in Montreal would never be realized.[68]

After seven years as Rector, Hingston departed from Loyola College. His was an impressive record. In every way, by 1925 the college was a radically changed academic institution. Along with the fundamental changes in the academic programmes, the Loyola School of Sociology and Social Service, the first of its kind in Canada, had been founded (1918) with classes held at 280 Mountain Street; the Loyola Scientific Society was set up; many scholarships were endowed; there was a greatly increased student enrolment; membership was gained in the Inter University Debating League; the Loyola Extension Lectures were introduced; an orchestra, usually around twenty-five pieces, and a Glee Club, had become reputable; the Loyola Dramatic Society was greatly enhanced, and Loyola's theatre flourished; an Officers Training Corps had been established; the college's basketball, football, and hockey teams had won several local championships; the Loyola Snowshoe Club had grown into a popular organization; the first edition of *The Loyola News* was published (12 November 1924); an advisory board of governors was organized by Thomas G. Lord

67   *Petition to Gaetano Cardinal Bisleti*, 12 April 1924; *Petition to His Holiness, Pope Pius XI*, 3 May 1924, ibid.

68   William H. Hingston, S.J., letter to Coadjutor Archbishop Georges Gauthier, 18 January 1932; Coadjutor Archbishop Georges Gauthier, letter to William H. Hingston, S.J., 20 January 1932, ibid.

Shaughnessy to assist the Jesuits in administering the college; the Loyola Club had been welcoming prominent speakers to the campus for several years, among whom were, in 1922, Julian Byng, 1ˢᵗ Viscount Byng of Vimy and governor general of Canada (1921–1926), and in 1923, Hilaire Belloc, the renowned English Catholic writer; and a few months after Hingston had left the college, his hope that it would become a "Collegium Maximum" was granted on 5 October by the Jesuits' Superior General.[69]

Additionally, Hingston's new arena/rink, Loyola Stadium, which had been under construction since 1922, was finally completed, and was formally opened on 19 January 1924 by the Rt. Hon. Narcisse Pérodeau, lieutenant governor of Quebec (1924–1929), with a packed audience of dignitaries, students, and alumni in attendance. Dedicated to the memory of the college's graduates who had taken part in the Great War, the stadium/hockey arena would become known popularly as the "Old Boys' Stadium". It would serve the college until after the 1960s.[70]

In every way, therefore, the long years of Hingston's rectorship were very productive. With the distinction between the academic programmes of the high school and the college in place, Loyola College took on an enhanced position among Canadian university colleges. As well, efforts were made so that the high school graduates could move seamlessly into college life without too many complications. During the decades from the 1920s through to the 1960s, a large percentage of graduates from Loyola High School became "eight-year men", taking Bachelor of Arts and Science degrees at Loyola College. To meet the demands from the yearly increase in student enrolment in the college, the number of lay faculty members had to be increased almost every year.

Without a doubt, when Erle G. Bartlett, S.J., succeeded Hingston on 31 July 1925, the future looked hopeful for Loyola College. It was set on a sound financial footing, and flourished during the mid to late

---

69   Wlodimir Ledóchowski, s.j., letter to John M. Filion, s.j., 5 October 1925, AJC, Box C-417; Slattery, 182–183. Later, in 1930, another famous English author and friend of Belloc, G. K. Chesterton, would also lecture at Loyola.

70   *Loyola College Review*, Montreal, 1924, 13.

1920s. The prosperity and general optimism of those years, together with the monies Hingston had raised, enabled Bartlett to complete in 1927 the Administration Building that McMahon had begun in 1916 and that Hingston had raised to three storeys in 1921. Due to reduced funds, the original plans were only partially realized; an indoor swimming pool was never built.[71]

Yet the confidence and buoyancy of that era quickly evaporated in the great stock market crash of October 1929. Faced with a new and increasingly difficult task of administering Loyola on fewer and fewer funds, Bartlett resigned the following summer, on 11 August. In his stead, Thomas J. MacMahon, S.J., was again called upon to lead Loyola College, this time as Vice Rector (1930–1935).

The Great Depression of the 1930s quickly became a different story from the successes during the 1920s. Those were among the hardest of times. As the country fell deeper and deeper into an economic morass, fewer young men enrolled at the college due to financial restraints. MacMahon struggled to keep Loyola's finances from collapsing. Fortunately, he was an experienced administrator and knew the stresses arising from fiscal shortfalls. While Rector from 1918 to 1922 in Regina, where he had established Campion College with limited funds and manpower, he had learned the art of fundraising and of never giving in to harsh conditions. Perhaps, too, with more good fortune than anything else, by means of the inheritance of Francis C. Smith, S.J., MacMahon was able to build a new chapel and auditorium/theatre at Loyola. That, at least, was cause for optimism.[72]

Indeed, ever since moving in 1916 to the Sherbrooke Street West campus, the plan was to have a chapel and auditorium large enough for the ever-growing number of students. Not only was the original temporary chapel too small, but the facilities on campus for public gatherings, debates, theatre, and concerts were greatly inadequate. After visiting Loyola in February 1925 as Provincial Superior, Filion wrote to Hingston, reminding him that "a fitting place of worship" was needed. Filion urged him to appeal for $50,000.00 from wealthy

---

71   DJB, vol. 1, 7; 139.

72   Ibid., 203.

friends to build the chapel, which had been envisioned in the original plans for the college, between the Administration Building and the Refectory Building.[73]

It would take, however, another eight years and two more Rectors before a chapel and an auditorium were realized. In midsummer of 1932, the ground was broken for a building to the right of the Administration Building. It opened on 2 April 1933. The new chapel quickly became a familiar fixture of simple architectural beauty, serenely facing Sherbrooke Street, a jewel in its neo-gothic design, its stained glass windows, its use of dark-stained wood for the interior, and its finely carved sanctuary space. Well situated, and connected by a small cloister to the Administration Building, the chapel and auditorium/theatre would serve generations of students and local English-speaking Catholics for decades to come.[74]

To many people, the successful completion of the long-awaited and much-needed chapel and auditorium gave the image that Loyola was surviving the depression. Yet as the depression deepened by the mid 1930s, that was only image. Even MacMahon's determination and sanguinity were sorely tested. Among the Jesuits at Loyola College, too, there was growing concern over whether they could continue to maintain the college. There were good reasons for that concern. Over the previous five years, several financial loans had to be taken out to cover the mounting debts. Every bit as alarming was the fact that the numbers of students had fallen noticeably from the level of the early 1920s. It would take almost twenty years before those enrolment figures would return to that earlier level.

In 1935, Hugh C. McCarthy, S.J., was appointed Rector. A man of immense energy and a matter-of-fact outlook, his main task was to pay down the enormous debt load. To that end, he established a Maintenance Fund Campaign with John T. Hackett, K.C., as chair. With the help of dedicated Catholic volunteers, they set out to raise

---

73   John M. Filion, s.j., letter to William H. Hingston, S.J., n.d. February 1925, AJC, Box C-417. The value of $50,000.00 would be approximately $670,000.00 at present.

74   The auditorium/theatre beneath the chapel was named The F. C. Smith Auditorium following the sudden death of Francis C. Smith, S.J., in 1945; at the time he was Rector of Saint Mary's University, Halifax.

the money to cover the debt and build up a reserve of funds. Their hope was that Loyola College would then have a resource not only for paying off the debt, but also for assisting future development and safeguarding against economic collapse. The campaign was successful; it also won several new friends as well as benefactors for Loyola.[75]

After Edward M. Brown, S.J., became Rector of Loyola College in 1940, another four years would pass before there would be any noticeable upward turn in enrolment. A skilful administrator and fundraiser with a pragmatic bent, Brown saw to it that the financial status of the college soon began to improve. He was an outward-looking, pleasant man who easily won friends and soon made a difference in spite of the war years that followed the ravages of the depression. In 1944, he initiated the construction of the much-needed Central Building. Completed in 1947, it complemented the architectural design of the other buildings. That was the last building designed in the collegiate gothic style at Loyola College.[76]

On at least three occasions between 1942 and 1948, Brown raised with Archbishop Joseph Charbonneau of Montreal (1940–1950) the long-standing issue of obtaining a university charter for Loyola College. However sympathetic the archbishop was towards Loyola, he advised Brown that there was no chance of obtaining such a charter. In 1947, therefore, Brown decided to approach Premier Maurice Duplessis (1936–1939; 1944–1959) himself. Along with two distinguished alumni of Loyola College, Major General Georges-P. Vanier and John T. Hackett, M.P., Brown presented the college's case to the premier. Although the three men were well received by him, Duplessis declined his support. He was aware of the strong voices against any advancement of an English-language educational institution in the province.[77]

Within a year, however, on 7 June, Archbishop Charbonneau indicated to Brown that his mind had changed; he supported the college's request. Later that autumn, the new Rector, John F. McCaffrey,

---

75   DJB, vol. 1. 216–217.

76   Ibid., 31–33.

77   Ibid., 32.

S.J., along with Hackett, visited Charbonneau, who urged them to approach the premier again. Hackett and Henry Mulvena, K.C., met Duplessis on 28 January 1949. They were turned down for financial and political reasons. The matter would have to wait until after the mid 1950s before being reintroduced.[78]

Even if the decade of the Great Depression, 1929 to 1939, and the subsequent years of the war, 1939 to 1945, notably strained the college's finances and enrolment, those were also periods of some consolidation and growth. In 1935, the Loyola Alumni Extension Courses were begun; in 1938, the "Loyola Lectures" for the general public were initiated; and the Mothers' Guild was founded in 1940 to assist the college in fundraising projects and in its many public social events. From the 1940s until into the mid 1960s, new buildings were completed or constructed: the foyer of the auditorium (1941); the Central Building (1947); the Drummond Science Building (1962), named after Lewis H. Drummond, S.J.; the students' residence, Hingston Hall (1963), named after William H. Hingston, S.J.; the Georges-P. Vanier Library (1964), named after the Loyola graduate and governor general of Canada; and the Bryan Building (1966), named after William X. Bryan, S.J., who came to Loyola College in 1931 and was a noted and outstanding professor for sixteen years.[79]

Of even more significance, well-established academic departments were added to with the establishment of new programmes, while new faculties were also founded. In 1943, a faculty of science and a department of engineering, which included the first three years of engineering (civil, mechanical, electrical, mining, chemical, metallurgical, and engineering physics) were formed, while honours programmes in chemistry and in mathematics were newly offered. Notably, too, with insufficient equipment, no money, and no professors except himself, Stanley P. Drummond, S.J., single-handedly established in 1944 the department of biology which, in time, through his direction, teaching, and hiring of excellent professors, became one of Loyola College's

---

78   Slattery, 282–283.

79   DJB, vol. 1, 33–34. Bryan taught economics, sociology, philosophy, French, and physics. As well, he served as Dean of Studies from 1945 until his death in 1947. Loyola's excellent tradition in dramatics was also greatly owed to him.

most renowned scientific teaching departments. For nearly sixty years, Drummond's biology course was attended by pre-medical students not only from Loyola College/Concordia University, but also from the other universities in Montreal, such as McGill University. Indeed, Drummond's courses were so important that Concordia University would allow him to remain as a professor in the department—with a reduced workload—for almost twenty years after the normal retirement age for professors.[80]

Of importance also was the founding in 1945, principally through the initiative and organizational skills of Henry F. Smeaton, S.J., of "The Veterans Refresher Courses", a special academic programme for war veterans returning from overseas that permitted them to begin or complete degrees. Later, in 1948, a faculty of commerce was added to the college's curriculum of studies. Five years after that, majors were introduced in history, English, and economics, with honours courses being added in those three departments in 1958. Evening division courses were introduced—among the first in Canada—which allowed students who were unable to be present at classes during the day to attend Loyola College. Among those evening courses were library studies and community health and nursing courses. As well, and following the trend during the 1960s in all-male Jesuit colleges and universities throughout North America, at the beginning of the academic year 1959–1960, women were admitted as students for the first time. Not only did this radically change the gender demographics of the college, but also enrolment noticeably increased in the following years.[81]

Over the decades, too, several departments were greatly strengthened by the presence of renowned Jesuit professors. R. Eric O'Connor, S.J., with a doctorate from Harvard University obtained in 1941, arrived in 1942 at Loyola College to lecture in mathematics. Brilliant, insightful, and curious of mind, he was never more enthusiastic than

---

80   Slattery, 275–277. Drummond died on 16 March 2012 at the Jesuit Infirmary, Pickering, Ontario, in his ninety-ninth year of age and in his eighty-first year as a Jesuit.

81   DJB, vol. 1, 323. Cf. also Slattery, 275–277, and Grace A. Pollock, *History of the Faculty of Commerce of Loyola College* (Montreal: M.B.A. Thesis, Concordia University, 1993). Loyola's evening division courses became in the mid 1970s the Center for Continuing Education of Concordia University.

when he was sharing ideas, planning projects, and searching for answers to questions. For the next thirty-two years, he taught at the college and at the Thomas More Institute for adult education, which, in 1945, along with other like-minded intellectuals, he had founded in central Montreal. From its beginning, the institute was a separate entity from Loyola College, a status that O'Connor determinedly guarded despite several efforts to integrate it with the college. Its reputation for academic excellence remains to this day.[82]

Likewise, there were many other professors, lay and Jesuit, who made an immense contribution to the academic life of Loyola College. Among the noteworthy Jesuits were the above-mentioned Stanley Drummond; J. Gerald MacGuigan, a distinguished humanist and superb lecturer in English literature and poetry from 1947 to 1972; J. Aloysius Graham, renowned lecturer in chemistry and a leading administrator both at Loyola College and at Concordia University, from 1952 until his retirement over thirty years later; and Cyril B. O'Keefe, historian, scholar, writer, teacher, and administrator, whose research, insights, and publications from 1962 to 1981 on the eighteenth-century French Church have become a major contribution to that historical period. Most impressive, too, was the new communication arts programme, the first of its kind in Canada, founded in 1965 by John E. O'Brien, S.J. Over the subsequent years, under his leadership as director and lecturer, that programme came to be recognized as among the best on the continent.[83]

As well, considerable efforts were made during the late 1950s and early 1960s to expand the department of theology with new professors and new courses. To achieve that end, the renowned writer in spiritual theology, lecturer, and researcher Elmer L. O'Brien, S.J., was assigned to Loyola College as chair of the department of theology (1962–1966). Under his resourceful leadership, the department grew rapidly in every way, with new course listings, public lectures and distinguished visiting professors, and by an augmented student enrolment. O'Brien's health, however, which had been never too certain at the best of times, began to decline noticeably, and in 1966

82   DJB, vol. 1, 266–267.

83   Ibid., vol. 1, 272; vol. 2, 179–183.

he had to leave the post of departmental chair to take on less strenuous responsibilities. That did not last long. Immediately he became the founding director of the Contemporary Theology Institute, and also accepted the position of research professor in the department of theology, posts he maintained until he left the theology department altogether ten years later.

O'Brien continued until 1969 to organize and oversee the internationally renowned Loyola Theological Colloquium, which he had established in 1964. It brought to the campus some of the greatest international theologians, scholarly figures, and distinguished ecclesiastics of the post–Second Vatican Council Church. O'Brien directed annually the colloquium in theology to about 160 priests, religious, and lay scholars. Among the many leading scholarly figures as well as *periti* of the Second Vatican Council that he attracted to Loyola were Walter J. Burghart, S.J., Jean Daniélou, s.j., James M. Gustafson, Bernard Häring, C.Ss.R., Hans Küng, Bernard J. F. Lonergan, S.J., Roderick A. F. MacKenzie, S.J., and Karl Rahner, s.j.[84]

Overall, there was more at Loyola College attracting students than the expansion of its buildings, the creation of new academic programmes and structures, and its reputation for excellent teaching, however significant those were from the 1920s to the 1970s in the historical life of the college. As in all Jesuit educational institutions of the day, the college's aim was to educate the "whole" person. In consequence, over the years there developed many extra-curricular activities for students that were characteristic of Jesuit institutions of higher education: sports (sometimes referred to during the college's early decades as "Physical Culture"), drama and music; dances and socials; public lectures and debates; the Canadian Officers Training Corps; and a wide spectrum of social programmes and charitable works, especially developed from those that Joseph Fallon, S.J., had begun during the 1920s and 1930s. Inspired by the papal social encyclicals *Rerum Novarum* (1891) and *Quadragesimo Anno* (1931), which challenged lay Catholics to become more socially active in helping the less fortunate, and along with the devastating consequences of

---

84   Ibid., vol. 2, 258–260.

the Great Depression on so many, over the years a large number of students at Loyola College voluntarily assisted these programmes in benevolent works. Among the several charitable organizations Fallon either founded or assisted others in founding were the Montreal Federation of Catholic Charities, the Catholic Men's Hostel, and St. Martha's House for destitute women and children. Each of those institutions also housed a clothing store and an unemployment bureau.[85]

As well, and ever true to its Catholic values and Jesuit ideals, of great significance was that Loyola College ranked the spiritual lives of its students uppermost in its responsibilities. A Sodality of the Immaculate Conception, the St. John Berchman's Altar Society, and the Apostleship of Prayer, all traditional Jesuit organizations, were well-established for decades; Masses were daily celebrated in the college chapel; annual and weekend retreats were offered; and spiritual counselling became a special feature of every academic year. In time, the college's graduates contributed immeasurably as Catholic laymen—and later, as laywomen—in parishes and dioceses, in the arts, in business, in politics, in law, in medicine, in international diplomacy, in the military, in education, and in governmental and industrial research projects. Over the years, too, many graduates became priests and Religious; several entered the Society of Jesus. Some returned as Jesuits to work at their alma mater.

Yet, if ever since the days of Hingston much of the excellent reputation of Loyola College had to do with its academic programmes, with its Jesuit and lay professors and administrators, and with its students' achievements and extra-curricular involvements, it was also due to the leadership given by its Jesuit Rectors and other administrators. Beginning with Bartlett, and followed by MacMahon, McCarthy, Brown, McCaffrey, Gerald F. Lahey, S.J. (1954–1959), and Patrick G. Malone, S.J. (1959–1974), each Rector strove to fulfil the Jesuit ideals of education; each brought his own vision and expectations to the college; each approached the furtherance of the college's aims with new and different insights and vigour; and each left a lasting mark on Loyola College.[86]

---

85   Ibid., vol. 1, 107–108; Slattery, 252–257.

86   DJB, vol. 1, 31–33; 177–178; 202–204; 215–217; vol. 2, 195–199.

Many Jesuits in other administrative positions likewise played an immensely significant role in creating and advancing the college's academic programmes and reputation as an undergraduate institution: de la Peza, prefect of studies (1920–1923); O'Keefe, academic vice president (1962–1969); Gerald F. Tait, S.J., registrar (1960–1967); John E. O'Brien, S.J., founder of the communication arts department in 1965, chair, and academic vice president (1969–1970); Graham, dean of the chemistry department (1969–1973); and J. Gerald McDonough, S.J., prefect of discipline (1961–1963) and dean of men (1963–1969). Each of these and many others besides, with their administrative skills, educational visions, and practical experiences, helped greatly in building the college's excellent academic standing, and in giving Loyola much needed direction in times of evolution or unrest.[87]

Nevertheless, and despite its fine reputation, its expanding departments and increased enrolment, always underlining the dreams for Loyola College was that of having its own university charter. Ever since Hingston's failure to gain one in the mid 1920s, the hope remained of reviving the request. As well as Brown's efforts to advance the discussion, unsuccessful efforts were made later by Gerald F. Lahey, S.J., when he was Rector. He worked tirelessly to move the cause forward, with Paul-Émile Cardinal Léger, archbishop of Montreal (1950–1968), with the Provincial Superior, George E. Nunan, S.J. (1950–1957), and with the French Canadian Jesuit Provincial Superior, Gérard Goulet, s.j., with Quebec government officials, and with Loyola College alumni.

At times, Cardinal Léger seemed not entirely clear about what the Jesuits and English-speaking Montreal Catholics wanted. To the surprise of many, he even proposed to Lahey in a meeting on 10 July 1957 that, after the government had granted Loyola a university charter—he was confident it would—the four Jesuit colleges in Montreal, Collège Jean-de-Brébeuf, Collège Sainte-Marie, Collège de l'Immaculée-Conception, and Loyola College, should form a single Jesuit university and use Loyola's new university charter for the granting of its degrees. He proposed what to many was the somewhat bizarre name *Institutum Canisium* for the new university. Needless to say,

---

87   Ibid., vol. 1, 272; 281; vol. 2, 209–211; 216–219.

however well-intentioned, the cardinal's proposal went nowhere. The French-Canadian Jesuits were not interested: they were never about to give over any authority to an English-speaking university, or use the name "Loyola", or, to them even worse, allow for any dominance by an English-language institution through means of a charter. Besides, Premier Duplessis was not interested. By the time Lahey stepped down from office in 1959, despite his many efforts, no further advancement had been made in obtaining a charter than during Hingston's time some thirty or more years earlier.[88]

In spite of such setbacks, however, by the 1960s the college was generally recognized as a first-rate undergraduate institution whose graduates were well educated and well formed. Many Canadian universities were accepting without question Loyola College's graduates into their programmes. That general recognition of excellence helped to give the college a new prominence on the Canadian academic scene. On 22 January 1960, it was singularly honoured by an invitation to become a member of the National Conference of Canadian Universities, one of the few denominational colleges at the time to be so recognized.[89]

As the college prospered in the post-war years, some thought was given during the mid to late 1950s, notably by Gerald F. Lahey, S.J., the Rector from 1954 to 1959, to separate physically the college from the high school, which was housed in the Junior Building. One

88 George E. Nunan, S.J., letter to Gérard Goulet, s.j., 11 August 1954; Gerald F. Lahey, S.J., letter to Archbishop Paul-Émile Cardinal Léger, 11 October 1954; George E. Nunan, S.J., letter to Jean-Baptiste Janssens, s.j., 18 October 1954; Gérard Goulet, s.j., letter to Gerald F. Lahey, S.J., 24 October 1954; George E. Nunan, S.J., letter to Gerald F. Lahey, S.J., 1 November 1954; Paul Vanier, s.j., letter to George E. Nunan, S.J., 7 November 1954; George E. Nunan, S.J., letter to Gerald F. Lahey, S.J., 8 November 1954; Gérard Goulet, s.j., letter to Gerald F. Lahey, S.J., 12 November 1954; Gerald F. Lahey, S.J., letter to George E. Nunan, S.J., 16 November 1954; Gerald F. Lahey, S.J., letter to George E. Nunan, S.J., 22 December 1954; Memorandum of Gérard Goulet, s.j., to the Rectors of the French Canadian Colleges in Montreal, 3 January 1955; Gerald F. Lahey, S.J., letter to George E. Nunan, S.J., 10 July 1957; Gerald F. Lahey, S.J., letter to George E. Nunan, S.J., 7 August 1957; Gerald F. Lahey, S.J., letter to George E. Nunan, S.J., 30 August 1957; Gerald F. Lahey, S.J., letter to Jean-Baptiste Janssens, s.j., 4 October 1957; Gerald F. Lahey, S.J., letter to George E. Nunan, S.J., 9 October 1957; George E. Nunan, S.J., letter to Gerald F. Lahey, S.J., 20 October 1957; Gordon F. George, S.J., letter to Gerald F. Lahey, S.J., 1 November 1957; Gerald F. Lahey, S.J., letter to Gordon F. George, S.J., 12 November 1957, AJC, Box C-414.

89 In 1965, the National Conference of Canadian Universities (NCCU) was renamed the Association of Universities and Colleges in Canada (AUCC).

such attempt by Lahey in 1958 to move more than 570 high school students from their building to the "South Campus"—the rather scruffy playing field south of Sherbrooke Street, opposite the main college building—seemed to many to be highly desirable, at first. Yet soon it was thought less so. Shortly, it became clear that any move of the school was Lahey's attempt to improve the useable space for the college by taking over the Junior Building for a faculty building and a college library, or for a science building. His plans met with stiff opposition from many quarters. On closer examination, and given Lahey's "Development Plan for Loyola College", which he had launched in 1957 to expand the college's academic facilities, most Jesuits preferred to leave well enough alone. There was always the ongoing shortage of money for them to be concerned about, and many feared Lahey's lack of practical sense and wondered whether he had thought through all the implications inherent in his development plan. Never a man to delegate authority, he governed as secretly as possible, consulted rarely, and generally controlled everything on campus. As information about his plans gradually spread, the opposition mounted. The majority of Jesuit and lay people alike preferred to leave the school where it was and to build a new college library at the corner of Sherbrooke Street and West Broadway Avenue, on the left side of the Administration Building, to balance the chapel on the opposite side.[90]

Whether Lahey ever hoped to implement his grand plan for development is not easy to judge. Certainly, for various reasons, sufficient numbers of people, including several fellow Jesuits, opposed his plans for the high school to have given him pause. By mid 1958, he had changed his mind about wanting to move the high school across the street and now wanted to leave that area for a new college building. He had become persuaded that a high school building on the South Campus would not help form what he called the new "image" of Loyola College that he was trying to create. Within that image he did not include a high school. In fact, as he eventually came to believe, a new science building on the South Campus would give a far better image to the English-speaking Catholic Montrealers of a progressing Loyola-College-to-Loyola-University than any high school building in

---

90   DJB, vol. 1, 32; 178.

that location ever would. "Image," he wrote on 27 June 1958 to Gordon F. George, S.J., the Provincial Superior (1957–1963), concerning the future use of the South Campus, "is important and will not be created if the new building is a High School."[91]

The end result was that by 1959, nothing had come of any of his plans, either of moving the school off the main college campus or of constructing a science building on the South Campus. That was due to the strong opposition to his plans for developing Loyola College, and to lack of finances. It was also greatly due to the fact that, under the guise of health reasons, Lahey was removed from office in the summer of 1959.

To a large degree, the long years under the rectorship of Patrick G. Malone, S.J., from 1959 to 1974, were among the most exciting and yet, for many, the most heart-breaking in the history of Loyola College. Greatly gifted in administrative skills, in elocution and in the art of calculated politics, Malone was an intelligent, forward-looking man, yet peppery and difficult at times to get on with, very determined and willing to take political risks. He was once described thus: "On all accounts, he was a powerful, somewhat daunting person, with a very strong personality and the will-power to match it. Anyone who had dealings with him had to learn quickly that he could be formidable, even difficult to contend with, and that confrontation was as much his style as anything else. It was well to be very prepared, with every detail in mind, before entering into any discussion with him."[92]

With his fiery temper and abrupt mannerisms, Malone was not always understood or liked, and was never popular in the minds of those who, to their dismay, watched Loyola College radically and rapidly changing from a college to becoming a university in all but name. He had to withstand some vigorous opposition, including from some of his fellow Jesuits who worried that the college was slipping from Jesuit control. Yet he seemed almost not to care what his detractors said. As he once remarked, "I am engaged in education, not in a popularity contest." It showed. By the mid 1960s, Loyola College was

---

91   Gerald F. Lahey, S.J., letter to Gordon F. George, SJ., 27 June 1958, AJC, Box C-414; DJB, vol. 1, 178.

92   DJB, vol. 2, 197.

scarcely recognizable compared to what it had been a mere decade previously.[93]

Indeed, immediately after Malone became Rector, the college began to expand rapidly in numbers. He searched increasingly for more space. With the Junior Building a physically intricate part of the college's building, Malone, not surprisingly, like Lahey before him, soon had his eyes on it for the college. Again as with Lahey, he faced rigorous opposition to taking over the Junior Building for the college. In the end, he gave up that idea and set out to carry out an extensive building plan that would last for another decade and more.

As Rector in the early 1920s, Hingston had made an effort to share some of the responsibilities of governing with an advisory board of prominent Montreal laymen. In the end, given the fact that the Jesuits saw themselves alone as the owners of Loyola, Hingston's efforts to form some kind of an external board never had much effect. Or at least, such an advisory board greatly depended on how much advice a Rector was willing to take. Certainly, the board that Hingston set up served Loyola well, especially in financial matters, and a board of advisers continued to meet with the subsequent Rectors during the following decades, frequently to help in fundraising and in certain legal issues pertaining to the provincial government. Yet the board was given no governing authority whatsoever.

By the late 1950s and early 1960s, therefore, nothing fundamentally had changed in that regard. Malone continued to govern as previous Rectors had governed, by accepting as little advice as possible from any board or often, for the most part, from anyone else, either. In fact, until 1969, he was the Chair of the Corporation ("Trustees") of Loyola College, which included the college, the high school, and the Jesuit Community, and whose membership consisted of Jesuits only.

Under mounting pressure, however, from several quarters within Loyola College and from within the Jesuits themselves, to have a more active voice in the governance of the institution, steps were taken in 1964 to clarify the distinction between the governance of the college, the high school, and the Jesuit Community. In that year, the Jesuits

---

93   Ibid., 196–197.

had all three of these entities incorporated separately. Each one was granted a different governing board which, at least theoretically, would allow each entity greater control over its own destiny. It would take, however, another five years before Malone, as Superior, would relinquish being chair of all three corporations, and several more years after that before there was a clear distinction made between the board of the college and the board of the high school.

Although that change of structure in 1964 had gained little attention beyond the Jesuits at Loyola, it was highly significant. In fact, it was the beginning of a fundamental rearranging of Jesuit governing structures at Loyola College. Nonetheless, even if after 1969 Malone was no longer in charge of the three corporations, he continued to hold enormous influence and power: he controlled the agenda. Among the more pressing issues was the untangling of finances so that the high school and the college would receive a balanced share. That took a long time, and Malone was a hard negotiator who favoured the college first and foremost. With the appointment on 1 August 1969 of Cecil C. Ryan, S.J., as Rector of the Loyola Jesuit Community, the situation began to clarify somewhat, since there was now a definite separation of the offices of the Rector of the college from that of the high school and that of the Jesuit Community. Malone became Rector, or President, of the college solely, but was also no longer chair of the corporation of the college or of the high school. J. Gerald MacGuigan, S.J., was appointed chair of the "Loyola Trustees" as of 1 August 1969, which in fact—however ambiguous it may have appeared at times—meant being chair of both separate corporations.[94] That situation remained until 1972, when two chairs were appointed: one for the college's corporation, and one for the high school's corporation. Some Jesuits, too, who sat on one board, often sat on the other. Yet that made for a conflict of interest, on occasion. Governance was never as simple or clear cut as many desired at the time.

Amongst Malone's greatest aspirations when he began as Rector was to develop the college academically by obtaining a university charter. No matter how long and unsuccessful, even, at times, tortuous, had

---

94   MacGuigan remained chair for two years, after which Stanley P. Drummond, S.J., became chair of both boards until 1972, when he resigned as chair of the high school board.

been the attempts to receive a university charter since 1899, Malone was never daunted by the history of those past failures. Perhaps there had been so many futile attempts in pursuit of a charter that his combative instincts were sharpened. Never one to back down from a challenge, he believed that if the college looked and acted like a university, it would become one. Not long after his arrival in the college, the letterhead on its stationery said it all: "Loyola of Montreal".[95]

Somehow he managed to maintain his optimism about obtaining a charter, an optimism that few others shared, and that many believed to be wrong-headed and an altogether unpromising undertaking. Malone thought otherwise. Indeed, within a year after his arrival at Loyola, he confidently wrote to Angus J. Macdougall, S.J., Rector of Campion College, that "I have had a number of meetings with people in high places. Both his Eminence [Cardinal Léger] and the Premier of the Province [Jean Lesage] are favourably disposed towards giving Loyola a Charter. In fact, it now seems as if we might have University Status during the current session [of the Quebec Legislature]." That was not to be.[96]

The matter of a charter eventually would be resolved by the Parent Commission, appointed by Premier LeSage (1960–1966). Mgr. Alphonse-Marie Parent delivered his "Le rapport de la Commission royale d'enquête sur l'enseignemente dans la province de Québec" in two stages during 1964 and 1966. A key recommendation was that Loyola College should form a Catholic university with the all-girls Marianopolis College, St. Joseph's Teachers' College, and the Thomas More Institute.

Despite Malone's effort to carry through the commission's recommendation, nothing came of it. The Sisters of the Congregation of Notre-Dame, who administered Marianopolis College, were rightly concerned and cautious. Given the size, prestige, and dominance of Loyola College and the Jesuits among the English-speaking Catholic population in Montreal, no doubt the Sisters had good reason to fear that their voice would scarcely get a hearing in such a union. Although

---

95   Ibid., 197.

96   Patrick G. Malone, S.J., letter to Angus J. Macdougall, S.J., 6 September 1960, AJC, Box C-256.

Saint Joseph's Teacher's College began drawing up plans to move close by Loyola's campus and to integrate its faculty and personnel, in the end it, Marianopolis College, and the Thomas More Institute, fearful of being engulfed by Loyola College, rejected Malone's efforts outright.

Earlier in 1960, and to achieve his plan of developing Loyola College into a university, Malone had set out to raise over $20 million for the construction of four buildings, to acquire four others, and to renovate existing ones, along with establishing several new departments. That was a necessity after the college became co-educational in order for it to cope with the yearly increase in students. From around 850 students in 1959, the enrolment increased rapidly, leaping to nearly 13,000 students in a few short years, along with the proportionate number of professors and staff to match such increases.[97]

The early to mid 1960s were the years of the Second Vatican Council. In the spirit of that council, Malone resolutely became an advocate of ecumenism, interfaith dialogue, and a wide international outlook. Although born in Belfast, he was never much given to the habit of many English-speaking Catholic Montrealers of maintaining overly sentimental links to Ireland, especially referring to themselves as "Irish". He had a deep respect for and pride in Canada, and refused to be a hyphenated "Irish-Canadian". At heart, he was determined to shift the college away from its rather narrow inward-looking Montreal English-speaking "Irish" Catholic base to a broader, more ecumenical, international one. He believed that Catholic values and theology had nothing to lose and much to offer in any academic exchange. To that end, he encouraged the establishment of Judaic Studies, one of the first of its kind in Canada, and a programme of East African studies—something then almost unknown in Canada—and invited philosophers and theologians of many faiths to join the faculty. As well, he encouraged and supported John E. O'Brian, S.J., in establishing the first permanent communication arts programme in the country.[98]

Whatever the physical and academic advances of Loyola College— and there were many—from the early 1960s to the mid 1970s, those

---

97   The amount of $20 million would have the value of over $155 million today.

98   DJB, vol. 2, 197.

were also difficult years. Not only was there a growing dissatisfaction at Malone's style of governance and the Jesuits' sole control of the board of trustees, there was considerable student and professorial unrest, which sometimes led to serious confrontations. In the midst of that general unrest, there arose the "Santhanam Affair".

Dr. Shankar Santhanam was a sessional lecturer in the department of physics who had received a succession of three one-year contracts. In time, the college made it clear to him that it was not going to re-new his contract on the grounds that his teaching was incompetent, and that he himself had assured the administration, in writing, that he would not remain after July 1969. Whatever the merits of his situation—even his own department had urged the college not to rehire him—his "case" became a flashpoint for extensive disruptions, confrontations, and turbulence on campus at the way the administra-tion was seemingly handling him. On 24 October 1969, most of the students went on strike in protest, while petitions, sit-ins, occupa-tions—even the foyer of the Loyola Jesuit Residence was "occupied" by students and a few faculty members—and gatherings on campus became a regular feature for months during late 1969. Rightly or wrongly, Malone and the Jesuits, along with a few lay faculty members, were painted as right-wing authoritarians, while, on the other side, the protesting faculty members and students were seen as left-wing radicals, "neo-Marxist conspirators", out to take over the college and oust Malone and the Jesuits.

Eventually, Santhanam appealed to the Canadian Association of University Teachers (CAUT) to take up his cause, and with little reason for doing so, CAUT clumsily demanded that Loyola College be censured. Yet Santhanam's case was never strong enough for a censure. CAUT then requested that the two sides submit themselves to arbitration. In turn, the college appealed to the Association of Universities and Colleges of Canada (AUCC) against CAUT. After a five-day occupation of the administration building, police were called in and 500 people were evicted. The end result was that during the week of 12 January 1970, Loyola College closed. Shortly thereafter, AUCC upheld Loyola's appeal, but did point out that "We are of the opinion that the recommendation of the CAUT committee for binding arbitration should not be accepted even though we deplore the fact that those who have encouraged Dr. Santhanam to seek a redress to which he is not entitled have left him in doubly difficult circumstances."[99]

Santhanam was not rehired. In April 1970, Loyola granted him a year's salary, letters of recommendation, and reimbursement for his legal costs. Nonetheless, the damage had been done to Loyola's reputation and to the Jesuits, and it was enormous.[100]

In the midst of all that turmoil, Malone carried on. Yet his reputation also had been damaged severely; even the Montreal newspapers had taken up the fight, publishing highly unflattering articles and cartoons of him. Whether it was a serious move or a ploy will never be known, but on 12 August 1970, Malone submitted his resignation to the board of trustees, which was to take effect on 21 August 1971. That never happened. He remained until Loyola College was no more.

While the negotiations unfolded during the early 1970s to unite Loyola College with Sir George Williams University to form a new university—in the minds of many at Loyola, a dreaded proposition—tensions mounted. Yet, despite the several stalling tactics tried, by 1972, Malone, the Jesuits, and Loyola College had to face the inevitable: there was no alternative but to amalgamate with Sir George Williams University or cease to exist. Protracted discussions and consultations ensued, often in an atmosphere of near hostility, one towards the other institution, each jealously guarding its domain and each considering itself better than the other, despite all the efforts of many to negotiate fairly and peaceably. The strain on Malone and several others took its toll; Malone's health deteriorated from exhaustion and over-indulgence in alcohol.[101]

During the month before he finally did step down as president of Loyola College in August 1974, a rumour was rife about whether he would insist on remaining as one of the chief administrators at the new Concordia University. He had no intention of remaining. When

---

99   *University Affairs*, 11, no. 3, March 1970, 3.

100   Edward F. Sheridan, S.J., letters to Pedro Arrupe, s.j., 23 January 1970; 29 January 1970; 5 June 1970, AJC, Box C-415.

101   DJB, vol. 2, 198.

he left office, he was dean among Canadian university presidents—having served at Loyola College for fifteen years—something rarely achieved by other presidents in Canadian universities. In later years, if Malone ever regretted anything or was disappointed with the outcome of the negotiations or with the final demise of Loyola College, he never admitted to it. Or at least he never did so publicly.[102]

Earlier, during the spring of 1974, and in some odd but inexplicable political manoeuvrings by some members of Loyola's board of trustees and others, the famed Canadian scholar and professor Marshall McLuhan was offered the post of president of Loyola. He certainly was interested, but on one condition: that he might become the chair of the communication arts department after Loyola College joined with Sir George Williams. Since that post of chair was not about to be given to him, nothing further was heard about his possible role at the college during its final months.[103]

In the end, and through it all, clear heads and balanced minds prevailed. The two institutions merged to become Concordia University, with the buildings and grounds of Loyola College becoming the "Loyola Campus" while those of Sir George Williams became the "Downtown Campus". In time, Concordia University was able to amalgamate the best of its two worlds, and developed into a first-rate international university.

Although Malone had stepped down as Rector on 16 August 1974, and left Montreal permanently, Jesuits remained as professors and in some administrative posts for some time at the newly formed Concordia University. Over the subsequent years, several other Jesuits were hired by the university as professors. It took several more years before some Canadian Jesuits would accept that Loyola College was no more and that there were justifiable reasons why it was no more. Indeed, many of Malone's Jesuit colleagues were considerably embittered at him for his failure, as they saw it, in not getting better terms in the amalgamation. They believed that the Jesuit Order had been

---

102   Ibid.; Patrick G. Malone, S.J., letter to J. Gerald MacGuigan, S.J., 12 August 1970, AJC, Box C-415.

103   Gerald W. Tait, S.J., letter to James W. Harmens, 18 March 1974, ibid.; *Loyola News*, 29 March 1974.

"sold out". Others were resentful that the Jesuits' academic presence in Montreal was so greatly diminished that there was no longer much hope for any future Jesuit "voice" in academic circles there.

Still other Jesuits felt disillusioned at all that had transpired during the period of negotiations, and dreamed of returning to the former and, as they imagined, glorious days of Loyola College either by re-negotiating the terms of amalgamation or by founding a new Jesuit Loyola College. Many graduates expressed similar sentiments. That was never going to occur. Even by the end of the 1960s, it had already become obvious to many that the days of Loyola College as a Jesuit-dominated institution were long past. The expansion of the college had seen to that, along with the fact that there were no longer sufficiently qualified or interested Jesuits available to fill the increasing number of available teaching and administrative posts at Loyola College. As the college grew, the Jesuit influence shrank. By 1970, the governing board of Loyola College reflected that new reality: it was principally composed of lay people, with the Jesuit numbers a minority and the Jesuit president, for the most part, answerable more to that lay majority than to his Jesuit Superiors.

Yet the truth remained: however disappointed and even angry so many felt, Jesuit and lay Catholics alike, in every way Loyola College, and especially Malone, had had no option but to negotiate an amalgamation. That was something Malone's fiercest critics never appeared to acknowledge. Indeed, the Quebec government had made it clear by the end of the 1960s: amalgamate or face extinction. In the heated, even at times turbulent political atmosphere of the 1960s and early 1970s in Quebec, there was no possibility that any Quebec government, separatist or federalist, would allow four English-language universities to continue in the province. Of those four, three were in Montreal. It also quickly became evident that McGill University would survive, whatever befell the other three. The well-respected undergraduate Bishop's University in far-off Lennoxville, Quebec, well away from the hurly-burly of the political debates in Montreal and Quebec City, was allowed to continue to serve a minority English-speaking population in the Eastern Townships.[104]

---

104   Terence G. Walsh, S.J., letter to Patrick G. Malone, S.J., 8 May 1973, AJC, Box C-415.

All the same, if the Jesuit presence and influence had waned on the campus of Loyola College by the mid 1970s, it did not become entirely extinct for another thirty years. In a city where the Jesuits had flourished among English-speaking Catholics for over 130 years, the opportunities for them were still there. It only took imagination and a desire to make the most of the situation. M. John Belair, S.J., as the then Jesuit Superior of the Loyola Jesuit Community—still in its residence on the edge of the Loyola Campus—had those qualities in abundance.

Belair set out in 1975 with a group of like-minded Jesuits and lay people to create a new forum on Concordia's Loyola Campus for intellectual reflection, discussion, and teaching. In company with Dr. Sean E. McEvenue, himself a Jesuit graduate, administrator, scholar, and professor at Concordia University, Michael A. Fahey, S.J., likewise a Concordia University professor, scholar, and theologian, Marc Gervais, s.j., a distinguished film critic, writer, and professor of film at the university, along with other Jesuit and lay professors, Belair helped establish, in 1979, Lonergan University College in a house owned by the Loyola Jesuit Community close by the Loyola Campus. Named after Bernard J. F. Lonergan, S.J. (1904–1984), the renowned Canadian theologian and international scholar, the college was set up in the style of an Oxbridge college. It opened during that summer, and in September received its first students and fellows. McEvenue became its first principal. Humanistic in orientation and non-denominational in character, with fellows principally drawn from the university's various departments, the objective of the college was to allow fellows, students, and visitors to engage in interdisciplinary dialogue around fundamental values in culture, history, art, science, philosophy, and religion.[105]

In short order, the college became an important intellectual centre on campus. It attracted large numbers from the campus and the city to its public lectures, seminars, and other events, such as the popular weekly "Thursdays at Lonergan" lecture and discussion series. Later, the renowned scholar Charles Davis served as the college's principal from 1987 until 1991. Over the years, too, among the many who were

---

105   DJB, vol. 1, 188–191.

elected fellows in the college were several Jesuits who were actively engaged in and greatly supportive of this scholarly endeavour, until its closing at the turn of the new century.[106]

From the mid 1980s onwards, the Loyola Jesuit Community again sought new ways of using its resources—intellectual and financial—at Concordia University. To that end, in late 1987 and early 1988, with the enthusiastic support of many at the university, the Jesuits explored the possibility of having on Loyola Campus a centre for the study of international peace, a growing area of academic interest in many Canadian universities at that time. Thus was founded in early September 1988, by Joseph B. Gavin, S.J., and Sandra De Rome, with the assistance of Gervais and Drummond, the Loyola Jesuit Institute for the Studies of International Peace (The Loyola Peace Institute) on the Loyola Campus of Concordia University. In 1990, David R. Eley, S.J., who had become a member of the chaplaincy's team on campus, also joined the institute's staff.

Financed wholly by the Loyola Jesuit Community and the Jesuit Province of Upper Canada, the institute was incorporated separately from the university, with its governing board made up of Jesuits and lay women and men. It rapidly became a place on campus for the study and reflection of peace and war. Set up somewhat similarly to Lonergan College, but without fellows, it offered frequent public lectures, forums, and seminars, and published several of those lectures. Among the institute's more significant achievements were an international symposium on peace and war and the establishment of an interdisciplinary credit course on international peace studies at the university.

The symposium was held in late September 1993 on the theme of armaments, children, and world population. Invited international scholars from France, Canada, Sweden, and the United States presented papers and held formal and informal sessions over a three-day period. The lectures and public discussions were published in book form in 1994.[107]

---

106 Ibid., vol. 1, 188–191; vol. 2, 11–13.

107 Joseph B. Gavin, S.J., ed., *Armaments, Children and World Population: An International Symposium* (Montreal: Loyola Peace Institute, 1994).

The course on international peace altogether proved to be both popular and long lasting. Under the supervision of Gavin and Eley, and in cooperation with Lonergan College, various professors of the university were invited to lecture weekly on a theme of war and peace from their discipline's perspective. The interdisciplinary course on peace studies shortly became a permanent choice among the university's optional credit courses. At present, it is offered in the department of political science, and continues to attract students every year.

When Gavin stepped down in 1996 after eight years as director, Eley succeeded him. Regrettably, however, growing financial restraints, a waning of interest on campus in the theme of peace and war, the curtailing of the institute's presence and profile on campus by some university administrators, and a lack of organizational focus and direction in time had reduced the effectiveness of the institute. It closed in the summer of 2004.

Over the years since 1974, other significant Jesuit academic contributions continued at Concordia University, most notably by individual Jesuits in the departments of communications, biology, theological studies, physics, and chemistry, and at the Loyola chapel and the chaplaincy. When, in early March 2004, the Jesuits departed from their residence, Concordia University, which had purchased the residence and extensive property from them in 2001, converted it to a residence for graduate students. Later, in 2006, to honour the Jesuits who had worked at Loyola College and Concordia University, the board of governors of the university formally named it "The Jesuit Residence".[108]

In addition, alumni and alumnae of Loyola College, and the Jesuits of English-speaking Canada, also desirous of marking the Jesuits' contribution to the university, refurbished the former Jesuits' refectory building on the Loyola Campus to serve as an alumni centre, lounge, conference centre, kitchen, and catering services. Completed in 1916, it had remained the Jesuits' refectory until February 1969, when they moved to their new residence nearby. Since that time, it had largely

---

108   The residence had opened on the edge of the college's campus in February 1969. At the time the university purchased it from the Jesuits, an agreement was reached whereby the Jesuits could remain in the building until March 2004.

served as space for the department of music. In a ceremony of dedication on 15 May 2008, the university officially named it "The Jesuit Refectory Building".

On that same day in 2008, the announcement by the university and the Loyola Alumni Association of *The Loyola Lecture Series* at Concordia University capped the long-standing efforts of many to keep alive the Jesuits' name and intellectual contributions in English-speaking Montreal. Established as a tribute to the Jesuit tradition of promoting education, both secular and spiritual, through excellence in research, learning, and service, the lecture series aims to address social and ethical contemporary issues. The first of these annual lectures was delivered in September 2009.

In 2005, after over forty years of teaching, Gervais left the university. A year later, the last Jesuit to teach at Concordia University, Gavin, also left his teaching post in the department of theological studies. With that, the Jesuits departed. The dreams for Loyola College of O'Bryan, Jones, MacMahon, Filion, Hingston, de la Peza, Brown, McCaffrey, Lahey, Malone, and many others may not have been fulfilled quite in the manner they expected. Nevertheless, the college still seems to remain in the hearts of hundreds and hundreds of its graduates and their descendants, and in the beautiful old college buildings on Sherbrooke Street West.

At the same time, it is important to recognize that the Jesuit educational ideals endure in Montreal in other institutions of higher education. Not only are they at the heart of Concordia University, through Loyola College as one of its founders, but they are also present through Collège Sainte-Marie at Université de Québec à Montréal, through the Thomas More Institute, which has become part of Bishop's University, and at McGill University, through monies granted it from the Jesuit Estates' settlement.

II

ONTARIO

SANDWICH (WINDSOR): ASSUMPTION COLLEGE, 1842–1859

"Embroiled in the uncertainties of far-off Sandwich"
—Jean-Baptiste Hus, s.j.

The belief that Catholics should be educated in Catholic universities and colleges was a fundamental part of Catholic thinking in nineteenth-century Canada. Establishing an alternative educational system at all levels was considered the only sure safeguard for the Catholic faith, notably against the perceived evils of the day: secularism, rationalism, modernism, liberalism, and Protestantism. That thinking remained inherent in Catholic culture, both French-speaking and English-speaking, for generations. Not surprisingly, therefore, many bishops were anxious to set up colleges in their dioceses. They frequently turned to the one Order in the Church that they believed could meet that educational challenge, the one with the reputation and record for running such institutions of higher learning: the Jesuits.

Michael Power of Toronto was one such bishop. Ever since he left Laprairie in 1842, he had hoped that the Jesuits would establish a college at Sandwich that would be a centre for the native missions in Canada West. In 1843, and in anticipation of founding such a college, he restored Assumption parish to the Jesuits; three years later, Pierre Point, s.j., completed the nave of the church that, it was hoped, would serve the new college.[1]

At the same time, the bishop had been wanting the Jesuits to open a college in Toronto. That was not to be during his lifetime. Instead, they had chosen a New York site. There, on the Old Rose Hill Farm in Fordham to the north of New York City, the Jesuits assumed direction of St. John's College (later Fordham University) in 1846, their first college of the newly established New York–Canada Mission.[2]

It was left to Power's successor, Armand François-Marie, Compte de Charbonnel (1850–1860), to pursue the possibility of founding a college with Jesuit assistance. Ever amenable to having Jesuits in his diocese, in 1850 he set out to persuade Rémi-Joseph Tellier, s.j., to open a residence for Jesuits in Toronto that in time would lead to their establishing a college. Again, that never happened, despite the follow-up efforts during the 1850s of a prominent Catholic convert, the Honourable John Elmsley, to attract the Jesuits to Toronto. He even offered a piece of prime property near Yonge Street and close by the new University of Toronto campus for a Jesuit college. They decided not to accept his offer.[3]

---

1   For Bishop Power, cf. Robert J. Scollard, C.S.B., *Historical Notes*, 29 (1964–1965), 29; 83. Sandwich is part of present-day Windsor, Ontario.

2   St. John's College had been founded in 1841 by Bishop John Hughes of New York. A seminary in all but name, the college received its charter in 1846, and a few months later the Jesuits arrived to staff it. Soon St. John's became principally an undergraduate college. It changed its name to Fordham University in 1907. The university remains an institution of higher education of the New York Province of the Society of Jesus.

3   DCB, vol. XII, 182–185; vol. IX (1976), 781; DJB, vol. 1, 20; 133; Lecompte, 248–251. Over 100 years later, there was another proposal to establish a Jesuit college there. In a letter of 27 June 1960, the Provincial Superior, Gordon F. George, noted to Archbishop Patrick J. Skinner, C.J.M., of St. John's: "This evening I am to attend a meeting of leading Catholics of Toronto whose aim it is to have a Catholic college in the new York University here in Toronto." That aim was never fulfilled. Gordon F. George, S.J., letter to Archbishop Patrick J. Skinner, C.J.M., 27 June 1960, AJC, Box C-256.

Bishop de Charbonnel opened St. Michael's College (later officially known as The University of St. Michael's College) on 15 September 1852; it was placed under the direction of the Christian Brothers. By February 1853, however, the Basilian Fathers, who had arrived in Toronto the previous August, took charge of the college. Later that Spring, they purchased lots on Elmsley's property in what is now central Toronto, and the college moved there. In time, it became the pre-eminent Catholic liberal arts college in English-speaking Canada during the nineteenth century.

To a degree, Bishops Power and de Charbonnel did get their Jesuit college, but not in Toronto. With the Jesuits already present in the Sandwich area, Bishop de Charbonnel approved the establishing of a college there in 1854, to be built under the guidance of Pierre Point, s.j. The bishop knew that Point had been strongly promoting the idea of Catholic education throughout that region of south-western Canada West since his arrival in 1843. His vision was that of the traditional Jesuit model: a college with a *cours classique* programme, an attached residence for Jesuits, and a collegiate/parish church. At first, his plans were modest. Although determined that a college would be established, and that in time the Jesuits might accept its administration, he wanted another religious congregation to administer and staff the college, since there were too few Jesuits at Sandwich. Over and above establishing the customary Jesuit humanistic college, therefore, Point's major intent was to help strengthen the presence of the French language in that isolated area of the colony.[4]

In 1854, he chaired a meeting to begin fundraising for a college building. The task had fallen to him of supervising the building's construction, recruiting teachers, and overseeing the general administration of the college and its finances. Before long, though, Bishop de Charbonnel became concerned that the new college, which had been named Assumption College, might compete with St. Michael's College in Toronto. He thus limited Assumption College to the status of a boys' Catholic high school. On 10 February 1857, it opened. Due

---

4   DJB, vol. 1, 286–289. For a history of the Catholic Church in Franco-Ontario of the nineteenth century, cf. Robert Choquette, *L'Église catholique dans l'Ontario français du dix-neuvième siècle* (Ottawa: Éditions de l'Université d'Ottawa, 1984).

to poverty and the small population, however, only twenty boarders and sixty day-students registered.[5]

Early in 1856, Pierre-Adolphe Pinsoneault, a Sulpician priest from Montreal, had been appointed the first bishop of the London diocese. Against considerable opposition, including that of Bishop de Charbonnel, he immediately moved the see to Sandwich, where he himself settled. Bishop Pinsoneault argued that the London area, which consisted mainly of English-speaking Irish immigrants, did not have a sufficient number of Catholics to justify having the see there, while Sandwich had a considerable French-speaking Catholic population. His removing the see to Sandwich and changing its name, however, were not helped by his clear antagonism to English-speaking people, especially the Irish immigrants.[6]

In every way, he quickly proved to be difficult and unpredictable, but even worse for the Jesuits, showed little sympathy towards their educational aspirations. Wishing to combine Assumption College with a minor seminary, and contrary to the advice and desires of Bishop de Charbonnel, Bishop Pinsoneault insisted that the Jesuits should expand the college to include a collegiate programme of studies. Since the Jesuits would not assume administration of the college, the bishop persuaded the Congregation of Saint Basil (Basilian Fathers) to send Joseph Malbos, C.S.B., to be in charge of the college. Even though Point had no responsibility for the college, he was not happy to see Malbos introduced on the scene. Before long, relations between the bishop and the Jesuits became complex and strained.[7]

To resolve the situation, in 1857 the Jesuits left the college by order of the Mission's Superior in New York, Jean-Baptiste Hus, s.j. After visiting the college earlier that year to assess the state of affairs, Hus had refused to supply more Jesuits, citing a lack of manpower. In truth, however, he was more intent on developing and staffing St. John's

---

5   Francis J. Nelligan, S.J., *Jesuits in Ontario a Century Ago*, unpublished manuscript, vol. 2, 7, AJC, Box C-401. By September 1857, twelve seminarians had registered.

6   Lecompte, 174–181. The see was later renamed the "London diocese" and returned to London after John Walsh became bishop in 1867.

7   Nelligan, op. cit. Malbos had been the treasurer for the Basilians at Saint Michael's College, Toronto, and arrived in Sandwich on 7 November 1857. He quit after a year. Scollard, 6 (1965), 103–112.

College in Fordham and St. Francis Xavier College in central New York than becoming embroiled in the political and financial uncertainties in far-off Sandwich.[8]

Notwithstanding Bishop Pinsoneault's lack of sympathy for the Jesuits, yet unable to attract any more Basilian priests or other teaching priests to Assumption College, he sought help directly from Pieter Jan Beckx, Superior General of the Jesuits (1853–1887). Nothing resulted from that request. In the end, though, and contrary to his predecessor's decision, the new Jesuit Superior of the New York–Canada Mission, William Stock Murphy, favoured the bishop's plans and decided to accept the college. By then, however, it was too late. Although Murphy had appointed two Jesuits to the college before he visited Sandwich in early September 1859, the day after his arrival, in a surprise move, Bishop Pinsoneault announced by means of a hand-delivered letter to Murphy that he had confiscated the college's property and the Jesuits' residence. In fact, he wanted the residence as his episcopal palace until he could construct a new and grander one. In that letter, he also issued an ultimatum: the Jesuits were either to assume responsibility for St. Peter's parish in London or leave the diocese altogether.[9]

They were not about to assume that responsibility. In effect, there-fore, the bishop dismissed the Jesuits from their parish and mission. Except for some three to five Jesuits remaining until 1874 at St. Joseph's parish in Chatham, they left the diocese for good in October 1859. Strangely, though, given Pinsoneault's vigorous support of French Canadians over English-speaking Canadians, he ordered that English would be the principal language at Assumption College "as in Toronto, [with] French the accessory."[10]

---

8   The Jesuits founded St. Francis Xavier College in 1847.

9   Nelligan, op. cit.; Scollard, 23 (1964–1966), 170; 29 (1964–1966), 35. In 1859, he had also in-vited the Basilian Fathers to teach at Assumption.

10   Scollard, 6 (1965), 107–108. Cf. John W. Keleher, "The Reverend Father John E. Holzer, s.j.," *Historic Guelph: the Royal City* (Guelph Historical Society, 1986–1987), 26; and John P. Comis-key, *My Heart's Best Wishes for You: A Biography of Archbishop John Walsh* (Montreal: McGill-Queen's University Press, 2012) for an account of Pinsoneault and the Jesuits, and those early years in Sandwich/London diocese. Eventually, and under the direction of the Basilian Fathers, Assumption College expanded considerably to become Assumption University in 1956, and then formed the nucleus of the University of Windsor when that institution was founded sev-en years later. Assumption University remains the Catholic presence within the University of Windsor.

GUELPH: ST. IGNATIUS COLLEGE, 1847–1864

"Dream unrealized"
—John Holzer, s.j.

During the years following their departure from Sandwich, the Jesuits received many requests to establish or assume responsibility for colleges in Canada West. An early proposal for a college in the Guelph area had been made around 1847, when Bishop Power succeeded in attracting some German-speaking Jesuit missionaries from the Continent. He had hoped that they would build a small college at St. Agatha (in the present-day Kitchener area). Nothing came of that, however.[11]

Since 1848, John Holzer, s.j., had been serving the scattered German-speaking Catholic population in that area. At the request of Bishop de Charbonnel, he settled in Guelph in 1852. Yet even before he had arrived in Guelph, he had had in mind to establish there several much-needed educational and social institutions to serve the local Catholics. What he found on arriving, however, was a small, poverty-stricken Catholic population, which was slightly more than 17 percent of the total households in Guelph, and St. Bartholomew's, an unfinished stone Catholic church, with an unsuitable presbytery, both of which were perched squarely at the front of "Catholic Hill", the highest piece of property in Guelph.[12]

At the time of the city's founding in 1827, the superintendent of the Canada Company, John Galt, himself a Presbyterian, had given the hill to the Catholics as a compliment to his friend Bishop Alexander Macdonell of Kingston (1826–1840). Macdonell Street, which leads directly towards "Catholic Hill", was named after the bishop. It remains thus to this day.[13]

---

11   For an account of the establishment of the Catholic Church in the area before the mid 1850s, cf. Arthur P. Monaghan, "Catholicism in the Hamilton Area before the Establishment of the Diocese in 1856," CCHA, *Report* 23 (1956), 29–39.

12   DJB, vol. 1, 146–147; Lecompte, 258–259. According to the census of 1860, the population of Guelph was 5,140, with 1,176 of those being Catholics.

13   Lecompte, 257.

The anti-Catholic Anglican establishment in Upper Canada was not pleased at that gift. As a result, the Catholics were feeling considerable duress from local anti-Catholic sentiment and violence, and they often were under siege by hostile members of the Orange Lodge and some local Protestant ministers who were determined to rout them off "Catholic Hill". Such displays of hostility fuelled considerable sectarian rivalry, and violent confrontations between Catholics and Protestants were not unusual in Canada West in the 1850s and 1860s.[14]

Stories abounded, some true, others highly overstated, that reflected the serious religious hostilities and tensions of the day. Rumours had been around ever since 1846, at the time St. Bartholomew's church was being constructed, that the Catholics had placed a cannon in the tower for protection against the local Orangemen and other Protestants. Later, a notorious incident—undoubtedly somewhat embellished—occurred in 1856, four years after Holzer's arrival, which again, it was said, involved a cannon. Some hot-headed, bigoted Catholics ambushed members of the Orange Lodge returning to Guelph from nearby Rockwood following a picnic celebrating 12 July. The militia at Guelph was called out to rescue the Protestants, who had been held captive in a hotel. A year later, the Orangemen planned revenge following the 12 July celebrations; they sent threatening messages to Holzer, promising to burn the church and schools to the ground after the day's festivities. According to a story later spread

---

14 Cf. Debra L. Nash-Chambers, "In the Palm of God's Hand? The Irish Catholic Experience in Mid Nineteenth Century Guelph", CCHA, *Historical Studies*, 51 (1984), 67–87. Such religious antagonism continued well into the twentieth century. The most infamous episode occurred beginning at 21.30 hrs on 17 June 1918. That was the so-called Guelph Raid that was made on the Jesuit Novitiate—situated on a farm at the edge of Guelph—on the pretence that the Jesuits were hiding men who should have been on the war front, and thus were violating the Military Service Act. It was clearly an anti-Catholic, anti-Jesuit incident spurred on by relentless attacks from national newspapers and Guelph's Protestant ministers—a Presbyterian minister, the Reverend Kennedy Palmer, was especially virulent—and headed by a particularly bigoted military leader, Captain A. C. Macaulay, Assistant Deputy Provost Marshall. He appeared at the novitiate in mufti demanding to search the place, but refused, when asked, to show identification papers. The Honourable Charles Doherty, the father of a novice, Marcus Doherty, was the Minister of Justice at the time; he was eventually contacted by telephone in Ottawa. In the end, and after an official investigation by a Royal Commission (September 1919), the Jesuits were exonerated while Macaulay was disciplined. The national scandal that erupted as a result of the raid lasted for years afterwards. Cf. Brian Hogan, C.S.S.B., "The Guelph Novitiate Raid: Conscription, Censorship and Bigotry during the Great War", CCHA *Study Sessions* 45 (1978), 57–80; and Mark Reynolds, "The Guelph Raid," *The Beaver* 82, no. 1 (2002), 25–30.

about, under his direction—and however riskily—the Catholics managed to haul a small cannon into the tower of the church. They pointed
it squarely down Macdonell Street, and thus dared the Protestants
to attack. In the end, the attackers—mainly local Protestant farmers
and some townspeople, who were armed with fiery torches, scythes,
firearms, and whatever they could lay hold of—thought better of it.
They retreated, their hopes thwarted of setting "Catholic Hill" alight
from the burning of Catholic buildings. Clearly, though, even if the
Catholics physically could have hauled a cannon—no matter how
small—into the church's tower, whose interior was made of wood, their
action was hazardous, given the possibility of the cannon plunging
through to the bottom of the tower.[15]

Undaunted by the conflicts and the local poverty, and determined
to inspire confidence and cohesiveness among the Catholic population, Holzer set to work with a wide-ranging educational and social
plan for the Catholics. He assisted in the building of two elementary
schools, St. Anne's, for girls (1854), and St. Stanislaus, for boys (1855),
and a girls' convent school, Loretto Academy (1856); he also purchased
twenty acres of land in 1859 for a proposed St. Joseph's hospital, which
would include a home for the elderly and an orphanage (1862).[16]

As well, by the early 1860s, St. Bartholomew's was greatly in
need of repair, and had become too small for the congregation.[17]
Consequently, and despite a heavy debt on the church, in 1864 Holzer
embarked on building a new and large church patterned in every
way on Cologne's immense mediaeval cathedral. His idea was that
the church would be the centre point on "Catholic Hill". Yet that plan
had to be abandoned due to the protests of the parishioners. It was
too costly and too elaborate for their tastes. Construction was soon
permanently called off.[18]

---

15   Lecompte, 264–266.

16   Cf. Nash-Chambers, 74ff.

17   Lecompte, 258. The first church on the site was set afire in 1846 by a firebrand, an Orangeman,
     or so it was believed by the parishioners.

18   Lecompte, 270. In short order, the debt ballooned to over $20,000.00, the equivalent at present
     to about $275,000.00. In the end, and however magnificent in size and in architectural beauty,
     the present neo-gothic French-style Church of Our Lady Immaculate, which was later built by
     Pierre Hamel, s.j., to replace the old St. Bartholomew's, is far more modest in size than Holzer's

Most important of Holzer's plans, though, would be the founding of a Jesuit college modelled on the Jesuits' classical college. Despite the initial opposition of the bishop of Hamilton to such a college, Holzer hoped that it would draw the young male Catholics of the area, mainly of German and Irish lineage, away from the Protestant schools and colleges to receive a Catholic education. To that end, and with the eventual approval of the bishop, the bill incorporating the College of Saint Ignatius was passed on 7 May 1862 in the legislature, and given royal assent on 9 June 1862. The act noted that a "college" had been founded in 1855, but without naming it. That was St. Stanislaus, the boys' elementary school founded by Holzer. The signees of the new college's corporation were Bishop John Farrell of Hamilton (1856–1873), John Holzer, s.j., John McGuaid, S.J., Francis C. Dumortier, s.j., and Hector Glackmeyer, s.j.[19]

The first meeting of the college's corporation was held on 12 May 1863. It confirmed the college's administrators and professors: Holzer, president, administrator and treasurer; Charles Petitdemange, s.j., prefect of studies; Mr. Francis Lynch, B.A., professor of rhetoric, Belles-Lettres, and English literature; Mr. John O'Connor, assistant professor of Latin and Greek; John B. Archibald, S.J., chaplain; Charles Petitdemange, s.j., librarian; Mr. John O'Connor, assistant librarian; Mr. Joseph Monde, teacher of music. Later, during that summer, Holzer opened the College of Saint Ignatius in the tumble-down presbytery.[20]

With that, all four educational institutions—St. Ignatius College, St. Stanislaus, St. Anne's, and Loretto Academy—sat almost defiantly atop "Catholic Hill", balanced on each side of St. Bartholomew's. Unquestionably for Holzer, the parishioners were expected to help

---

original plans called for and, despite beliefs to the contrary, has no resemblance to Cologne cathedral whatsoever. Designed by the renowned architect of the day, Joseph Connolly, and built between 1877 and 1888—the two front towers were completed in 1926—it was dedicated on 10 October 1888 and renamed the Church of Our Lady Immaculate.

19 DJB, vol. 1, 146–147; 98–99; Pierre Point, s.j., letter to William S. Murphy, S.J., 1 June 1859, AJC, Box C-401; Pierre Point, s.j., *Histoire de Sandwich*, 69ff; Lecompte, 269–271.

20 DJB, vol. 1, 280–281; AJC, Box C-401; Lecompte, 269–270; J. George Hodgins, *Documentary history of Education in Upper Canada from the Passing of the Constitutional act of 1791 to the close of Rev. Dr. Ryerson's Administration of the Education Department in 1876* (Toronto: Warwick Bros. & Rutter, 1894–1910), vol. xvii, 43; 45; 51; 55–57.

finance the four buildings. Instead, they objected to the accumulating debts. After only one year, in the summer of 1864, St. Ignatius College had to close, partially from a lack of interest and support by local Catholics, and greatly from a lack of funds and Jesuit professors. Holzer's dream of a permanent Catholic, Jesuit classical college there was never to be realized.[21]

KINGSTON: REGIOPOLIS COLLEGE, 1837–1971

"The impossible dream"
—Henry Keane, S.J.

Kingston seemed somewhat a more promising location for a Catholic college directed by the Jesuits than did Sandwich or Guelph. Five years before they had arrived in Canada, Bishop Macdonell had already incorporated the College of Regiopolis on 4 March 1837, and two years later, laid the cornerstone of a five-storey building in Kingston on 11 June 1839. His intention was that the college would educate men for the priesthood. To that end, he was eager to persuade the Jesuits to assume responsibility for it, but never lived to see that happen. While visiting Scotland in January 1840 to raise funds to complete Regiopolis College, he died suddenly from pneumonia.[22]

It took almost another ten years before his successor, Bishop Rémi Gaulin (1840–1857), convinced the Jesuits to involve themselves at Regiopolis College. Rémi-Joseph Tellier, s.j., became director there, but after only one year, he left the college in 1849, due mainly to the inability of his Superior in New York to supply any Jesuits to assist him. It would be a further eighty-two years before the Jesuits would return to Regiopolis College to accept responsibility for it.[23]

---

21 DJB, vol. 1, 147; Lecompte, 270.

22 Lecompte, 248. The original college was enclosed by Brock, Bagot, Johnson, and Sydenham Streets in what at the time was known as Selma Park. Macdonell's building survives as the Sydenham Street wing of Hotel Dieu Hospital.

23 Ibid., 248; DJB, vol. 2, 333. In 1896, the college moved to King Street, and finally in 1914 to Division and Russell Streets into newly constructed and elegant limestone buildings. It was into those buildings that the Jesuits moved in the summer of 1931. After they left in 1971, the beautiful old buildings at Regiopolis College eventually were wantonly destroyed, in the minds of many, and then replaced by a rather tasteless, non-descript school building. By then it was known as Regiopolis-Notre Dame Catholic Secondary School. Regiopolis had amalgamated with the girls' school in 1967.

That acceptance in 1931 to direct and staff Regiopolis College rested on the dream of William H. Hingston, S.J., during his time as Provincial Superior (1928–1934), to establish a Jesuit "Catholic University of Canada" by means of Regiopolis College's university charter. During the nineteenth century, efforts were made to affiliate Regiopolis College, along with other religious colleges in Ontario, with the University of Toronto, and for a time the rector of Regiopolis College sat on the university's senate. Yet for many reasons, not least being the antagonism of many Protestants to such an educational arrangement, along with the unwillingness of the bishop of Kingston to give up any of the college's autonomy, Regiopolis College never affiliated. It had sought, and was granted on 18 August 1866, its own royal charter as a degree-granting college.[24]

For six years, that dream of a Canadian Catholic university dominated Hingston's thoughts, plans, and actions. He was ever optimistic that, whatever the hurdles, he could make a major advancement in Catholic higher education by establishing such a national Catholic university. He also hoped to establish a college of education to train Catholic teachers. During January and March 1934, he had Regiopolis College federally and provincially incorporated, which granted it the status of "University of Regiopolis". That, however, was not met with universal approval. Indeed, Queen's University, a staunch Protestant establishment, was not at all pleased at the idea of having a Catholic university next door. Nor were most English-speaking Canadian Jesuits supportive of the idea. Financially, it was difficult to see how such a college could survive, and Jesuit manpower was already stretched to its limit.[25]

Notwithstanding all objections, on behalf of the Canadian English-speaking Jesuits, and having received permission from the Superior General, Wlodimir Ledóchowski, Hingston had purchased Regiopolis College from Richard Michael J. O'Brien, the coadjutor archbishop of Kingston, in the spring of 1931.[26] At the same time, the

---

24   DJB, vol. 1, 140–141.

25   Ibid., 92; 100. The college was federally incorporated on 4 January 1934, and provincially incorporated on 16 March 1934.

26   Richard M. O'Brien was coadjutor archbishop of Kingston from 1929 until he became archbishop in 1938. He died in 1943.

university charter and the authority for appointing members to the board of governors were passed over to the Jesuits from the archbishop. Meanwhile, to help finance his dream of a University of Regiopolis, Hingston sold the Church of Our Lady Immaculate, Guelph, to Bishop John T. McNally of Hamilton (1924–1937). The Jesuits departed on 6 September 1931 from that parish. Many Jesuits and lay people found it hard to forgive Hingston for withdrawing from one of the oldest Canadian ministries of the English-speaking Jesuits, and for decades afterwards, the "loss" to the Jesuits of the Church of Our Lady Immaculate was greatly regretted and not forgotten.

To move his argument for a University of Regiopolis along, Hingston set out to obtain a pontifical charter from the Congregation of Seminaries and Universities in Rome. To that end, in 1933 he proposed to the Superior General that the Jesuit Scholastics studying in Toronto should transfer to the new university in Kingston. The General Superior thought otherwise. The Jesuit seminary in Toronto had been opened three years previously, and there was no possibility that Ledóchowski would approve having the Jesuit Scholastics in Kingston.[27]

Since 1914, the college had been situated in north Kingston, on Russell Street. In Hingston's mind, that "campus" did not come near to fulfilling his expectations for a large university campus. During 1933, therefore, he purchased over 300 acres on Princess Street at what was then the north-western edge of the city. A detailed plan by the famed architect Noulan Cauchon was drawn up with facilities for faculty, staff, and 6,000 students on a beautifully laid-out campus. Separate residences for 3,000 women and 3,000 men, gymnasiums, golf courses, playing fields, student buildings, along with buildings which would house offices, lecture halls for schools of education, arts and science, medicine and dentistry, engineering, geology, offices, an art gallery, and a museum were all envisioned on the plan. With these, too, were sketches for a stadium, a hospital, and other facilities. The entire campus would include gardens, reflecting pools, and restful oases for study and reflection. In every way, had the plans ever been

---

27   William H. Hingston, S.J., letter to Wlodimir Ledóchowski, s.j., 19 February 1933, AJC, Box E-618.

developed, Hingston's university would have been among the most beautiful of Canadian university campuses.[28]

Ownership of the campus was a further issue in Hingston's mind. Unlike the Jesuit universities in the United States, which were owned by the Jesuits and not by the local episcopal authorities, Hingston thought that the Canadian bishops should be the proprietors of the university. In that way, he believed, the bishops would have the responsibility for the financial burdens of the institution, while the Jesuits would maintain academic control. Thus, the bishops would acquire the property from the Jesuits, raise the funds, construct the buildings on the new campus, and assume all responsibility for financing and maintaining the university.[29]

Hingston and Archbishop O'Brien pursued those plans in early October 1933 with the other English-speaking bishops of Canada who were meeting in Quebec City at the invitation of Jean-Marie-Rodrigue Villeneuve, cardinal archbishop of Quebec (1931–1947). During the meeting, Archbishop O'Brien invited the English-speaking bishops to dinner at the Château Frontenac on 4 October. Hingston was the guest speaker. He spoke eloquently and persuasively of his plans for a Catholic and Jesuit university in Canada that would help strengthen the Catholic Church in the country by means of a well-educated laity. The bishops were impressed with his speech and with his fervent presentation, and were generally enthusiastic at the idea of such an independent Catholic institution in Kingston. Many of them expressed their hope that their own colleges and seminaries could affiliate with this new university. Both Hingston and Archbishop O'Brien believed that an important advance forward had been made to their plans.

Yet, it was not to be, for in the end the bishops were not willing to support financially such an educational adventure. Nor did they have the same vision for the university as did Hingston. The bishops' model was to have their own colleges, but affiliated to Regiopolis, while Hingston's model was to have everything on the Kingston

---

28   Noulan Cauchon was a founder of the Town Planning Institute of Canada and of the Ottawa Town Planning Commission. He played a significant role during the early twentieth century in the planning of Canada's capital.

29   Ibid.

campus. In fact, between 1931 and the spring of 1933, many of the archbishops and bishops had been petitioning Hingston to open a college in their dioceses, and in April 1933, the Provincial Superior of the Lower Canada Province had even offered his college in Edmonton to Hingston so that it might become the English-language college that the archbishop there desired. The bishops of Vancouver, Calgary, Winnipeg, Edmonton, and St. John had all been hoping for a favourable response from Hingston to found colleges; others, such as the bishops of Charlottetown and Sault Ste. Marie, proposed an affiliation of their colleges to the new University of Regiopolis. Hingston was not interested in anything but a single campus at Regiopolis College.[30]

During the latter months of 1933, everything appeared to be moving smoothly for Hingston towards the fulfilment of his dream. Near the end of November, he paid a visit to Arthur H. U. Colquhoun, Ontario's deputy minister for education, to discuss the founding at the future Catholic university of a Normal School for Catholic teachers and a college of education as well. Colquhoun was supportive of Hingston's plans for education, and believed that these were possible to achieve. He introduced Hingston to several ministers of the government and arranged for a meeting with George S. Henry, the premier of Ontario (1930–1934), for 12 December. By the new year, Hingston was filled with optimism that, even if his university might not be completed until 1936, his plans would continue to unfold.

Unfortunately, however, during all his planning he did not take into consideration the strong opposition that was building among Jesuits, including among some of his Jesuit Consultors, towards his grand plans for Kingston and what to many seemed like a reckless disregard for finances during a severe national depression. To make the general situation even more disheartening to everyone but Hingston, the Canadian Jesuit Vice Province was itself labouring under heavy debts, and was all but bankrupt. Hingston's estimated cost of building

30   Archbishop Richard Michael J. O'Brien, letter to Andrea Cassulo, 28 September 1933; William H. Hingston, S.J., letter to Andrea Cassulo, 1 October 1933; "Meeting of the English-Speaking Bishops of Canada in the City of Quebec regarding Regiopolis College", William H. Hingston, S.J., address to Arthur H. U. Colquhoun, 15 January 1934, ibid.

the University of Regiopolis was $1 million, at that time an unattainable sum of money for the English-speaking Canadian Jesuits.[31]

Hingston's dream was quickly and finally shattered by a letter of 10 March 1934 from the Superior General, informing him that his six-year term of office as Provincial Superior was ending and that a *terna* of three candidates was to be submitted to Rome. Hingston was shocked at the idea of leaving office and fretted about the future of his educational plans. Yet he had no choice but to step down and leave the future to his successor. By early June, Rome announced that it had not accepted the *terna*. In the end, the Superior General appointed Henry Keane, an English Jesuit, to straighten out the administrative and financial difficulties left by Hingston. One of Keane's first acts as Provincial Superior was to quash any hope for a Jesuit Catholic university in Kingston. Concerned at the enormous sum proposed by Hingston—some $3 million—for a fundraising drive, Keane and his Consultors deferred any further efforts to establish a university. Ever optimistic until his final days, Hingston firmly believed that, had he been given the opportunity, he could have raised the money.[32]

Yet the idea of Regiopolis College granting its own degrees did not entirely disappear. That was especially true during the late 1930s, when Archbishop O'Brien proposed to the Jesuits that, by using Regiopolis' charter, they establish an undergraduate programme for educating seminarians in philosophy. He also hoped that the young Jesuits studying philosophy in Toronto would move to Kingston. As a result, for a time there followed discreet but unofficial negotiations with Queen's University for affiliation. Even Loyola College, although long since desiring its own charter, became interested in forming a union with Regiopolis College, through which Loyola's degrees might be granted. Nothing resulted from any of those efforts except for an arts course that began on 26 September 1938.

Late that summer, Erle G. Bartlett, S.J., was appointed dean of studies with the responsibility for organizing and introducing a Bachelor of Arts programme. Four years later, it had to be abandoned due to

---

31   That sum of money would be over $17 million in today's dollar value.

32   DJB, vol. 1, 160–161. The "campus" in Kingston was sold in 1939 to the Aluminum Company of Canada.

lack of interest and resources. Bachelor of Arts degrees were granted in 1941 to T. J. Raby, B. McAline, F. McAllister, and J. Brennan, and in 1942 to C. Parker and R. Smith. Other than the college's granting these six degrees, and despite the hopes of its founder and many others, during its entire history Regiopolis College remained first a school and for a brief time a seminary, and then a high school.

Brief attempts to resuscitate the university charter occurred in 1950 and again in 1957, in the hope that Loyola College and Campion College might become affiliated with Regiopolis College. Joseph V. Driscoll, S.J., was keenly trying to activate the notion of a University of Regiopolis with Loyola and Campion as affiliated Jesuit colleges. Such efforts, however, quickly died out. The Provincial Superior, George E. Nunan, S.J., was cool to the idea. The Jesuits left Regiopolis College in 1971.

III

Atlantic Canada

CHARLOTTETOWN:
ST. DUNSTAN'S COLLEGE, 1880–1881

"Rift without remedy"
—George B. Kenny, S.J.

In the colony of Prince Edward Island, Bishop Bernard MacEachern (1829–1837), desiring to respond to the educational needs of Catholics on the island, founded St. Andrew's College in 1831. It was the first institution of higher learning in the colony. By 1855, under his successor, Bishop Bernard McDonald (1837–1859), the college had not only changed its name to Saint Dunstan's, but also its location—nearer to Charlottetown—and its purpose, that is, to become a seminary as well as a college. Student enrolment, however, remained small for years, fluctuating by the 1860s and 1870s between thirty-seven and seventy-two students. There was, as well, a large turnover of teaching staff, along with many complaints among Catholics about the poor quality and high cost of education offered. Additionally, a considerable part of the college's problems had arisen from the unsatisfactory administration of its rector, James MacDonald

(1869–1880). Dissatisfied and at odds with the rector, three priests of the college resigned their teaching posts in 1880.[1]

Twenty years earlier, and shortly after he had become bishop, Peter McIntyre (1860–1891) had petitioned the Jesuits in Rome for help in the college. They had demurred, citing lack of manpower. Later, on 11 November 1877, Hector Glackmeyer, s.j., gave the first parish mission in the diocese. The overwhelmingly favourable reaction by Catholics to Glackmeyer's preaching, and his success in convincing them to abstain from alcohol, greatly impressed the bishop. So effective, in fact, was Glackmeyer's mission in every way that the bishop managed to convince himself to prevail once again upon the Jesuits to take over St. Dunstan's College.

From every perspective, therefore, it seemed fortunate for Bishop McIntyre that Glackmeyer's mission had been so successful. Were the Jesuits to take charge, he could look to a resolution of his chief worry: the college's mounting debts. Thus he hoped that by placing the college under Jesuit control, its future, which seemed especially bleak, would be secured. That was dubious, however, given the financial chaos and physical shambles of the college.[2]

Determined to improve the situation in the college, while on his way to his *ad limina* visit to Rome in 1880, the bishop successfully convinced the Jesuits' Superior General, Pieter Jan Beckx, then staying in Paris, to supply Jesuits for Saint Dunstan's. It had not been easy, however. Knowing that during the previous year the Canadian Jesuits had become part of the Jesuit Province of England, the bishop stopped in England before reaching the Continent to speak with Edward I. Purbrick, the newly appointed Provincial Superior there, with the hope of getting his support and a letter of introduction to Beckx. Purbrick was lukewarm in his reaction, although he agreed to consider the matter.[3]

---

1   For a history of Saint Dunstan's College, cf. G. Edward MacDonald, *The History of Saint Dunstan's University, 1855–1956* (Charlottetown: Saint Dunstan's University, 1989).

2   DCB, vol. XII, 637–640.

3   DJB, vol. 1, 297–298.

In Paris, initially, the Superior General was also hesitant to approve the Jesuits' taking over Saint Dunstan's. The need to staff St. Mary's College in Montreal and the other established works in Canada were already a great strain on manpower and finances. In the end, Bishop McIntyre was persuasive. Beckx finally agreed to the bishop's request. There were, however, stringent conditions. All the debts of the college would be assumed by the bishop; the Jesuits would take responsibility only for its annual financial upkeep; they would maintain Saint Dunstan's as a college of higher education for at least five years; and the academic programme would consist of the ordinary classical and philosophical courses.

During the late summer of 1880, nine Jesuits arrived at Saint Dunstan's prepared to assume charge of the college: three priests, three Scholastics, and three Brothers. George B. Kenny, who had already been instrumental in establishing St. Peter's College, New Jersey, was appointed Rector, and Pierre O. Racicot, his assistant. Almost at once there were difficulties between the Jesuits and the bishop. For his part, as ordinary of the diocese, Bishop McIntyre was nothing if not sternly determined that his college would flourish, and was never amenable to any suggestion that he was not still in charge. In every sense he believed that, except for the college's operational costs, he was responsible for Saint Dunstan's. When someone once suggested that he should close the college due to its severe financial drain on the diocese, he firmly rejected any such idea: "Close my eyes first, then close the college."[4]

On the other hand, and contrary to all their expectations, the Jesuits found a much different situation than they had anticipated. Having been traditionally responsible for the teaching, administering, and planning of their own colleges, they were not used to having a bishop so closely involving himself in the minutiae of college life. They found him meddlesome and difficult. They also felt deceived. The bishop, so Kenny believed, had not been forthcoming originally

---

4   Ibid., 120; 160; 169–170; 300; Lawrence Landrigan, "Peter MacIntyre, Bishop of Charlottetown, P. E. I.", CCHA, *Report*, 20 (1953), 81–92. The three priests were Kenny, Racicot, and David Plante; the Scholastics were Alfred Brosnan, William F. Gagnieur, and Lawrence J. Kavanagh; and the Brothers were Daniel Riordan, Joseph Hould, Matthew Dunne, and Michael Hogan.

about the poor condition of the college's building and about the local poverty. Whatever the truth of the matter was, in fact the physical state of the college was appalling, and the Catholic population was greatly impoverished. Kenny quickly calculated that the funds for repair—some $3,000.00—would be impossible to raise, given the penury among Catholics and the meagre resources of the Canadian Jesuits. Yet the bishop was unwavering, and held resolutely to the contract. He was responsible for the college's debts, and it was up to the Jesuits to look after the college's upkeep.[5]

In the end, the rift between the bishop and the Jesuits was without remedy. Although enrolment in the college had increased noticeably after the Jesuits arrived—there was general approval among Catholics with their presence in Charlottetown—at the close of the academic year of 1881, and greatly disenchanted at their unfilled dreams, the Jesuits withdrew from St. Dunstan's College. They never returned. The college reverted to the care of the diocesan clergy. The Jesuits would not go back permanently to Atlantic Canada for nearly sixty years.[6]

HALIFAX: SAINT MARY'S UNIVERSITY, 1841–1974

"Age quod agis"
—Motto of Saint Mary's University

In 1940, the Jesuit Province of Upper Canada accepted from the archdiocese the responsibility of Saint Mary's College on Windsor Street, Halifax. Founded in 1802 by Edmund Burke, the college was originally located in what was known as Glebe House on the corner of Spring Garden Road and Barrington Street in central Halifax. Nearly forty years would pass, however, before Saint Mary's was formally established. In 1841, Saint Mary's College received its degree-granting

---

5   The equivalent value at present would be about $65,000.00.

6   In time, St. Dunstan's flourished, and became a small but prominent liberal arts college serving the Catholics of Prince Edward Island. Over the next hundred years, and well into the twentieth century, came a steady number of young men from the college. Very many of these became priests, serving the Church not only in Prince Edward Island but also across Canada and beyond. A proportionally high number of those graduates became Canadian Jesuits. In 1969, St. Dunstan's College merged with Prince of Wales College to form the new University of Prince Edward Island, although the college still retained its Catholic character and purpose within the university.

charter from the legislature of Nova Scotia. Over the subsequent years, the college remained small and in every way greatly dependent upon the archbishops of Halifax for survival. Its existence was always uncertain, but never more so than in 1881, when its annual grant from the provincial government was cancelled. The college was forced to close. In February 1881, a wealthy Catholic politician and merchant in Halifax, Patrick Power, bequeathed a substantial sum to the archdiocese of Halifax, part of which was to be used to bring the Jesuits to the city to work in education.[7]

The revival of Saint Mary's College was dear to the heart of the new archbishop, Cornelius O'Brien (1882–1906). During the year before becoming archbishop, he had been at Saint Dunstan's College when the Jesuits were there. As well as having come to know the Rector, George B. Kenny, S.J., O'Brien had been sympathetic to their situation. With the monies of Power's estate in mind, he began negotiations with the Jesuits to take charge of Saint Mary's College. On 22 February 1884, he wrote to Kenny, who was working at the Church of the Gesù in Montreal, inviting them to consider the matter. In reply, Kenny regretfully noted that after "due consultation", they would not be able to accept his offer.

Still wanting to attract them to Halifax, four years later the archbishop wrote to the Jesuit Provincial Superior of the English Province, Edward I. Purbrick, requesting his help. The reply was not encouraging. Canada was, he pointed out, an independent Jesuit mission dependent on no other Province, and therefore "England has no word in the matter. Fr. General [Anton Maria Anderledy, s.j.] would not allow our Province to take charge of any college on your side of the Atlantic, north, at least, of the West Indies."[8]

The archbishop had to abandon those plans. He next turned to other religious orders for assistance, but was still hoping to use

---

7   Cf. "Patrick Power", DCB, vol. XI, 709–710. His will also left money for an orphanage and a boys' home in Halifax.

8   Archbishop Cornelius O'Brien, letter to George B. Kenny, S.J., 22 February 1884; George B. Kenny, S.J., letter to Archbishop Cornelius O'Brien, 15 April 1884; Archbishop Cornelius O'Brien, letter to Edward I. Purbrick, S.J., n. d. 1888; Edward I. Purbrick, S.J., letter to Archbishop Cornelius O'Brien, 3 July 1888, AJC, Box, F-624; Desjardin, 284.

Power's legacy to support Saint Mary's College. Difficulties arose, however. The bequest had clearly stated that it was to be used by the Jesuits for educational purposes in Halifax. The benefactor's son and a co-trustee of the estate, Lawrence Geoffrey Power, refused to allow any money to be used for the college unless the Jesuits were placed in charge. Archbishop O'Brien successfully challenged his position in the Nova Scotia courts, but the decision was overturned by the Supreme Court of Canada in 1903. Saint Mary's College was eventually reopened that year, mostly staffed by laymen, and without money from Power's estate.[9]

In 1913, under Archbishop O'Brien's successor, Edward J. McCarthy (1906–1931), the Christian Brothers of Ireland assumed the administration and staffing of Saint Mary's College. The bishop arranged with the executors of the Power estate—now more obliging, despite the court's order—to release the money for the college. For the next several decades, under Archbishop McCarthy and his successor, Archbishop Thomas O'Connell (1931–1936), Saint Mary's flourished as a liberal arts college. Among its development was an expansion of the undergraduate programmes, most notably in 1934 with the opening of a faculty of commerce. It was among the first of its kind in Canada.[10]

Yet, however supportive the archbishops had been in the past, the relations between the Christian Brothers and the new archbishop, John T. McNally (1937–1952), quickly deteriorated. He had a reputation of being firm, if not pugnacious at times, and ever sure of his own judgment and watchful of his authority. He swiftly made his mark on Halifax. Fully determined to assume charge of Saint Mary's College, he soon concluded that the Christian Brothers, whom he accused of acting independently of his episcopal authority, were showing no enthusiasm for his position that the college belonged to the archdiocese

---

9   DCB, vol. XIII, 772–774. Lawrence G. Power (1841–1921) was the son of Patrick Power. Educated at Saint Mary's College, he was appointed a Senator in 1877 by Prime Minister Alexander MacKenzie. Cf. David Allison and Edwin C. Tuck, *History of Nova Scotia* (Halifax: A. W. Bowen, 1916), vol. 3, 225–336.

10   In August 1992, the faculty was renamed the Sobey School of Business to honour Frank H. Sobey, founder of Sobey's grocery store chain. Four years later, a new building for the school, the Sobey Building, was opened on campus.

no matter who staffed and administered it. In effect, that meant for him that he had a hand in the college's appointments and administration. The Brothers disagreed.[11]

After a bitter wrangle with the Brothers involving the money from the Power estate and the Brothers' refusal to allow a minor seminary at Saint Mary's, Archbishop McNally took his case to Rome. He had enjoyed a long friendship with Eugenio Pacelli, Vatican Secretary of State and soon-to-be Pope Pius XII. Having eventually received a decision against the Brothers, on 14 July 1940 the archbishop expelled them from both the college and the archdiocese. Shortly before, the Brothers unanimously had agreed that, given the tension between themselves and the archbishop, they should withdraw from Saint Mary's. Needless to say, the archbishop did not endear himself to many Catholics in Halifax; the Brothers were greatly loved and admired, and reaction to their treatment and to their departure was anything but positive.

With the Brothers assuredly about to depart from the college by the end of the term, the archbishop was inclined to appoint his own priests to administer and staff Saint Mary's. Instead, however, he offered it to the Basilian Fathers. Their superiors declined it. He turned to the Jesuits. At first, he considered offering them the college for a six-year trial period. His long-time friend Alfred A. Sinnott, archbishop of Winnipeg, by then very accustomed to dealing with the Jesuits at St. Paul's College, advised against it. On 18 October, Archbishop

11   From the time of his being named the first bishop of Calgary in 1913, through his years in Hamilton (1924–1937) and then in Halifax, Archbishop McNally put up with no insubordination, as he saw it, from both Religious and diocesan priests. His attitude especially towards members of Religious Orders and Congregations was clear: when he perceived that an Order or Congregation was not fully cooperating with him, he was unrelenting in his efforts to remove it. In Calgary he soon became embroiled in a bitter struggle with the French-speaking Oblate Fathers over control of two of their churches. Very quickly he secured the expulsion of the Oblates from his diocese. Later, in 1944, he expelled the Congregation of the Resurrection (Resurrectionists) from Bermuda—then part of his archdiocese—for what he considered to be their disloyalty. Cf. M. B. Venini Byrne, *From the Buffalo to the Cross: A History of the Roman Catholic Diocese of Calgary* (Calgary: Calgary Archives and Historical Publishers, 1973); Robert Choquette, "John Thomas McNally et l'érection du diocese de Calgary," *Revue de l'Université d'Ottawa* 45, no. 4 (1975), 414ff; Robert N. Bérard, "Archbishop John T. McNally and Roman Catholic Education in Canada," *Vitae Scholasticae: The Bulletin of Educational Biography*, VII, no. 2 (1988), 255ff; Bérard, "Cardinal for English Canada: The Intrigues of Bishop John T. McNally, 1930–1937," CCHA, *Historical Studies*, 63 (1997), 82ff; Sheila Ross, "Bishop J. T. McNally and the Anglicization of the Diocese of Calgary, 1913–1915," CCHA, *Historical Studies*, 69 (2003), 85ff.

McNally wrote to another friend, William Dunn, S.J., requesting him to approach the Jesuit Provincial Superior, Thomas J. Mullally, about assuming responsibility for Saint Mary's College, "for, say, nine years as a beginning." On that same day, McNally also wrote to Mullally offering him the college. Its debt was $80,000.00, which the archbishop would assume. The Jesuits would have to pay the interest. In his letter acknowledging the archbishop's offer, Mullally reacted cautiously; he would have to refer the matter, he informed the archbishop, to the Superior General in Rome.[12]

In response to Mullally, on 4 January 1940 the Superior General cryptically telegrammed Mullally: "Halifax negative Ledóchowski".[13] Because part of the quarrel between Archbishop McNally and the Christian Brothers had been over the archbishop's efforts to establish a minor seminary at Saint Mary's College, the Superior General was not interested, since the archbishop was still insisting that a minor seminary had to be established there. Nor was the cardinal archbishop of Quebec, Jean-Marie-Rodrique Villeneuve (1931–1947), an Oblate priest, sympathetic to Archbishop McNally; he had sided with the Christian Brothers in their quarrel with the archbishop, and likewise opposed a seminary at Saint Mary's.[14] The Superior General followed his telegram with a letter to Mullally on 13 January pointing out that, since the archbishop wanted to establish a minor seminary at the college, the Jesuits could not accept it ("non possumus"). In a follow-up letter of 21 January to Mullally, Adelard Dugré, s.j., the English Assistant, informed him that, "le P. Général incline à approuver votre

---

12   DJB, vol. 1, 99–100; Archbishop John T. McNally, letter to William Dunn, S.J., 18 October 1939; Thomas J. Mullally, S.J., letter to Archbishop John T. McNally, n.d.; Archbishop John T. McNally, letter to Thomas J. Mullally, S.J., 31 October 1939, AJC, Box F-624. The $80,000.00 would be more than $1 million in today's value. Long before becoming bishop of Hamilton in 1924, McNally had known Dunn. From 1926 to 1931, Dunn had served on the staff at the Church of Our Lady Immaculate in Guelph, and was there during the negotiations between the Jesuits and Bishop McNally to transfer the parish to the diocese of Hamilton. Dunn was implacably opposed to that transferral on 6 September 1931. For the rest of his life, he bitterly blamed the Provincial Superior, William H. Hingston, S.J., for—as Dunn and many Jesuits at the time viewed it—"selling us out".

13   Wlodimir Ledóchowski, s.j., telegram to Thomas J. Mullally, S.J., 4 January 1940, AJC, Box F-624.

14   McNally's ousting of the Oblate Fathers in Calgary in 1913 had angered many French-Canadian clergy, including Archbishop Villeneuve. As a result, some considered McNally to be anti–French-Canadian.

proposition [not to accept the college]: il est bien possible qu'il vous ait maintenant donné sa réponse."[15]

Disappointed at the Jesuits' reaction, the archbishop went to Rome in early February to argue his case with Ledóchowski. His visit paid off. The Superior General changed his mind and agreed to accept Saint Mary's. Yet, concerned about the soured relationship between the archbishop and the Brothers, Ledóchowski insisted that there were two conditions that had to be met in order for the Jesuits to accept the college. He requested his Vicar General, Maurice Shurmans, s.j., to outline these to the archbishop, which Shurmans did in a letter dated 26 February: the Jesuits would not accept responsibility for the college until after the Christian Brothers had left completely, "so that the differences between them and the archdiocese will be settled," and thus the Jesuits "will have no fear of litigation"; and "the archbishop would have the Apostolic Delegate [Ildebrando Antoniutti] let the Cardinal Prefect of the Congregation of Seminaries [Giuseppe Pizzardo] know that he approves that the college is ours, and has no objections." On 28 February, Archbishop McNally agreed to the two conditions. Later, on 9 April, the apostolic delegate informed McNally that the entrusting of Saint Mary's to the Jesuits had been granted.[16]

To confirm his approval, on 5 March Ledóchowski wrote to Mullally expressing his contentment at the agreement with the archbishop. Nonetheless, given the ruckus that had ensued between the Christian Brothers and the archbishop, the state of affairs remained, not surprisingly, most delicate for the Jesuits. Some unease lingered. In fact, the Jesuits were guarded for good reason. On 19 March, Dugré wrote to Mullally advising that the Jesuits must avoid any friction with the Brothers, or with the archdiocese, as the Brothers had had. It was advice well directed.[17]

---

15 Wlodimir Ledóchowski, s.j., letter to Thomas J. Mullally, S.J., 13 January 1940; Adelard Dugré, s.j., letter to Thomas J. Mullally, S.J., 21 January 1940, ibid. See also John L. Swain, S.J., letter to Jean-Baptiste Janssens, s.j., 16 July 1947, ibid., for a summary of the negotiations between the Jesuits and the archbishop.

16 Maurice Shurmans, s.j., letter to Archbishop John T. McNally, 26 February 1940; Archbishop John T. McNally, letter to Maurice Shurmans, s.j., 28 February 1940; Ildebrando Antoniutti, letter to Archbishop John T. McNally, 9 April 1940, ibid.

17 Wlodimir Ledóchowski, s.j., letter to Thomas J. Mullally, S.J., 5 March 1940; Adelard Dugré, s.j., letter to Thomas J. Mullally, S.J., 19 March 1940, ibid.

A month later, the bishops of Canada met in Winnipeg. While there, Archbishop McNally, on behalf of the archdiocese of Halifax, and Mullally, on behalf of the Jesuits of the Upper Canada Province, signed an agreement on 8 April. Archbishop Sinnott witnessed the signing. True to his earlier verbal promise, McNally reduced the amount of the debt on which the Jesuits would have to pay interest from $80,000.00 to $50,000.00. That was more agreeable to them.[18]

Even if the Superior of the Christian Brothers, Michael J. Lannon, C.F.C., had assured Mullally that the Brothers would vacate Saint Mary's College by the end of June, they were slow in departing.[19] Still smarting because of their sudden ejection from the college and the archdiocese, by late May they had yet made no show of moving out. For some people, that was causing problems. On 23 May, J. Leo Day, the parish priest of St. Joseph's Glebe at Bridgewater, confusing Thomas J. Lally, S.J., director of Martyrs' Shrine, Midland, with Mullally, wrote to Lally complaining that an annual garden party that was to be held from 19 to 21 June on Saint Mary's campus was being jeopardized by the Brothers. He had written Lannon for permission to use the college's grounds, but the response, as Day noted, was frosty and unhelpful: "There would be no garden party on the College Campus while he [Lannon] was in charge; and that the archbishop had no right to give me [Day] such permission. I only made matters worse when I tried to find out when the Brothers were leaving, since he told me 'that was none of my business.'"[20]

Day requested from Lally permission to postpone the garden party until 19 to 21 July. Whether Mullally gave Day permission for the dates in July is not clear. Certainly, according to the archbishop, the Jesuits were well settled in by the time of Day's proposed new date.

Yet, however administratively skilled the first Rector, Christopher J. Keating, S.J., was, it had been an awkward time for the Jesuits because of the considerable uncertainty throughout June over whether the Brothers would vacate the university by the agreed departure date.

---

18   *Agreement between the Roman Catholic Episcopal Corporation of Halifax and the Jesuit Fathers of Upper Canada*, 8 April 1940, ibid.

19   Michael J. Lannon, C.F.C., letter to Thomas J. Mullally, S.J., 26 March 1940, ibid.

20   J. Leo Day, letter to Thomas J. Lally, S.J., 23 May 1940, ibid.

In the end, they did not leave then; they departed on the morning of 14 July. Within a half-hour, the Jesuits took over the direction of Saint Mary's College.[21]

Immediately following their arrival, and despite the fact that they had nothing to do with the matter, the Jesuits faced widespread resentment among Catholics, who blamed them not only for "ousting" the Brothers, but also for purchasing a building on Barrington Street for the college. In fact, the Jesuits had done neither; they were not involved in the Brothers' departure and had known little or nothing about the purchase of property until it was confirmed. Nonetheless, there was not much the Jesuits could do to dispel the resentment.

Despite the archbishop's positive impression of the Jesuits' arrival at Saint Mary's, they were not as settled as he had supposed. What they found at Windsor Street were appalling living and working conditions. Their communal quarters especially were run-down, cramped, and physically inadequate, with scarcely the minimum space for a Community of ten men. Among other notable complaints were that the personal rooms were not only in every way shabby, but were scarcely large enough to accommodate a bed, while if a toilet was flushed on the second floor when someone elsewhere was taking a shower, the water suddenly became scalding in the shower. As well, the classrooms and laboratories were small and ill-equipped, and the students' quarters were inadequate for young men. The archdiocese had the responsibility for the upkeep of the college's buildings and the Jesuits' living quarters. Yet nothing had been done by the archbishop to improve the state of affairs.

During the summer of 1943, Francis C. Smith, S.J., had replaced Keating as Rector. He, too, soon felt the strain of the office.[22] Archbishop McNally's constant interference in the ordinary administration of the college and his attempts to force the Jesuits to hire his clerical friends to professorial posts, however unqualified they were, brought the Jesuits close to abandoning the college altogether. When Mullally became Rector following Smith's sudden death on

21   Archbishop John T. McNally, letter to Thomas J. Mullally, S.J., 20 July 1940, ibid.; DJB, vol. 1, 162–163. Keating became Rector on 13 July, but stepped down from the office in 1943.

22   DJB, vol. 1, 325–326.

23 December 1945, he was shocked at the college's state of disrepair and at how the archbishop had failed to fulfil his side of the bargain to maintain the building. Matters did not improve. Before long, the fire chief of Halifax, J. C. MacGillivray, had condemned the college building, calling it a "fire-hazard".[23]

Following his Visitation of the Halifax Jesuit Community in March 1947, the Provincial Superior, John L. Swain (1945–1951), pointed out to Mullally that the living conditions of the Jesuits were "increasingly inadequate and [there] was no talk of new accommodations" for the fourteen Jesuits who lived there.[24] A month later, Swain wrote to McNally about the many serious shortcomings at Saint Mary's. He noted the difficulties surrounding the Jesuits' quarters, which, although "fair", had "inconveniences".[25] Of greater concern to Swain, however, was that "The [students'] dormitories are overcrowded, unhygienic, dangerous in case of fire. Classroom and laboratory facilities are very inadequate. In the circumstances it is hard to maintain standards of scholarship, discipline, conduct and character formation." Even though he assured McNally that the Jesuits in Halifax were "loyal" to the college, Swain was not at all happy about the inadequate quarters and other matters at Saint Mary's, especially the fact that the archbishop was doing little to change the mistaken impression among Catholics that the Jesuits had been the ones responsible for removing the Brothers.[26]

Swain insisted with the archbishop that these several issues had to be cleared up before the Jesuits would sign a new contract with the archdiocese to remain at Saint Mary's: "Yet precisely because there are only two more years for the present agreement to run, it would not be fair to give the impression to Your Grace—or to Father General—that the situation is satisfactory and then, after two years, to balk about entering into a new agreement if Your Grace then wishes us to do so.[27]

---

23   J. C. MacGillivray, letter to Archbishop John T. McNally, 10 June 1947; Thomas J. Mullally, S.J., letter to John L. Swain, S.J., 12 June 1947, AJC, Box F-624.

24   John L. Swain, S.J., letter to Thomas J. Mullally, S.J., n. d. March 1947, ibid.

25   Swain was being very careful in his choice of words.

26   John L. Swain, S.J., letter to Archbishop John T. McNally, 2 April 1947, ibid.

27   Ibid.

The archbishop was furious at Swain's letter and, according to Swain, complained bitterly to Mullally that there would be no question of a renewal of contract with the Jesuits, and that they "could leave now" if they wished. He also complained that the Jesuits were criticizing his policies, and protested that they did not promote vocations to the secular clergy.[28] Yet despite those strained relations between Archbishop McNally and the Jesuits, a year later the archbishop had mellowed somewhat towards them. Swain had assured him that the Jesuits were more than willing to share in the pastoral needs of the diocese, and for that he was most grateful.[29]

Within three years of the Jesuits' having taken over Saint Mary's, because of the sizable increase in enrolment, it had become evident that the needs of the college were outgrowing the facilities. Soon the archbishop had plans for "his" university. Under his vigilant eyes, in 1943 the archdiocese had purchased for a new campus thirty acres of the southern side of the Gorsebrook Golf Course in the south (and wealthy) end of Halifax.[30] That, however, only caused additional problems: most Haligonian Catholics were not used to contributing to higher education. Besides, the majority of them were of modest means, and felt they ought not to pay for the property. Yet the archdiocese owned the college and the new property, and the archbishop was determined to keep himself involved and the Catholics in the parishes contributing financially to Saint Mary's. He drew up plans for a new campus.

Due to the war effort and the post-war shortage of steel, however, the move onto the Gorsebrook campus at 35 Robie Street, and into the new building—named in honour of the archbishop—had to be delayed until the autumn term of 1952. In every way, although by no means a handsome building, the new campus was a vast improvement over what the Jesuits and students had had to endure during the previous twelve years; it was considered at the time to be the

28   John L. Swain, S.J., letter to Jean-Baptiste Janssens, s.j., 18 July 1947, ibid.

29   Archbishop John T. McNally, letter to John L. Swain, S.J., 26 August 1948, ibid.

30   The archdiocese purchased the property from the Gorsebrook Golf Club, which had served a wealthy clientele of Halifax. It originally had been the estate of Enos Collins (+1871), a businessman and ship owner who was considered to be the wealthiest man of his day in Atlantic Canada.

most modern and innovative university campus in Atlantic Canada. The McNally Building included a library, a chapel, a gymnasium, classrooms, laboratories, offices, and accommodations for boarders and the Jesuits. During its construction, the archbishop announced that he planned to retire to "his" building in a penthouse that he was planning to construct on the fifth floor. That news was not greeted with much enthusiasm by the Jesuits in Halifax. He died, however, on 18 November 1952. The penthouse was never built.[31]

Even though it would take another few years before the new building was entirely completed, Catholic critics of the archbishop's "grand plans" were especially irate; the building was, for them, a "white elephant". It was too large, they argued, and would never be filled. Even more irritating for them was that the parishes had to assume the cost of its construction along with costs arising from moving the college from Windsor Street in the north to Robie Street in the south, and were also expected to help raise the money to cover a good deal of those costs. Not unexpectedly, that only created more resentment among Catholics towards the Jesuits. It mattered not that the archbishop had not informed the Jesuits in advance about his purchasing of the property. The Jesuits were still blamed for the parishioners' new financial burdens.

The Rector, J. Frederick Lynch, S.J. (1950–1956), set about countering this lack of enthusiasm for the Jesuits among the Catholic population of the city. A discreet, astute man, he succeeded remarkably in that endeavour, quietly and resolutely. He took every opportunity to point out that, although the Jesuits were not responsible for purchasing the property, the fact was that the college needed the space because it would have double the enrolment within ten years. It did, and indeed within less than a decade the need for more space and new buildings were again pressing issues.[32]

---

31   The archbishop had also laid plans to be buried in front of the McNally Building on the grounds of the university. In the end, however, he was buried in Holy Cross cemetery in the section reserved for archbishops and priests. A story that lived on among the Jesuits from those years at Saint Mary's was that, when the archbishop first saw the elevator that would take him to his future penthouse, he commented that a coffin could not fit into it. Evidently he had intended to die in his penthouse.

32   DJB, vol. 2, 167–168. The pressure for more space at Saint Mary's was so great by 1961 that it became a major factor in the Jesuits closing the high school sector of Saint Mary's in 1963.

Under Lynch's leadership—he was also dean of studies from 1950 to 1951—and most especially that of Patrick G. Malone, S.J., who was dean of studies from 1951 to 1956 and Rector from 1956 to 1959, the academic programmes expanded considerably. Although courses in adult education had been set up by M. John Belair, S.J., in 1950, Malone was keen on developing those further.[33] Additionally, a co-educational evening division was established in September 1951, offering credit courses that led to a Bachelor of Arts degree. William A. Stewart, S.J., taught the first class. To reflect the growing importance of Saint Mary's, the college was given the status of a university on 10 April 1952.[34]

Malone also planned to introduce pre-law, pre-dentistry, and pre-medicine courses; although it would take some time before those were admitted, eventually they would become part of the curriculum.[35] Of considerable importance to Malone was his intention to reform the journalism programme. The university had already begun to participate in the Halifax School of Journalism. Malone wanted to develop further Saint Mary's programme in order to make a strong contribution. To that end, and along with the classes in journalism leading to a diploma, he added public relations and advertising to the curriculum at Saint Mary's.[36]

Yet his intentions went well beyond that. He had in mind the establishing of courses leading to a diploma in communication arts that would include advertising, radio, TV, newspaper and magazine production, speech, debating, and public relations. Had he introduced this to the extent that he had hoped, the programme would have been the first of its kind in Canada.

In contrast, the Provincial Superior, George E. Nunan, was adamantly opposed to such a programme. He had noticed, he wrote to Malone with more than a little irritation on 15 April 1954, a reference

---

33   Ibid., 11–13. Belair would continue as the programme's director until 1970.

34   "An Act to Amend Chapter 140 of the Acts of 1918: an Act to Amend the Law Respecting Saint Mary's College, Halifax", 10 April 1952, AJC, Box F-264.

35   Patrick G. Malone, S.J., letter to George E. Nunan, S.J., 11 June 1952, ibid.

36   Patrick G. Malone, S.J., letter to George E. Nunan, S.J., 23 June 1953, ibid., Box F-625. The Halifax School of Journalism was an inter-university—Mount Saint Vincent, King's, and Saint Mary's—effort that had been organized in 1948.

to this new programme "in one of your small folders." He was not pleased that Malone had not referred the matter to him first. In consequence, Nunan insisted that the proposed communication arts diploma course should not go ahead.[37]

In truth, however, Nunan feared that such a programme would eventually lead to the secularization of Saint Mary's, because it would move the university away from the traditional Jesuit role of teaching theology and philosophy along with the humanities. Nunan's fear was a general one among most Catholic educators of the day. It was not so for Malone; he had no fear whatsoever about the direction Catholic education might take. As was his wont, he deftly sidestepped Nunan by pointing out that he had already been informed of the matter by the Rector. That, for Malone, was sufficient. Effectively, he ignored Nunan's concerns and introduced a number of measures that eventually would lead to a communication arts programme.

Other new steps were taken that helped to widen Saint Mary's academic influence. Off-campus credit courses—a new feature for universities—were offered in Dartmouth and faraway Kentville and Truro. Additionally, J. Arthur Nelson, S.J., introduced between 1951 and 1954 a programme for the teaching of French conversation by means of cassette tapes; it was among the first such offerings in Canada. In 1953, Saint Mary's established an engineering faculty. Two years later, a school of education opened; the university became the degree-granting institution for the two Jesuit houses of formation, Ignatius College, Guelph, and Regis College, Toronto; and Mildred Harrington was appointed to the faculty, the first woman to be appointed to the faculty of a Jesuit university or college in Canada. In 1957, the school of education was established, while during 1959, an electronic digital computer (a Royal McBee LGP-30) was installed under the guidance of James W. Murphy, S.J., the first such computer in Atlantic Canada.[38]

To the unease of several people, however, the university seemed to be growing too rapidly. A man of vision and ambition, Malone was not

---

37   "Proposed Curriculum for Communications Arts", 20 February 1953; George E. Nunan, S.J., letter to Patrick G. Malone, S.J., 15 April 1954; Patrick G. Malone, S.J., letter to George E. Nunan, S.J., 10 May 1954, ibid.

38   DJB, vol. 2, 195–199; 245–249; AJC, Box F-624.

one to consult much, if at all. He was highly intelligent, single-minded, and not patient with those who did not agree with him or accept his understanding of what a modern university should be. When he became dean in 1951, Saint Mary's was a small undergraduate college of about 400 students; when he stepped down as Rector eight years later, it had grown into a university with over 1,300 students and several departments and schools.

Following Malone's departure to become Rector at Loyola College, Montreal, on 31 July 1959, Clair J. Fischer, S.J., assumed the office of Rector at Saint Mary's. He had a very different personality than Malone. Unflappable and gentle of nature, he believed in governing more by consensus and dialogue than by confrontation and single-mindedness. Consequently, although the university had to face some campus unrest during the 1960s, as did most Canadian universities, he managed to keep the campus calm during the next eight years.

Saint Mary's especially prospered due to the upsurge in the public's need for higher education. For that reason, the university developed new programmes and increased the number of faculty members and students accordingly. In 1961, a business administration major was offered to commerce students for the first time; the O'Donnell-Hennessey Student Centre was constructed in 1962; that same year, Archbishop J. Gerald Berry (1953–1967), who had succeeded Archbishop McNally, announced an "Expansion Programme" for Saint Mary's, a fundraising effort by the archdiocese for new buildings and academic programmes; and in the autumn of that year, and with the archbishop's approval, the first women were admitted to Saint Mary's on a full-time basis.[39] In 1965, Fischer opened the Alumni Arena as well as the Bishop Burke Education Centre/Burke Library, which provided much-needed space for two large classroom theatres, an art gallery—a special project of Fischer, who was himself a painter—a library and a music room.

The organizing of the new library was greatly due to the efforts of E. Gibson Hallam, S.J. During 1957 and 1958, he had taken his Master

---

39   William A. Stewart, S.J., letter to Gordon F. George, S.J., 11 January 1961, AJC, Box F-625. In time, the faculty of commerce became, under the deanship of Dr. Harold Beasley, among the very best in the country.

of Arts degree at Columbia University in New York City. Five years later, during the summer of 1963, he was appointed librarian of Saint Mary's. Immediately, he set out to bring order to a rather disordered library. While organizing the library's holdings, he also gave consider-able leadership to librarians elsewhere who often lacked experience and resources. With them, Hallam was able to establish a combined catalogue of all the local university libraries. Because he was an ef-fective co-ordinator and was dedicated to his field, many librarians in the Maritimes sought his advice during a time of rapid expansion of all the universities' libraries. During 1967 and 1968, he worked on several special library projects for Dalhousie University.[40]

In the end, however, Saint Mary's library was physically small, while its holdings, neglected for years, were without focus and largely insufficient to support a full-fledged university programme. Hallam's efforts to convince the university's administrators that a larger build-ing, along with a considerably higher annual budget to increase its holdings, was needed were rebuffed. Fischer was clear: there were other priorities on campus, and he was not about to build a larger library or spend more money on updating its holdings. By 1968, Hallam had become disillusioned; he left Saint Mary's exasperated and disheartened.[41]

Because of the mounting debt the university and archdiocese had to bear, beginning in 1962 Fischer opened preliminary discussions with Archbishop Berry and Mount Saint Vincent University, the Catholic women's university in Halifax administered by the Sisters of Charity of Saint Vincent de Paul, to form some kind of union between the two institutions to lessen the cost of education for the archdiocese. At the request of the archbishop, a meeting was held in the board room at Mount Saint Vincent's on 8 February 1963 to consider some kind of closer cooperation between the two institutions. Discussions centred on the idea of federation or affiliation, something greatly favoured by the archbishop and his vicar general, Monsignor William Smith. It was decided that Fischer would put together a preliminary proposal

---

40   DJB, vol. 1, 127–128.

41   He died four years later from a heart seizure.

that would demand no commitment on either side, other than that of seriously considering the matter and promising further discussions.[42]

Following that meeting, Fischer prepared a preliminary brief entitled "A Proposal for the Unification of Catholic Higher Education in the Archdiocese of Halifax". On 18 February, he circulated the brief among the individuals involved. In effect, and so that there would be a better use of finances and personnel, his brief consisted of an invitation for Mount Saint Vincent's to federate with Saint Mary's.[43]

The Sisters, who saw the matter quite differently, were unsympathetic to his proposal. For them, Fischer's plan was nothing but an attempt to absorb Mount Saint Vincent's. Its faculty and board of governors likewise rejected his plan; they, too, saw his recommendations as a move towards a complete takeover by Saint Mary's.[44]

During the autumn of 1963, in a further effort to reach some acceptable procedures for working together, Saint Mary's and Mount Saint Vincent's agreed to have more planning committees. After further discussions about federation, those committees merged with one that had been established by the archbishop, who was exploring once again the feasibility of such a union. As a result, Laurence K. Shook, C.S.B., was appointed to undertake a study of the matter and come up with some proposals for unification. He was instructed to include in his study all four Catholic institutions in Halifax: Saint Mary's, Mount Saint Vincent's, Sacred Heart Convent, and Holy Heart Seminary. The hope was that these might be formed into some kind of Catholic federated university.

---

42 Present, along with Archbishop Berry and his vicar general, Monsignor William Smith, were Gordon F. George, S.J., Provincial Superior, Maria Gertrude Farmer, C.S., Superior General, Clair J. Fischer, S.J., president of Saint Mary's, and Francis d'Assisi Murphy, C.S., president of Mount Saint Vincent's.

43 Clair J. Fischer, S.J., letter to Gordon F. George, S.J., 18 February1963, AJC, Box F-624. Fischer's *A Proposal for the Unification of Catholic Higher Education in the Archdiocese of Halifax* was included in that letter. Cf. also Mary Olga McKenna, C.S., *Charity Alive: Sisters of Charity of Saint Vincent de Paul* (Lanham, Maryland: University of America Press, 1998). 163–165.

44 Francis d'Assisi McCarthy, S.C., letter to Archbishop J. Gerald Berry, 20 August 1962; Clair J. Fischer, S.J., letter to Francis M. d'Assisi McCarthy, S.C., 18 February 1963; Gordon F. George, S.J., letter to Maria Gertrude, S.C., 10 July 1963, AJC, Box F-624. Sister Maria Gertrude was the Mother General of the Sisters of Charity.

Shook's report of 29 June 1964 was wide-ranging, and for many was positive enough about unification. He proposed the establishing of a co-educational "Catholic University of Halifax" that would be made up of four federated institutions. Following the model of certain colleges at the University of Toronto, Saint Mary's and Mount Saint Vincent's would hold in abeyance their degree-granting powers in favour of the new Catholic foundation.[45] Nonetheless, and however sensible from many perspectives Shook's proposed new federated university seemed to be, it remained far too ambitious, even risky, for some. There was still an ingrained reluctance, not only by the archbishop and the Holy See, towards having a fully co-educational Catholic university; Mount Saint Vincent's also remained cool to the whole idea of federation or of unification of any sort. It interpreted Shook's proposal as another way for Saint Mary's to "swallow up" Mount Saint Vincent's. For the Sisters, that was not about to happen.[46]

Disappointed and tired, and with his dream of unification un-fulfilled, Fischer left office in 1967. Yet, during his time as Rector, despite plenty of financial and other pressures, he had brought Saint Mary's through most of the turbulent 1960s without too many mis-haps. As with so many universities of the day, it continued during the latter 1960s to expand physically and academically to meet the ever-increasing demands of enrolment, especially after 1968, when the university admitted women into every faculty as full-time students. That demanded new separate residential facilities for men and women, along with a new science building and more classroom space and of-fices, as well as a new stadium for the university's highly successful football team, the Huskies.[47]

At the beginning of the autumn term of 1968, fifty women regis-tered at Saint Mary's. After that, the numbers increased rapidly. Not everyone was pleased, however, at the university's move towards co-

45   "Report on Catholic Higher Education in the City of Halifax, having in mind ways and means of encouraging fuller co-operation among existing institutions, by Reverend L[aurence] K. Shook, C.S.B., submitted to Archbishop Joseph Gerald Berry", 29 June 1964, ibid.

46   McKenna, op. cit., 165.

47   Robert L. MacDougall, S.J., telegram to Angus J. Macdougall, S.J., 17 September 1968, ibid. Huskies Stadium was opened during the summer of 1968 to provide a fitting playing field for the Canada Summer Games.

education. The Sisters at Mount Saint Vincent's continued to object that Saint Mary's would draw women away from them. At the same time, some faculty members at Saint Mary's, along with a large number of male students, were opposed to having a co-educational university. They caused some minor disturbances within the university to show their opposition to women on campus.[48]

Still believing that a merger of the Catholic universities in Halifax into some kind of a federation would be beneficial to Catholic education and to the archdiocesan finances, Archbishop Berry's successor, Archbishop James M. Hayes (1967–1990), decided to explore the matter again. To that end, he established a committee during the summer of 1968; it held a series of meetings between Mount Saint Vincent's and Saint Mary's over that summer. After extensive discussions, a preliminary plan for "cooperative effort" between the two institutions was agreed upon. Yet the board of governors of Mount Saint Vincent's rejected even this plan. After that, the hope for unification of the Catholic universities was abandoned.

With their manpower declining by the end of the 1960s in Canada, the Jesuits decided to relinquish the responsibility for directing Saint Mary's University. On 31 July 1970, it was newly incorporated as a public university under a non-Jesuit board of governors and a senate. By that, the university was given complete academic autonomy from the Jesuits and the archdiocese.[49] Over time, the archdiocese also transferred its ownership of the buildings and property to the board. Representatives of the Jesuits and the archdiocese sat on the board, and the archbishops of Halifax remained the university's chancellor along with the vicar general as vice chancellor.

Among the first items of business of the new board of governors in September 1971 was to announce the name of the first non-Jesuit president, Dr. D. Owen Carrigan. Since he was unable to undertake the duties of the office until the following year, Mr. Edmund Morris became interim president. After Carrigan assumed the office in 1972,

---

48   E. G. Jarvis, letter to Archbishop James M. Hayes, 16 August 1968, ibid.

49   "An Act to Amend and Consolidate the Acts Relating to Saint Mary's University; Bill no. 102, House of Assembly, Nova Scotia, Session 1970", ibid., Box F-625. The bill was signed on 31 July 1970.

his attempts at improving the academic standards of the faculty members led to protests and disruption on campus, especially when he tried to fire three long-standing faculty members, one of whom was head of the faculty association. In the final analysis, the whole episode was responsible not only for the protests but also for the forming of a faculty union in 1974.

With the Jesuit Community having become a separate corporation in August 1970, and with the change at the same time in the governance of Saint Mary's from a Jesuit board to a non-Jesuit board and from a Jesuit president to a lay one, concern arose again among the Jesuits over the use of the revenues from the Power estate.[50] For many years, this matter had been rather contentious, but never more so than during the mid 1950s. The two executors of the estate, D. F. MacIsaac and the Honourable R. A. Donohue, the attorney general of Nova Scotia, were opposed to granting the Jesuits the monies. As a result, the executors were not distributing annually any revenues as they were required to do. Archbishop Berry challenged them for allowing the yearly income to accumulate rather than disposing it in conformity with the 1903 judgment of the Supreme Court of Canada, which had forbidden any accumulation of the income. When no change in procedure was forthcoming, to make his position clear, the archbishop threatened legal action against the executors of the estate for not acting properly. That prompted them to act. Between December 1956 and 5 April 1957, they sent to the archbishop revenues from the estate to the amount of about $40,000.00. In turn, he forwarded a cheque of $29,000.00 to Saint Mary's, part of which went towards completing the university's auditorium/gymnasium.[51]

The question of those revenues was not resolved then, however. For the following decade and more, legal arguments continued over whether the original will had granted the money to the Jesuits solely, to

---

50   Edward J. Dowling, S.J., letter to M. John Belair, S.J., 5 August 1970; M. John Belair, S.J., letter to Edward F. Sheridan, S.J., 15 September 1970, ibid. Dowling was the assistant or Socius to the Provincial Superior.

51   George E. Nunan, S.J., "The Power Estate", 6 April 1957, ibid. At the time, Nunan was the Provincial Superior. In drawing up the document, he had written that "It might be noted that it is the Jesuit Fathers, and not St. [sic] Mary's University, who are the beneficiaries of the will." Not everyone would have agreed with him on that point then or for the next many years.

the Jesuits working at Saint Mary's, or to Saint Mary's alone. Naturally enough, by the early 1970s, the Jesuits came down on the side of the first argument; to them should go the revenues. Nevertheless, the trustees still remained implacably opposed to allowing the Jesuits any money from the estate. Attempts were made in 1971 by the then Jesuit Superior in Halifax, M. John Belair, S.J. (1970–1975), to have some revenue made available to the Jesuits of Halifax for their academic purposes within the university. He did not have much success at first. Certainly "the matter of the Power Estate has reached an impasse," the Provincial Superior, Edward F. Sheridan, S.J. (1969–1972), noted on 8 June 1971.[52]

Indeed it had. At an acrimonious meeting of the estate's trustees a few days earlier, at which a Mr. MacInnis, the Jesuits' lawyer, was present to argue their case, "Mr. R. A. Donohue, the senior trustee, and his two lawyer sons, insisted that we [Jesuits] had no title to anything." Nonetheless, Belair informed the Provincial Superior, the Jesuits "have not given up." In fact, "Mr. MacInnis has obtained a copy of the whole will and is studying it to see if Donohue's interpretation has any grounds."[53] Belair then approached Archbishop Hayes concerning the matter. His response a few months later in a letter to the Provincial Superior was that the estate should endow the chaplaincy at Saint Mary's in order that a Jesuit might be hired. Eventually, under pressure from the archbishop, the trustees relented. By 1976, the Power estate was contributing $12,000.00 per annum to "assist Jesuit projects" in Halifax.[54]

---

52   Edward F. Sheridan, S.J., letter to M. John Belair, S.J., 8 June 1971; M. John Belair, S.J., letter to Edward F. Sheridan, S.J., 5 August 1971; Memo of a telephone conversation between Edward F. Sheridan, S.J., and M. John Belair, S.J., concerning the Power Estate, 17 September 1971; M. John Belair, S.J., letter to Edward F. Sheridan, S.J., 20 September 1972, ibid.

53   M. John Belair, S.J., letter to Edward F. Sheridan, S.J., 10 June 1971, ibid. Belair suggested that Donohue's antagonism to the Jesuits stemmed from his having been retired from the university's board of governors. Perhaps so, but that did not explain fully the reasons for his antipathy towards the Jesuits during the several years previously.

54   M. John Belair, S.J., letter to Edward F. Sheridan, S.J., 5 August 1971; Memo of a telephone conversation between Edward F. Sheridan, S.J., and M. John Belair, S.J., concerning the Power Estate, 17 September 1971; M. John Belair, S.J., letter to Edward F. Sheridan, S.J., 20 September 1972; Archbishop James M. Hayes, letter to Edward F. Sheridan, S.J., 24 January 1972; "Concerning the Power Estate", 31 December 1976, ibid.

With the Jesuits participating less and less in the university by the early 1970s, the archbishop sought other ways for them to become involved in Halifax. During March 1972, he explored with Belair the possibility of their assuming responsibility for St. Patrick's parish, principally to work in the inner city among the poor. There seemed little likelihood of that happening; Jesuit manpower was not available to take on that ministry. Thus, Belair's response to the archbishop was not entirely encouraging. On 25 March, Belair wrote the Provincial Superior: "I said [to the archbishop] I doubted strongly if we would want to take it over, and that we would just have to await further developments." Certainly Belair was correct in his assessment of the situation about Jesuit manpower and their hesitation in assuming the responsibilities of another parish in the city.[55]

Yet alternatively, the Provincial Superior recognized that there could be a wider possibility at St. Patrick's than parochial ministry. On Sheridan's behalf, his assistant, Edward J. Dowling, S.J., proposed to Belair that St. Patrick's might become "a residence for the team of chaplains looking after all the university and college people in Halifax." With that too, there might be a Jesuit "devoting his time to spiritual animation and renewal work with priests and Religious and, perhaps, for one man looking after what parochial responsibilities are still present at St. Patrick's." Although nothing ever came of that suggested use of St. Patrick's at the time, from many viewpoints the proposal had merit. In the end, however, due to a manpower shortage, the Province of Upper Canada was reluctant to assign any Jesuits to such a team.[56]

Over the years since 1940, many Jesuits who served at Saint Mary's could be singled out for their contributions to the university. Of those, two deserve special mention: M. Walter Burke-Gaffney, S.J., and

---

55   M. John Belair, S.J., letter to Edward F. Sheridan, S.J., ibid. The Jesuits already had staffed Canadian Martyrs parish since 31 July 1952.

56   Edward J. Dowling, S.J., letter to M. John Belair, S.J., 28 March 1972, ibid. Ironically, eventually the Jesuits did assume significant responsibility for St. Patrick's parish. Although assigned to other ministries in the Halifax area, George P. Leach, S.J., served in the parish as a sacramental minister from 1995 to 2000, as the presbyteral moderator from 2000 to 2002, and again as the sacramental minister from 2008 to 2009. During those years, other Jesuits also assisted in the parish from time to time. Beginning in 2009, Jean-Marc Laporte, s.j., assumed the responsibility of sacramental minister at St. Patrick's, and in 2011 was appointed priest-in-charge of the parish.

William A. Stewart, S.J. Deeply committed to higher education and to Saint Mary's, their dedication and years of service were outstanding. Both worked long years there; both were excellent teachers; both participated extensively in the life of the university; and both were greatly involved in the wider Halifax community.

Intelligent, scholarly, and a first-rate pedagogue, Burke-Gaffney was assigned to Saint Mary's in 1940; he remained there until his death in 1979. Along with being dean of engineering (1940–1948) and dean of science for four years, he was professor of applied science (1948–1955) and then professor of astronomy until 1965, at which time he became a professor emeritus and special university lecturer. During his years at Saint Mary's, he also oversaw the renovation of the science laboratories and the installation of a telescope, and had a principal role in preparing the scientific curriculum for the Nova Scotia Technical College. In the course of his academic career, he also produced several internationally acclaimed articles on astronomy, mathematics, and engineering, which appeared in scholarly journals in Canada, Europe, and the United States; he also wrote two books, *Kepler and the Jesuits* (1944) and *Daniel Seghers, 1590–1661* (1961). As well, he had membership in eleven distinguished Canadian and international scientific, mathematical, and astronomical societies; he attended as many annual meetings of those societies as he could; and he delivered papers at sundry national and international conferences. On account of his renowned contributions to science and astronomy, he received distinguished awards and acknowledgements from a number of those societies.[57]

Because of his interests in celestial mechanics and in tracking the orbits of *Sputnik* I and II and *Echo* I, in eclipses of the sun and moon, in investigating the superstition surrounding UFOs, in demonology, in meteors and comets, as well as in writing poetry and collecting flowers, Burke-Gaffney was in great demand as a public lecturer. It was once said of him, by someone who had heard him speak, that he spoke in the silky intonations of an Irish gentleman. Highly intelligent, witty, and speaking with a slight Dublin accent—he was born there—and

---

57   DJB, vol. 1, 38–39.

given his ease in explaining in ordinary language the most intricate of scientific phenomena, he was in demand as a public speaker and became a popular resource-person for the Halifax media. He had a gift for elucidating the most abstruse of scientific principles and complex technology to the uninformed; he especially enjoyed speaking about space-age technology at a time when it was still in its infancy. To honour his scholarly achievements at Saint Mary's and his contribution to the international scientific and astronomical communities, in 1972 the Reverend Michael Walter Burke-Gaffney Observatory was installed on the top of the Loyola Residence on campus.[58]

William A. Stewart, S.J., arrived at Saint Mary's ten years after Burke-Gaffney. A humanist through and through, and an exceptional teacher, he involved himself in many academic and extra-curricular activities on campus. In everything he did, his was a simple, direct approach, based on his belief that if one loved a subject and was passionately committed to it, not only would one do well in it but one would also greatly influence others to become involved. Throughout his years at Saint Mary's, Stewart held numerous positions: professor of philosophy, librarian, dean of arts and science, academic vice president, and eventually professor emeritus.

Stewart was passionate about English literature and poetry, drama, music, art, the sea, and Saint Margaret's Bay. Most especially, though, he loved the theatre. In many ways he became best known at Saint Mary's and in Halifax as a promoter and director of drama. After arriving at the university, he was reluctant at first to participate in its theatrical life—he was aware how time-consuming that could be—yet in the end he could not resist. Before long he became fully engaged in the SMU Dramatic Society, and in short order was appointed the society's moderator. Eventually, he became greatly involved in the promotion of drama throughout the city and in many parts of Nova Scotia. As well, he was a long-time member of the Nova Scotia Drama League and of the Theatre Arts Guild; participated regularly in the Dominion Drama Festival; was a member of the board of directors of

---

58   Ibid.

Bit Players; and served two terms as chair of the board of governors of the Cultural Federation of Nova Scotia.

In 1983, Stewart retired from teaching, at which time he was granted the status of professor emeritus and awarded an honorary doctorate for his exceptional service to the university and to the community at large. That same year, the University Alumni Association established the Father William A. Stewart, S.J., Medal for Excellence in Teaching, an annual award given to a Saint Mary's professor who has distinguished herself or himself as a professor inside and outside the classroom. The several other awards and medals he received— including the Queen's Silver Jubilee Medal (1977) and the Dramatist of the Year Award (1981)—also commemorated his outstanding achievements and unqualified contributions to teaching, to university life, and to theatre in Halifax and in Nova Scotia. Stewart died on 5 March 2009 at the René Goupil House (Jesuit infirmary), Pickering. He was ninety-three years of age, and had been a Jesuit for over seventy-two years; he had spent fifty-six of them at Saint Mary's. On 20 May 2009, the university announced the establishment of a scholarship in his name: the Father William Stewart, S.J., Memorial Scholarship. Altogether, these remain a fitting testimony to his life's work at Saint Mary's.

Following the shift in governance to a non-Jesuit board in 1970, the university effectively became secular in nature, although it continued to foster some ties with the Catholic Church by maintaining a Catholic chaplain and supporting the department of theological studies, which became the department of religious studies to reflect the intentions of the university to move away from its Catholic historical roots. As well, an Institute for the Study of Values had been established in 1968. Later, in 1975, it became The Institute of Human Values, the only such institute in Canada at the time. Those Jesuits already with professorial appointments would remain there until their retirement. Because of the dearth of manpower, since 1970 no more Jesuit professors were appointed full-time to Saint Mary's. The last two Jesuit professors, William P. Lonc, S.J., and Lawrence Murphy, S.J., both retired in 1996. Lonc was the last Jesuit appointed to a full-time position at Saint Mary's University when he joined the department of physics in 1969.

Jesuits continued to be assigned to the university's chaplaincy until 1976; during the subsequent twenty years, none were appointed. From 1996 to 2009, a Jesuit was once again either the university's chaplain or a member of the chaplaincy team. The last Jesuit chaplain, Daniel Kelly, left Saint Mary's in 2009. Thus ended sixty-nine years of Jesuit presence at Saint Mary's University.

IV

Western Canada

ST. BONIFACE: ST. BONIFACE COLLEGE, 1885–1924

"Bonitatem et disciplinam et scientiam doce me"
—Motto of St. Boniface College

For generations, the First Nations people—the Ojibway, Cree, Sioux, Dene, Mandane, and Assiniboine—had lived in sparsely settled agricultural areas along the Red River in what is now Manitoba, principally growing corn and other seed crops. Only in the late eighteenth and early nineteenth centuries, with the fur-trading posts of the Hudson's Bay Company and the North West Company arising along the river valley, did the first pockets of European settlements develop nearby. Later the Métis—those who have both European and First Nations heritage, the majority of whom identified with the French-speaking Catholic population—mainly inhabited what became Saint-Boniface and the French-speaking areas in the Red River valley to the south.

In 1812, a small group of Scots, sponsored by Thomas Douglas, 5th earl of Selkirk, established the first permanent European agricultural settlement in what became the Red River Colony (or Selkirk

Settlement). In time, descendants of these various peoples—First Nations, French, English, Scots, Métis—founded the province of Manitoba in 1870.[1] At first, the province's demographical mixture remained fairly balanced between the First Nations, the Métis, the French-speaking and the English-speaking inhabitants. That would begin to shift, however, during the early 1880s, with the advance of the Canadian Pacific Railway into Manitoba and onwards towards the Rocky Mountains, when English-speaking Protestant farmers from Ontario and elsewhere were attracted by the offer of free land. On the other hand, far fewer French-speaking people from Quebec, New Brunswick, or Ontario were enticed to move westward.

By the end of the century, due to the federal immigration policy of Sir Clifford Sifton, the change in the demographical balance would rapidly increase. As minister of the Interior in Sir Wilfrid Laurier's first cabinet of 1896, Sifton set out to populate the prairies with a productive agricultural people who would contribute significantly to the settlement of western Canada. Anti-Catholic and anti–French Canadian, he favoured Protestants, as he said, those who would farm, and especially those who spoke or would learn to speak English. For nearly a decade after 1896, he vigorously wooed to the prairies Midwestern American farmers, people from Scotland and northern England, Protestant farmers from Ontario, and Scandinavians to settle on the prairies. That brought about a sizeable increase in the English-speaking population, along with a major shift to a Protestant dominance. With these groups came peasant farmers from Eastern and Central Europe, few of whom spoke English, and who were not Protestant.[2]

---

1 DCB, vol. V, 204–269. For an account of the Selkirk Settlements, cf. John M. Bumstead, *Lord Selkirk: A Life* (Winnipeg: University of Manitoba Press, 2008), 192–195; 208–213; 345–355. At the time of entering Confederation in 1870, the Province of Manitoba—excepting the First Nations people who were not included in the census—had a population of 12,228 inhabitants. Of that number, the area of Winnipeg was around 8,000 people. By 1891, the population of Winnipeg had increased to more than 27,000, to 45,000 ten years later, and to over 130,000 in 1911.

2 DCB, vol. XV, 941–948. David J. Hall, "Clifford Sifton: Immigration and Settlement Policy, 1896–1905" in Howard Palmer, ed., *The Settlement of the West* (Calgary: University of Calgary, 1977), 50–85; Jean Burnet with Howard Palmer, *Coming Canadians: An Introduction to a History of Canada's People* (Toronto: McClelland and Stewart, 1988), 27. A member of a prominent Winnipeg family, Sir Clifford Sifton's immigration policy was instrumental in around three

Even when there was still a demographical balance in population between the French-speaking and English-speaking inhabitants, the French-speaking people desired their own Catholic educational institutions. That was essential, they believed, in order to preserve their Catholic faith and the French language. With the steady growth of Protestantism in Manitoba during the years following 1870, that desire became ever more pressing.

The first such French-language post-secondary Catholic college founded in western Canada was Collège de Saint-Boniface.[3] The origins of the college are imprecise, but can be placed at approximately 1818, when two priests from Quebec, Joseph-Norbert Provencher and Sévère Dumoulin, and a seminarian, Guillaume Edge, arrived to take up missionary work in the vast area known as the "Pays d'en haut" far to the west of the French settlements along the St. Lawrence River.[4] During that year, Provencher established a small French-speaking school for boys of white settlers and Métis, with a view to educating them as priests for the western mission.[5]

Later, in 1841 and 1842, despite his many efforts, Provencher was unsuccessful in attracting Jesuits to administer and teach in his classical college, situated in Saint-Boniface opposite the confluence of the Red and Assiniboine rivers. Instead, the Oblate Fathers accepted to direct it, from 1860 to 1866. They were succeeded by the Christian Brothers, then followed by the Oblates again, from 1870 to 1879, next by the secular priests and, finally, by the Jesuits in 1885, when Archbishop Alexandre-Antonin Taché (1853–1894) of Saint-Boniface invited them to assume responsibility for the college. Five Jesuit priests, three Scholastics, and four Brothers were assigned there; Hippolyte Lory, s.j., was appointed the first Rector.[6]

---

million people settling in western Canada between 1896 and 1914.

3   Incorporated on 3 May 1871 as Collège Saint-Joseph, it became known as Collège de Saint-Boniface. Today it is entitled Université de Saint-Boniface.

4   DCB, vol. VIII, 249–250; 718–723.

5   Joseph-Norbet Provencher had been appointed auxiliary bishop of Quebec in 1819, and head of the newly established vicariate apostolic of Hudson Bay and James Bay when it was established in 1844. When that became the diocese of the North West in 1847, Provencher became its first bishop. The name of the diocese was changed to Saint-Boniface in 1851.

6   DCB, vol. XII, 1002–1012.

For some time, Collège de Saint-Boniface had tried to maintain the traditional core eight-year programme of a classical course in philosophy, religion, history, Latin, Greek, English and French literatures, composition, grammar, mathematics, geography, and music. Many of those courses were given in both French and English. When, in 1878, the provincial government set out to found the first university not only in Manitoba but in all of western Canada, Collège de Saint-Boniface became one of the three founding institutions of the new University of Manitoba.

After 1885, the Jesuits aimed to replicate their bilingual classical course programme in the humanities and commerce at St. Mary's College, Montreal. Thus they added further French and English courses over the years, in science, botany, chemistry, physics, medicine, law, and seismology. As well, the Jesuit professors worked closely with L'Hôpital Général de Saint-Boniface, founded by Les Sœurs Grises in 1871 near Collège de Saint-Boniface, notably teaching in the area of medical ethics, and later with the hospital's School of Nursing, after it was established in 1897.

Among that first group of Jesuits at the college was Lewis H. Drummond, S.J. Altogether, he would serve in different capacities for some twenty-four years, with the exception of two years as Rector of St. Mary's College, Montreal (1890–1892). It was most especially as prefect of studies, professor of philosophy and languages, and public speaker that he was renowned. Although an anglophone, he furthered the French and Jesuit causes in his lectures, sermons, speeches, and writings with considerable eloquence. From the mid 1880s, he involved himself in all the broiling issues of the day, notably those concerning the rights of French- and English-language Catholic schools in the province (the Manitoba Schools Question). As the controversies increased, he became the primary spokesman for the Catholic position. He published many articles on the topic in the Catholic weekly *Northwest Review*, of which he was editor, along with a number of pamphlets and tracts, including "The French Element in the Canadian Northwest" (1887), "True and False Ideals in Education" (1888), "The Jesuits" (1889), and *Acadia, Missing Links of a Lost Chapter in American History* (1895).[7]

In the late 1890s, the University of Manitoba began planning fundamental structural changes, from being a university made up of degree-granting colleges to a degree-granting university with affiliated colleges. At its foundation, the University of Manitoba was not, in itself, a teaching university. The original provincial legislative act allowed the university to confer degrees only on students graduating from the three founding colleges: St. Boniface College, St. John's College, and Manitoba College. In 1900, the Manitoba legislature changed the University Act to allow the University of Manitoba to do its own teaching instead of relying solely upon the teaching of the three founding colleges. At the time, the fear—however ungrounded—was that the university would not accept the courses of the colleges, and therefore not accept their students for a degree. Drummond played a leading role as the representative of St. Boniface College and the archdiocese during the long negotiations that, in 1900, brought about the reorganization of the University of Manitoba and its colleges.[8]

All through the years following his arrival at the college, Drummond also ministered to the small but growing English-speaking Catholic population in the area. Eventually, he took charge of an English-speaking parish in the Fort Rouge area of south Winnipeg between the rivers. There, on 16 February 1908, in a vacant store on Osborne Street, he celebrated the first Mass for what would become the Jesuits' St. Ignatius Parish in 1909.[9]

From the time the Jesuits assumed charge of St. Boniface College, the student enrolment generally remained low, and continued thus during the final two decades of the nineteenth century; enrolment fluctuated annually from seventy to about ninety students. By the early twentieth century, however, the numbers increased rapidly, partially due to the economic recovery on the prairies following the economic depression of the 1880s, and partially due to the general

---

7   DCB, vol. XV, 303–305; DJB, vol. 1, 93–96.

8   DCB, op. cit.; DJB, vol. 1, 94.

9   DJB, vol. 1, 94–95.

population growth rising from the Sifton immigration policy. The college's enrolment eventually reached well over 300 French and English male students, and remained somewhere in that range for many years afterwards. Due to that increase, the college constructed extensive additions between 1904 and 1906.[10]

Several scholarships were available to students at the college. These aimed not only to assist a student financially during his years at the college, but most importantly to help him maintain a high general average in order to gain admission into the University of Manitoba. Admission was based on a student's academic standing received in an individual college, and was very competitive. In general, St. Boniface's students did well, as was noted on 10 June 1896 in the *Northwest Review*: "St. Boniface has once more maintained its reputation for thoroughness in pass subjects and for a high general average." The writer went on in a somewhat ironic manner, however, to indicate what that might have implied: "There is no hot-house forcing of budding geniuses at the expense of the general improvement of each class.... No University candidate from St. Boniface College has ever made a total failure and that partial failures have been comparatively few." The general results seemed brighter the following year, as the same newspaper pointed out on 8 July 1897: "The students of St. Boniface College came off with even more than their usual success.... Not one of the St. Boniface men failed in anything."

The college's unofficial policy of bilingualism was often a source of serious tension between the two language groups by the turn of the new century. The complaints among English-speaking students about the college were several. The college was too far away; the English-language students, usually fewer in number, were not treated as equal to the French; the English-language courses were poorly presented by French-speaking professors; the eight-year classical course education was not what they wanted. It should be noted, however, that from 1886 to 1924, despite the complaints about French-speaking Jesuits and their poor English, many English-speaking Jesuits were professors at St. Boniface College and lectured in English in a number of courses.[11]

---

10   *Northwest Review*, 10 June 1896.

11   Gérard Jolicoeur, *Les Jésuites dans la vie manitobaine, 1885–1922* (Saint-Boniface: Centre

Félix Martin, s.j. (1804–1886), founded Collège Sainte-Marie/St. Mary's College, Montreal, in 1848 as a bilingual college, and became its first Rector.

Collège Sainte-Marie/St. Mary's College, Montreal, opened in 1848 and moved to rue Bleury in 1851 into this building, designed and built by Félix Martin, s.j.

Arthur Jones, S.J. (1838–1918), was among the greatest Canadian scholars of the nineteenth century. His pioneering archaeological work in Huronia led to the first identification of its principal Jesuit sites.
He was archivist of the Canadian Jesuits for thirty-six years.

3

Gregory O'Bryan, S.J. (1858–1907), was responsible for establishing Loyola College, Montreal, in 1896, and served twice as Vice Rector and briefly as Rector.

Prominent on "Catholic Hill", the Church of Our Lady Immaculate, Guelph, Ontario, was constructed between 1877 and 1888 (the two towers were completed in 1926). It replaced an earlier church, St. Bartholomew's, on each side of which were the first schools and the short-lived St. Ignatius College established by John Holzer, s.j. (1817–1888).

William H. Hingston, S.J. (1877–1964), was Rector of Loyola College,
Montreal (1918–1925), and Provincial Superior of the Vice Province
of Upper Canada (1928–1934).

Loyola High School Archives

A refugee from the persecution in Mexico, Eduardo de la Peza, s.j. (1878–1953), came to Loyola College, Montreal, in 1919, served as Prefect of Studies (1920–1923), and assisted in revising the academic programme into two sectors: the college and the high school.

Opened in 1896, Loyola College, Montreal, moved to the Tupper Building, 68 Drummond Street, in 1898, where it remained until 1915.

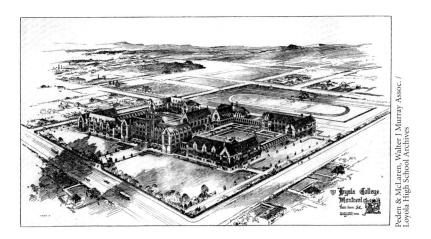

Drawing by the Montreal architects Peden, McLaren, and Walter Murray,
Associate in 1913 for the new Loyola College buildings on Sherbrooke Street.

Refectory and Junior Buildings, Loyola College, Montreal, 1916.

William Argan, artist, Campion College Archives

Established in 1917, Campion College, Regina, was under the direction of Thomas J. MacMahon, S.J. (1918–1921), and opened in these two houses on 13th Avenue during September 1918.

William Argan, artist, Campion College Archives

Campion College, Regina, moved into its second building at 1400–1414 Argyle Street in 1919.

The third building of Campion College, Regina, was designed by
the Regina architect James J. Puntin and opened in 1921
on the corner of 23rd Avenue and Albert Street.

Designed by the Vancouver architect Peter Thornton, Campion College
moved to this new building on the Regina Campus, University of Saskatchewan
(later University of Regina), in 1968.

The Chapel, Loyola College, Montreal, at the time of its opening in 1933.

St. Paul's College, Ellice and Vaughan, Winnipeg, 1950s. The college opened on Selkirk Avenue in 1926, and moved to Ellice and Vaughan in 1931. The Jesuits assumed responsibility for the college in 1933.

Regiopolis College, Kingston, Ontario, 1960s. Established in 1837, the Jesuits taught at and administered the college from 1931 to 1971.

Saint Mary's University, Halifax, the McNally Building, 1960s.
After occupying a site on Windsor Street, the university moved
to this new building at 35 Robie Street.

The Chapel, Campion College, University of Regina,
during a Eucharistic liturgy, 2010.

University of Regina Photography Department

The Chapel, St. Paul's College, University of Manitoba, Winnipeg,
with its splendid mosaic of Christ the King in Glory by Lionel Thomas of Toronto,
remains the jewel of the university's campus.

That tension at St. Boniface College reflected the rising conflict between the two language groups throughout the Winnipeg area, and was seriously affecting the Catholic Church in Manitoba.[12] By the early 1900s, as the Catholic English-speaking population increased across the Red River in Winnipeg, the demand for more English-speaking priests was being raised due to the dissatisfaction from being served by bilingual French priests in the English-speaking parish, St. Mary's. On 25 November 1906, a committee of parishioners—clergy, business people, and other professionals—from St. Mary's petitioned the archbishop, Louis-Philippe-Adélard Langevin (1895–1915), to establish an English-speaking diocese in Winnipeg along with more English-speaking parishes that would be served only by English-speaking priests, and to establish a separate English-language Catholic college, also in Winnipeg.[13]

Seven parishioners met with the archbishop on 2 December. He was sympathetic to their petition, but he was not in a position to satisfy all their demands, notably that of establishing an English-language diocese in Winnipeg. Instead of founding a separate English-language college, the archbishop officially confirmed once again the bilingual status of Collège de Saint-Boniface/St. Boniface College, and emphasized his successful efforts to persuade the Jesuits there to establish a separate English-language programme leading to a Bachelor of Arts degree. That had begun the previous September. His intention was, he assured the English-speaking Catholics, to serve satisfactorily both French and English Catholic students.[14]

Nevertheless, his assurances were not satisfactory. The fact was that during the first decade of the twentieth century, the English-speaking Catholics of Winnipeg were fundamentally less and less at ease with having a dominantly French-speaking college as the only

---

d'études Franco-Canadiennes de l'Ouest, 1985), 163–174; André-N. Lalonde, "L'Église catholique et les Francophones de l'Ouest, 1818–1930," CCHA, *Sessions d'études*, 50 (1983), 485–497; DCB, vol. XIV, 597–601.

12   Cf. John M. Reid, "The Erection of the Roman Catholic Archdiocese of Winnipeg," (Winnipeg: University of Manitoba, unpublished M.A. Thesis, 1961), for an account of those years of conflict.

13   Ibid., 12–15.

14   Ibid., 16–17.

institution for higher education. Many of them were determined not to be content until they had their own college. In response, some English-speaking Jesuits at St. Boniface College even suggested that, given the large number of English-speaking students at the college, it should be declared an "English" college. That was not about to happen, however.[15]

For some time, too, the public struggle between the two language groups arising from the Manitoba Schools Question continued to be intense, with the issues of language and schools greatly debated on all sides. The conflict was being observed from afar by many Catholics with more than a little interest. In fact, it had been keenly noticed especially from Ontario and Quebec, and raised considerable problems between the two provinces. The tensions had come to a boiling point in the passing of the controversial provincial legislation in 1890 that altered Manitoba's French-language school system and abolished French as an official language in the province. Along with those difficulties caused by French and English education in Manitoba, the developing and heated discussions in Ontario over the establishing of bilingual Catholic schools—which in the end split the Catholic hierarchy—had also become a point of friction between Ontario and Quebec as well as between Protestants and Catholics in the country, especially during the federal election of 1896.[16]

It did not help matters that Bishop Michael F. Fallon of London (1909–1931) involved himself in the fray. A powerful figure among English Catholics in Ontario and a leader of the anti-bilingual movement in Ontario's Catholic colleges and schools, he encouraged the

---

15   Jolicoeur, 167.

16   For studies about the Manitoba Schools Question, cf. Paul Crunican, *Priests and Politicians: Manitoba Schools and the Election of 1896* (Toronto: University of Toronto Press, 1974); Manoly R. Lupul, *The Roman Catholic Question and the North West School Question: A Study in Church-State Relations in Western Canada, 1875–1905* (Toronto: University of Toronto Press, 1974); Raymond J. A. Huel, "The Irish-French Conflict in Catholic Episcopal Nominations: the Western Sees and the Struggle for Domination," CCHA, *Study Sessions*, 42 (1975), 51–70; Francis Russell, *The Canadian Crucible: Manitoba's Role in Canada's Great Divide* (Winnipeg: Heartland Associates, 2003); Roberto Perin, *Rome in Canada: The Vatican and Canadian Affairs in the Late Victorian Age* (Toronto: University of Toronto Press, 1990); Vincent J. Jensen, S.J., "The Manitoba School Question of the 1890s", in Friesen and Lebrun, 284–301; Raymond J. A. Huel, *Archbishop A.-A. Taché of St. Boniface: The "Good Fight" and the Illusive Vision* (Edmonton: University of Alberta Press, 2003); and DCB, XII, 1010–1011; XIV, 598–600.

English-speaking Catholics in Winnipeg to persist in their opposition to the dominance of the French-speaking population and to agitate for their own diocese and Catholic college. Rightly or wrongly, he was accused of being anti-French and of stirring up animosity between the language groups. At heart, however, Bishop Fallon was not anti-French. He himself spoke fluent French, and believed that a fluency in both languages was important, indeed essential, for educated Catholics. At the same time, however, he held strong objections to bilingual education in Catholic colleges and schools. Although intelligent, well-educated, and articulate, he was not always careful of how he expressed himself. As a consequence, his French-Canadian episcopal colleagues, including the archbishop of Saint-Boniface, along with some English-speaking bishops, took offence at some of his anti-bilingual speeches and at his generally outspoken, intransigent stand against bilingualism that they interpreted as being anti-French.[17]

Eventually, the requests of the Catholics in Winnipeg to have their own English-speaking bishop and college would be granted, although not before some years would pass. Yet even that did not settle the matter entirely. English-speaking Catholics in Winnipeg were determined that their bishop would be an English-speaking archbishop having equal status with the French-speaking archbishop of Saint-Boniface. Bishop Fallon and other English-speaking bishops saw to that with Rome when the archdiocese of Winnipeg was established on 4 December 1915, with Alfred A. Sinnott (1915–1952) as its first archbishop.[18] In the meantime, though, and given that in Manitoba there was no Catholic higher education alternative to St. Boniface College, English-speaking Catholic young men—however reluctantly, in some cases—continued to attend the English-language courses until

17   For detailed accounts of Bishop Fallon's crusade against bilingual colleges and schools, and of the English-French conflict in the Catholic Church, cf. John K. A. Farrell, "Michael Francis Fallon, Bishop of London, Ontario-Canada, 1909–1931: The Man and His Controversies," CCHA, *Historical Studies*, 35 (1968), 73–90; Robert Coquette, *Language, Schools and Religion: English-French Conflict in Ontario* (Ottawa: University of Ottawa Press, 1975); Chad Garfield, *Language, Schools and Cultural Conflicts: The Origins of the French-Language Controversies in Ontario* (Kingston: McGill-Queen's University Press, 1987).

18   Robert Choquette, "Adélard Langevin et l'érection de l'archidiocèse de Winnipeg," *Revue d'histoire de l'Amérique française*, 28 (1974–1975), 187–207. Winnipeg is not a metropolitan see. Thus, it is not an ecclesiastical province, and does not have suffragan bishops.

the founding in 1926 of an English-speaking male Catholic college, St. Paul's College, by Archbishop Sinnott.[19]

No doubt the most distressing event in the life of the college occurred on Saturday, 25 November 1922, when tragedy struck at two o'clock in the morning: a devastating fire ravaged the college. Nine students and one Jesuit Brother, Frederick Stormont, perished in the fire. The 40,000-volume library, the dormitory building, the chapel, the classrooms, and the college's registries and archival records of Franco-Manitoba were lost. Neither the Jesuit Community nor the students were prepared for such an emergency. The college had not employed a night watchman, there were no fire escapes on the building, and regular fire drills in the college had not been introduced. Further, the fire ladders were too short to reach the fourth floor of the college building, which, despite their heroic efforts to save as many in the burning building as possible, left the firemen accused of "cowardice and incompetence."[20]

Several conspiracy theories circulated, with foul play alleged. Two explosions, it was immediately asserted, had started the fire. Indeed, because there had been a number of recent fires in Religious houses, especially French-Canadian ones, arson by discontented anti-French English-speaking persons from Winnipeg was highly suspected. Supporters of the Ku Klux Klan, which was active in Winnipeg at the time, were also blamed. According to a report in *The New York Times*, a Mrs. Charles Loiselle reported seeing a "mysterious" man carrying a rope on the grounds of the college at eight o'clock on Friday evening; two hours later, she declared, she saw him again in the same vicinity. Nothing was ever proven. Even the Jesuit Provincial Superior, John M. Filion, s.j., reported to the Superior General in Rome that the fire was caused by explosions set off by English-speaking Protestant extremists. His accusation was never proven, either. In the final report by Charles Heath, the provincial fire chief, on 7 February 1923, careless smoking in a boys' washroom was cited as the cause.[21]

---

19   Reid, 97–96.

20   DJB, vol. 1, 329; Vince Leah, *Alarm of Fire: 100 Years of Fire-fighting in Winnipeg, 1882–1982* (Winnipeg: Fire-fighter's Burn Fund, 1982), 37.

21   *The New York Times*, "Mystery in College Fire," 1 December 1922.

Despite the devastation, however, academic life continued. Archbishop Arthur Béliveau (1915–1955) made available to the Jesuits the nearby Le Petit Séminaire de Saint-Boniface, located at 200, rue de la Cathédrale, and in early January 1923, the bilingual classes resumed. Later, in 1924, the archbishop sponsored a drive among the francophone population in Manitoba and Quebec to raise funds for a new college wing. It was completed within the year, and provided recreation areas, classrooms, an assembly hall, and dormitories.[22]

At the division of the Jesuit Province of Canada on 27 June 1924 into the La Province du Bas Canada and the Vice Province of Upper Canada, Collège de Saint-Boniface became the sole responsibility of the French-Canadian Jesuits.[23] They remained at the college until 1967, at which time it was turned over to the archdiocese of Saint-Boniface. Even if, by the twenty-first century, Jesuits no longer were involved with the college's administration or teaching, true to its origins, Collège de Saint-Boniface remains the centre of the francophone cultural and educational life in Manitoba, and still is situated in Saint-Boniface, despite the fact that both the University of Manitoba and all its constituent colleges moved in 1958 from central Winnipeg to the southern part of the city, the Fort Garry Campus. As a constituent college in the University of Manitoba, Collège de Saint-Boniface remains the sole French-speaking university college in western Canada.

EDMONTON: EDMONTON JESUIT COLLEGE, 1913–1924

"Le collège s'adapte aux exigences de l'Alberta"
—From *Xavier*, the student newspaper

During the opening decade of the twentieth century, several attempts had been made by the archbishop of Edmonton, Émile-Joseph Legal, O.M.I., and by several prominent Catholics to found a Catholic college in that city. In 1906, Édouard Lecompte, s.j., Superior of the Canada Jesuit Mission, contemplated a request of 28 March from Legal to found such a college. In August, Lecompte dispatched to

---

22 The college's original site is the present-day Parc Provencher in Saint-Boniface.

23 In 1933, the English-speaking Jesuits would assume the direction of St. Paul's College, Winnipeg.

Edmonton Jacques Dugas, s.j., Rector of Collège de Saint-Boniface, and Philip Bournival, s.j., a professor of philosophy there, to visit the archbishop and assess the situation. Lecompte himself travelled to Edmonton later that autumn, but in the end deemed that it was more appropriate to wait awhile. The archbishop, however, persisted in pressing his request on the Jesuits.[24]

Consequently, six years later, on 10 August 1912, Théophile Hudon, s.j., professor of rhetoric, classics, and history at Collège de Saint-Boniface, arrived in Edmonton with instructions from Joseph Carrière, s.j., Lecompte's successor as Provincial Superior (1912–1918), to meet with the archbishop to decide whether to found a college there. The Jesuits accepted to open a college. With the backing of the archbishop and several prominent laymen, money was promised to construct a building on land donated by John Norris and Joseph Scott, strong supporters of Catholic education. The college's three-storey building was begun in December 1912. On the following 25 March, the Alberta Legislature accorded Collège Saint-François-Xavier/Edmonton Jesuit College civil recognition with a bilingual charter. Situated on 114th Avenue between 127th and 128th Streets, the college became generally known as "Collège des Jésuites/Edmonton Jesuit College".[25]

Hudon became its first Vice Rector on 1 June 1913; later that summer, five Jesuit priests and three Brothers arrived, among whom was Lewis H. Drummond. The college opened as a bilingual classical college on 1 October with fifty-two English and French students. By year's end there were ninety-six students. Eight years later, in 1921, the college achieved its maximum enrolment of 221 students.

Not having its own degree-granting facilities, the college affiliated in 1917 with Université Laval, and in 1919, the first class of Rhetoric sat the examination for Laval. The first students graduated through Laval in June 1921. Indeed, the Rector of the university let it be known that he was pleased at the "très beaux succès" of these first graduates. That

---

24   Moreau, Joseph-P. "Le collège des Jésuites (1913–1942)". *Aspects du passé franco-albertain: témoignages et* études, ed. Alice Trottier (Edmonton: Salon d'histoire de la francophonie albertaine, 1980), 21.

25   DJB, vol. 1, 95–96. Its building was demolished in 1967.

was an important moment for the reputation of both institutions, as the Rector at Laval pointed out: "De si beaux succès sont une preuve non équivoque de la bonne instruction donnée au Collège."[26]

From its beginning, Collège des Jésuites/Edmonton Jesuit College was plagued with financial problems. Fundraising turned out not to be easy. There were wholehearted but none-too-successful attempts by lay people to raise $50,000.00 for the college. Not only were the French-speaking and English-speaking Catholic populations small and generally of modest means, but to make matters more difficult, there was a serious economic slump in Alberta during the war years, while Edmonton's population was in decline, from 72,500 in 1914 to 53,000 two years later. In consequence, during the post-war years—the 1920s and, in particular, during the Great Depression of the 1930s—life continued to be hard economically for most families. In every sense, therefore, the college never recovered financially from those years of want and the subsequent fall-off in enrolment.[27]

Further complications had ensued as well during the early 1920s. The newly appointed archbishop, Henry J. O'Leary (1920–1938), was keen on founding in Edmonton a college solely for English-speaking Catholic young men based on the four-year arts and science collegiate model, and thus distinct from the Jesuits' bilingual classical college. He hoped that English-speaking Jesuits would staff it, and so raised the matter on several occasions with the Jesuit Provincial Superior, John M. Filion. Filion was none too sympathetic to the idea.

Nonetheless, in 1926 the archbishop decided to open his English-speaking Catholic college, St. Joseph's, which would be affiliated with the University of Alberta. Filion, who since 1924 was the Provincial Superior of the newly formed Vice Province of Upper Canada, again would not accept the archbishop's invitation for the Jesuits to direct the college. He was rightly concerned that, since St. Joseph's would be in the north end of the city, near Collège des Jésuites/Edmonton Jesuit College, such proximity might raise difficulties with the French-

---

26 Moreau, 21–22.

27 Edmonton's population had increased only slowly until oil was discovered nearby at Leduc in 1947, after which its population surged from 83,000 to 134,000 within six years. The sum of $50,000.00 in today's value would be approximately $800,000.00.

speaking Jesuits. Their college had been admitting English-speaking students since its establishment. Already under financial duress, understandably the French-speaking Jesuits did not want any competition for students from an English-speaking Jesuit college. Their disquiet was justified. Many English-speaking Catholics did not want to be educated in a mainly French-speaking classical college, and were eager to switch to St. Joseph's College and to its four-year undergraduate programme.

As Filion also knew, there was scarcely sufficient money and English-speaking Canadian Jesuits to staff the colleges they already had. For those reasons, he had refused requests from the bishops of Sault Ste. Marie, Victoria, Vancouver, Winnipeg, and Toronto to open colleges in their cities. Indeed, the Archbishop of Toronto, Neil McNeil (1912–1934), especially had been pressing Filion during the summer of 1924 to open a college for "the boys of the aristocratic families," as the archbishop told Filion, "who would not send their boys to the ordinary schools." In Filion's mind, that was definitely out of the question.[28]

Making the situation in Edmonton even more complex was the fact that by the mid 1920s, the Oblate Fathers—who had in 1908 opened a junior seminary in Edmonton for French-speaking boys, Collège Saint-Jean, which was affiliated with the University of Ottawa—were planning to offer some university courses. That would present strong competition for French-speaking students with Collège des Jésuites/ Edmonton Jesuit College. Given the small francophone population in Alberta, there seemed not to be room for two French-language colleges. With the financial troubles of Collège des Jésuites mounting yearly during the 1930s, along with the fact that the college's degrees through Université Laval were not recognized by the Province of Alberta, eventually the Provincial Superior of the French-Canadian Jesuits announced, on 23 November 1942, that Collège des Jésuites/ Edmonton Jesuit College would close. With that, the Jesuits left Alberta permanently.[29]

---

28   DJB, vol. 1, 113.

29   Jolicoeur, 177–178.

REGINA: CAMPION COLLEGE, 1917–2013

"Sapientia Regina"
—Motto of Campion College

The two western Jesuit bilingual collegiate foundations, Collège de Saint-Boniface/St. Boniface College and Collège des Jésuites/ Edmonton Jesuit College, differed in significant ways from a third Jesuit college in western Canada, the Catholic College of Regina (Campion College). Although bilingual, Collège de Saint-Boniface/ St. Boniface College and Collège des Jésuites/Edmonton Jesuit College were established principally to serve French-speaking populations seeking an opportunity for higher education. Both followed the Jesuits' Canadian *collège classique* model, both remained relatively small, usually with around 200 students, and both became part of the French-Canadian Jesuit Province when, in 1924, the Province of Canada was separated into La Province du Bas Canada and the Vice Province of Upper Canada. On the other hand, Campion College never followed the *collège classique* model, it was never bilingual but served an English-speaking population exclusively, and it remained in the Vice Province of Upper Canada after 1924.[30]

From the time of his arrival as bishop of Regina in 1911, Olivier-Elzéar Mathieu (1911–1929) had hoped to establish two Catholic post-secondary educational colleges in southern Saskatchewan: one French-speaking, the other English-speaking. Yet the immediate years after 1911 seemed not propitious for such an undertaking: Catholic numbers were small, the times were economically unfavourable, diocesan resources were meagre, and the Catholic population itself was not overly favourable to the idea. The archbishop decided not to proceed with his plan of founding the two colleges.

In the end, it would be George Daly, C.S.s.R., the rector of Holy Rosary Cathedral in Regina, and Abbé Louis-Pierre Gravel, the parish priest of French-speaking Gravelbourg, who would persuade Archbishop Mathieu to proceed. They were convinced not only that there was a need for such colleges but that, despite the potential obstacles, the colleges would prosper. At Mathieu's request, therefore,

---

30   On 12 March 1939, the Vice Province of Upper Canada became the Province of Upper Canada.

and by an act of the Saskatchewan Legislature, on 15 December 1917, both colleges were incorporated under the auspices of the archdiocese: The Catholic College of Regina for English-speaking Catholic men, and Collège Catholique de Gravelbourg for French-speaking Catholic men.[31] The legislative act clearly expressed the college's mandate in Regina. The archdiocese of Regina was authorized "to establish, maintain and conduct at the city of Regina a college and school where students may obtain a liberal education in the arts and sciences."[32]

Even before gaining this incorporation, however, Mathieu had requested that Daly invite a male Religious Congregation to assume control of the college. First Daly asked the Society of Mary (Marist Fathers) if they would take charge of any future college in Regina, but they were not able to take in hand that responsibility. Then he turned to the Holy Cross Fathers, who also declined. Next he sought out the Benedictines, but they likewise demurred. Finally, in September 1917, Daly wrote to Gregory Féré, s.j., the Rector at St. Boniface College, enquiring whether the Jesuits might take charge of a college.[33]

In Féré's response of 14 September, he indicated that he was referring the matter to William I. Power, S.J., a Visitor to the Canadian Jesuits from 4 April 1917 to 8 July 1918 who at that time was visiting St. Boniface College. Power had been given the usual authority of a Jesuit Visitor, that is, to be "an extraordinary Superior for how long and with what authority as the General [Superior] wishes." To fulfil his mandate, he was to examine all aspects of the Province du Canada/Province of Canada, to conduct official visits to the various Jesuit Communities, and to consult the members of the Province in order to acquire a sense of and insights into the affairs of the Jesuits in Canada.[34]

---

31   Although the original names of the colleges remained the legal titles, The Catholic College of Regina was renamed Campion College on 5 September 1918, while Collège Catholique de Gravelbourg was renamed Collège Mathieu in 1922 in honour of its founder. Gravelbourg was named after Abbé Gravel.

32   *An Act to incorporate The Catholic College of Regina*, 5 December 1917, Saskatchewan Legislature, Second Session, Chapter 76, 0. 34. According to the act of incorporation, all members of the governing body ("owners") must reside in the province of Saskatchewan. The diocese of Regina had become an archdiocese on 4 December 1915. George Daly, C.S.s.R., was an uncle of Hector Daly, S.J. (1900–1969). DCB, XV, 434–436; DJB, vol. 1, 77–78.

33   DJB, vol. 1, 110–111.

34   Ibid., 291–292.

As a result, while on his way to Edmonton, Power stopped in Regina on 5 November and again on 17 November, on his return trip. During Power's first visit, he showed some support for opening a college and indicated that he would visit again after his time in Edmonton. Following that first visit to Regina, and encouraged by Power's positive response, Daly contacted François-Xavier Renaud, s.j., Power's assistant or Socius, for advice on the wording of any future written contract between the archdiocese and the Jesuits. Renaud sent a draft contract on 8 November 1917.[35]

Clearly impressed with the opportunities in Regina, Power decided to pursue the possibility of the Jesuits accepting responsibility for a college. After returning to Montreal, he wrote to convey his gratitude to the archbishop and to Daly for their interest in having the Jesuits in charge of a new college. Yet he still had misgivings. He knew that assuming responsibility for a new college in Regina would be anything but easy: the number of English-speaking Jesuits was small, while financial resources seemed scarcely adequate for such a venture. At the same time, too, in Montreal the Jesuit Consultors of the Province of Canada were especially apprehensive at the slowness of reaching a satisfactory agreement between the archbishop and the provincial government about the college's academic status. Over the opening months of 1918, Power sought ways to settle with the archbishop the contractual terms for establishing a college, for its financial security and its location.[36]

On the other hand, and despite whatever uncertainties Power may have felt, after he returned to Montreal during mid November 1917 from his western visit, he had instructed Joseph Carrière, s.j., the Jesuit Provincial Superior, to explore how the Jesuits might assume responsibility for a college in Regina. In response, Carrière appointed Féré to confer in person with Mathieu and Daly. While in Regina, Féré was impressed with Daly's plans, and concluded that

---

35 Gregory Féré, s.j., letters to George Daly, C.S.s.R., 27 October 1917; 31 October 1917; 5 November 1917, AJC, Box D-516.

36 William I. Power, S.J., letters to George Daly, C.S.s.R., 18 December 1917; 16 January 1918; 4 March 1918; 30 March 1918; 21 April 1918; George Daly, C.S.s.R., letter to William I. Power, S.J., 3 April 1918, ibid.

such an institution would be a worthy venture. He recommended that Carrière proceed with it. As a result, and having consulted Power, Carrière asked Thomas J. MacMahon, S.J., to visit Regina to promote the merits of a Catholic secondary and collegiate education. At the time, MacMahon was completing his term as Rector of Loyola College. Among his Jesuit colleagues, his reputation as an administrator and fundraiser was unequalled.[37]

Meanwhile, in Montreal, Power remained anxious to sign a contract. In fact, a written agreement between the Jesuits and the archbishop would not be signed until 7 January 1922. According to the archbishop, a verbal contract between him and the Jesuits would have to suffice because of problems he was encountering over the purchase of property. He had been hoping to buy some vacant land at the corner of College Avenue and Broad Street that was owned by the provincial government. Although it was reasonably well situated, the whole area had marshland, and thus was considered by many to be greatly overvalued at $2,000.00 per acre. The archbishop and his advisors refused it at that price. Yet the government would not negotiate for anything less.[38]

MacMahon arrived in Regina on 13 June 1918. He recounted in his diary: "Arrived in Regina via C.P.R. this a.m.... Father Daly took me in his car through the city. We visited the site of the future college. I find it admirable." That "site of the future college" was the government land on Broad and College that the archbishop had been reluctant to purchase.[39]

MacMahon spent several weeks travelling throughout the archdiocese, speaking and preaching in parishes and to Catholic lay groups about the advantages of having a Catholic college in Regina. In general, he received a positive response. With Power's authorization, therefore, on 31 July 1918, Carrière asked MacMahon to establish a college and

---

37 DJB, vol. 1, 203.

38 30 March 1918; 21 April 1918, AJC, Box D-516. The value of $2,000.00 in today's dollars would be approximately $26,000.00. It remains unclear on which side of Broad Street the property was located. If it was on the south-west side, south of the Normal School, the present-day building of the Canadian Broadcasting Corporation is on the property; if on the south-east side of Broad Street, it would have been immediately west of the old St. Chad's Anglican College.

39 Thomas J. MacMahon, S.J., *Diary*, 13 June 1918, ibid.

appointed him Superior. With him would be a Scholastic, L. Gwynne, S.J., and a Brother, William H. Laflamme, S.J.[40]

From the outset, negotiations to buy property for a college had been tangled. As early as 1903, four prominent Catholic laymen, John Murphy, William Fabyean Windeatt, John McCarthy, and his brother Edward, had purchased shares of a property for "Catholic educational purposes" between Dewdney Avenue and 7th Avenue, known as Block 164. Each of them had agreed to dispose of their sections of the land together. In time, however, and despite the protests of the other two owners, the McCarthy brothers refused to hand over their share of land to the Oblates in 1905 when that Congregation had considered establishing a college in Regina. The Oblate Fathers never did open a college, and in time handed to the archdiocese their share of the property that Murphy and Windeatt had given them. Block 164 was subsequently divided into six lots. Of these, the archdiocese transferred to the Jesuits lot 218 on Argyle Street, referred to as the "Murphy Land", in 1919.[41]

During the early summer of 1918, with the approval of the archbishop, MacMahon had begun an extensive search for funds in addition to continuing his quest for a suitable location. Yet by August, he still had no property and almost no money. The new Provincial Superior, John M. Filion, s.j., became concerned. In a letter of 3 August, he cautioned MacMahon about continuing without resources: "If you do not meet with the response that would warrant your going on with the hope of covering your expenses this year—then you must not open a class this year. Do not incur any expenses which you are not morally certain of being able to meet." Nonetheless, to help MacMahon out, Filion enclosed a generous cheque for $368.00.[42]

---

40   DJB, vol. 1, 175–176. Born in the United States, Laflamme had worked in a circus before entering the Jesuit Novitiate at Guelph in 1914. At Campion College, where he remained as cook and infirmarian for nearly ten years, he became renowned for his tricks of magic with which he endlessly entertained whoever happened to be on hand. Gwynne, also an American, belonged to the New Orleans Province of the Society of Jesus. He lasted less than a year in Regina before returning to the United States to leave the Jesuits.

41   AJC, Box D-516. Contrary to the agreement, eventually the McCarthys sold separately their share of the property, the west half of Block 164, which was known as "The College Reserve".

42   John M. Filion, s.j., letter to Thomas J. MacMahon, S.J., 3 August 1918, ibid. The equivalent value of $368.00 in today's money would be over $5,000.00.

Despite how discouraging the situation might have appeared, MacMahon was not about to give up. All through August he accepted ministry in parishes and convents and gave retreats and days of recollection. The stipends he received went to fund the college. By early September, he had managed to raise a sufficient amount to rent two houses for $100.00 per month opposite the cathedral at 3136 13th Avenue.[43]

On 12 September 1918, he opened the college in the two houses. Tuition and board was $300.00 per annum; tuition alone was $50.00 per annum. However inadequate they were, the houses included offices and residences for the Jesuits and space for boarders. A prominent Catholic businessman in the city, Frank Smith, offered his nearby property at 3232 13th Avenue as a "campus" for the students. At times, the basement of the cathedral served as a classroom. Although Daly had suggested that, since they were considering Loyola College, Montreal, as a model, the college in Regina should be named "Western Loyola", MacMahon thought otherwise. Without legally changing the title "The Catholic College of Regina", he renamed it "Campion College" on 5 September 1918, before a large gathering of clergy and Catholic lay people assembled to honour him and the Jesuits.[44]

From the beginning, MacMahon intended to establish a college that would one day offer a full course of studies, from Grade Nine to a college degree. That would take some time. When the college opened, there were only two boarders and four day-students present. By New Year's Day, 1919, however, that number had increased to twelve boarders and six day-students, and by June the enrolment was eleven boarders and nine day-students. Following the opening of the new academic year the following September, enrolment had reached twenty-four; by Christmas, it was forty-one. After that, the numbers increased steadily each year, with the goal set that a new class would be added every year until the full eight years of high school and collegiate studies were realized. That was achieved by 1926.[45]

---

43   The value of $100.00 would be over $1,300.00 in today's currency.

44   Before moving to the residence on 13th Avenue, MacMahon had been living with Daly at 2161 Cameron Street. Edmund Campion was an English Jesuit priest martyred under Elizabeth I on 1 December 1581. He was beatified in 1886 and canonized in 1970.

45   *Advertisement for the opening of "The New Jesuit College, Regina, Sask"*, n.d., ibid.

The college remained for one year on 13th Avenue before moving to larger but temporary quarters on lot 218 at 1400–1414 Argyle Street near 8th Avenue ("Murphy Land") while a more permanent location could be found. A building opposite, on the corner of 8th Avenue and Argyle Street, was rented for the college's use as well. The teaching staff was composed of three Jesuits: MacMahon, E. Leo Burns, S.J., and James F. Carlin, S.J. During 1919, efforts were made, with the assistance of the Knights of Columbus, to organize a fundraising drive for a building somewhere in the south end of the city, "to be built on plans of Loyola College, Montreal." Such plans were grandiose, to say the least, given the lack of funds, students, and Jesuit staff, indeed even of interest among many Catholics for higher education.[46]

During his three years at Campion, MacMahon struggled to make ends meet. Yet he never gave up. He travelled endlessly throughout the province, sometimes in appalling winter conditions, to address Catholic groups about the importance of Catholic education. Despite his well-known eloquence and charm, it was not always easy; various groups, especially among Protestants, were strongly opposed to the establishing of Catholic colleges and schools in the province. Sometimes the opposition could become intense. For years, the *Regina Daily Star* carried on a rabid anti-Catholic, anti-French campaign, ranting endlessly on about the need of freeing "the province from the grip of Rome." The Ku Klux Klan, which was especially opposed to what it called the "unassimilable" [sic] immigrants and to the Catholic Church for its "subversion" of the public educational system, thrived in the province after the Great War until the early 1930s. It, too, was virulently anti-Quebec. Only when the Grand Keagle left the province to escape arrest was the Ku Klux Klan eventually rooted out of Saskatchewan.[47]

MacMahon was appointed Vice Rector of the college in 1920. He was still searching for property worthy of his dreams for a college. Finally, after having considered several locations, he settled on an

---

46   DJB, vol. 1, 39–40; 43–45; *Regina Post*, 21 June 1919; 8 December 1920.

47   For a history of the Klan in Saskatchewan, cf. William Calderwood, "The Rise and Fall of the Ku Klux Klan in Saskatchewan" (Saskatoon, University of Saskatchewan, unpublished M.A. Thesis, 1968), and "Religious Reaction to the Ku Klux Klan in Saskatchewan," *Saskatchewan History Magazine* (1974), vol. 26, 103ff.

offer of twenty acres from Walter Hill of McCallum-Hill Company at $1,000.00 an acre. The land was surrounded by open prairie in an undeveloped area south of the legislative building at the corner of Albert Street and 23rd Avenue. It was somewhat isolated, with only a few residences along the west side of Albert Street from Wascana Creek to 23rd Avenue. The area was served by rickety streetcars on a one-track line. These travelled occasionally along Albert Street— which was little better than a dirt path—from the city's centre to the Wascana Golf Course beyond Campion's property. They were rather unreliable machines, with an overhead electrical power source, and would travel in one direction and then on the same tracks return backwards into town.[48]

A few months later, MacMahon also purchased three further acres from the Sisters of the Missions whose property abutted the college's land to the south. He was hoping to establish a campus similar to that which had been developing since 1913 at Loyola College in Montreal, with a college building, a Jesuit residence, and a collegiate church. Indeed, as part of the original arrangement with the Jesuits, Archbishop Mathieu had promised to establish a parish for them at the college. Although the proposed parish was reconfirmed by the archbishop on 7 January 1922, nothing ever came of it, or of a western-style Loyola campus.

The first building on the new campus was an unimpressive small frame structure that served as a Jesuit residence.[49] Although MacMahon was involved in the location of the new college and its building, until 1921 all the negotiations about the college-to-be were conducted by the chancery office, while the title to all of Campion's assets and debts were in the name of the archdiocese. The Jesuits, however, were responsible for raising the funds to operate the college and to construct new buildings. By selling for $10,000.00 the one city

---

48   The college's students quickly learned that they could pester the conductor by crowding into the rear seats, which forced the front end of the car to rise off the tracks, disconnect from the power line and stop. Complaints to the college's authority over such behaviour never prevented the students from forcing the cars to jump the tracks; their "fun" continued well into the late 1930s, when a new, modern and more reliable streetcar system was constructed.

49   The building was later faced with brick, and for years afterwards served as a carpenter and maintenance shop.

block of "Murphy Land" that the archbishop had given them, they were able to fund partially the purchase of the property in the south end for a building that would hold seventy boarders and fifty-five day-students. On 25 November 1921, the foundation of the new college, designed by James H. Puntin, a prominent Regina architect of the time, was blessed by Archbishop Mathieu. The following March, he transferred the ownership of the college to the Jesuits. The original members of the corporation—the archbishop, Daly, and G. E. Grandbois—resigned. Four Jesuits were elected sole members of the corporation: MacMahon, Féré, Burns, and Carlin.[50]

By then, MacMahon had accomplished what he had been assigned to do: to found a Jesuit college in Regina. On 24 August 1921, Joseph Leahy, S.J., replaced MacMahon as Vice Rector. Leahy had a reputation as an excellent overseer for building low-cost but solid structures. Within a short time, he had completed the college's single building with $14,000.00 collected by the Knights of Columbus and $10,000.00 donated by Mathieu. From the beginning, the Knights had given their generous support to MacMahon. In 1919, their councils of Regina, Moose Jaw, Weyburn, and Yorkton sponsored a fundraising drive that raised the $14,000.00.[51]

The college moved on 2 November 1922 to the new site at the corner of Albert Street and 23rd Avenue. Only twenty boarders and ten day-students were registered. The college would remain there for forty-seven years until, on 1 January 1968, a new college building opened on the campus of the University of Saskatchewan: Regina Campus (later University of Regina).

Gregory Féré, s.j., who had been greatly instrumental in the Jesuits accepting Campion College in the first place, was appointed to the college in 1920 as professor of German and French literature and grammar, and, most importantly, as librarian. There was, however, no

---

50   DJB, vol. 1, 184–185; "Conventio inter Archiepiscopus Regina, RR. DD. O-E. Mathieu et Patres Societatis Jesus"; Archbishop Olivier-Elzéar Mathieu, letter to John M. Filion, s.j., 31 March 1920; "Transcript of Legal Transfer of the Catholic College of Regina, 25 August 1920", AJC, Box D-516. For a summary of those negotiations between the archbishop and the Jesuits, cf. John M. Filion, s.j., letter to Henry J. Keane, S.J., 27 June 1936, ibid.

51   DJB, vol. 1, 184. The equivalent value of $14,000.00 at present would be over $180,000.00.

library. Unfazed, he set out to assemble one. For months he scoured the small towns and villages throughout southern Saskatchewan where he had been invited to preach, in search of used books. In time, his patient efforts were rewarded. By 1927, he had single-handedly laid the basis of what would become an impressive college library.[52]

From its beginning, the college was unable to grant its own degrees. The attempts to have the University of Saskatchewan recognize the new Campion College as a junior college seemed not too promising. The university would not permit any college situated away from its campus to give courses leading up to and including the Bachelor of Arts degree. As a result, Campion also held negotiations with Université Laval and with Université de Montréal. In the end, persistence paid off. In 1924, the University of Saskatchewan agreed to accept Campion as a junior college, while eventually St. Boniface College at the University of Manitoba agreed to accept the last two years of Campion's studies. That meant that if students at Campion wanted to transfer to the University of Saskatchewan with advanced standing, they could do so because their courses carried credit. In effect, a Campion student could enter the second year of a three-year Bachelor of Arts programme at the University of Saskatchewan. The college could promote itself as a college where a student might obtain a "Bachelor of Arts, while at the same time receiving a complete course of religious instruction in a Catholic atmosphere." That arrangement lasted with Saskatoon until 1939.[53]

The prosperity of the mid 1920s arising from exceptional crops and high grain prices provided excellent financial security for the college. Being the only unilingual English Catholic college in the west, it attracted residential students from Saskatchewan and from the other western provinces. Several programmes were introduced after 1921

---

52 Ibid., 110–111. Gregory Féré, s.j., F.R.S.C., had graduated as a gold medallist from the faculty of medicine at the University of Toronto. He did further studies in medicine at Edinburgh University, and later taught anatomy at the University of Toronto's Medical College before joining the Jesuits on 30 July 1892. In time he became a valued member of the Province of Saskatchewan Library Board. He died on 29 February 1952 and is one of two Jesuits buried in Regina Cemetery, the other being Michael A. Leonard (died 27 June 1958), who taught chemistry at Campion for many years.

53 *The Campion*, 1926, No. 2, 26.

to enhance the cultural, physical, and intellectual life of the students. Music teachers were hired to teach piano, organ, and violin; eventually, a small college orchestra was organized. Dramatic, debating, and literary societies, a student library committee, and a yearbook committee were all established. As well, the Sodality of the Blessed Virgin Mary, the St. John Berchman's Altar Society, and the Apostleship of Prayer became prominent in students' spiritual development each school year. Under the direction of Thomas J. Lally, S.J., and, after 1928, of John M. Filion, s.j., those spiritual activities became a traditional part of the moral and religious training of students. The expansion after 1923 of the athletic activities was the college's most attractive feature to the majority of students. Boxing, wrestling, track and field games, football, tennis, skating, and interclass and intercollege hockey games allowed for excellent physical sports and competition during any season. To record the student events of each year, a college yearbook, *The Campion*, was founded in 1925. It continued to be published for the next four decades.[54]

In June 1926, with George F. Bradley, S.J., Campion's third Rector (1924–1930), presiding, the college's first graduation exercises took place. Leonard Kusch and Orville Kritzweiser received their Bachelor of Arts degrees. They were the first two among the 100 who graduated with Bachelor of Arts degrees between 1926 and 1942. Their graduation gave the college the distinction of being the first academic institution in Regina through which students earned such a degree. Both of them had been prominent and active students in the college, and both went on to become successful: one in business in Regina, the other as a medical doctor in Vancouver.[55]

By 1926, the college had 150 students, but lack of space was becoming critical. Bradley organized a fundraising drive for constructing more college buildings. Although the drive was well supported at first, with the collapse of the financial markets on 29 October 1929

---

54   DJB, vol. 1, 111–114; 178–180. Lally organized the first edition of *The Campion*.

55   DJB, vol. 1, 26–27. Cf. also Joseph G. Schner, S.J., "Campion College: A History," in *Heritage and Hope: The University of Regina into the 21st Century*, ed., K. Murray Knuttila (Regina, University of Regina, Canadian Plains Research Center, 2004), 66–68. The arts programme was suspended in 1942.

and the beginning of the Great Depression, the fundraising drive had to be abandoned. Saskatchewan was hit hard by the crisis; the price of wheat fell to below the price of seed, and the fallout smothered Saskatchewan with poverty and unemployment. To worsen the situation, 1930 was the start of what became known as the "Dust Bowl" years or the "Dirty Thirties", when severe drought and dust storms all but swept away the rich prairie soil, destroying as it went the farms and people's livelihood. The drought and the depression lasted until about 1940. Yet despite such miseries, so great was the desire for higher education, when Bradley stepped down in 1930, enrolment had been rising, and continued to rise, even if parents were finding it more and more difficult to pay tuition and board for their sons.[56]

On 9 August 1930, John S. Holland, S.J., succeeded Bradley as Rector. He was only thirty-seven years of age, had been ordained for five years, and had been teaching at Loyola High School in Montreal since 1928. He had had no experience in higher education, nor any in administration. His task was enormous. Not only did he have to contend with the complex affiliation issues with St. Boniface College—the University of Manitoba was increasingly unenthusiastic about having affiliated colleges outside the province—but more significantly, Campion College was penniless. There seemed almost no hope of any resolution to the financial crisis. Unable to pay with cash, many parents paid tuition and boarding fees in kind, with food, raw materials, or clothing, or with whatever else they could put together, or by credit. Along with almost everyone else in the city, Holland and the other sixteen Jesuits at Campion College suffered considerable poverty and hardship. The students' dormitories and the Jesuits' quarters were sometimes without heat, despite the harsh winter climate, and food was scarce and of poor quality. The college struggled to survive.[57]

In the mist of such extreme adversity, Holland remained calm and determined not to succumb to the crisis. In the end, his serene temperament and mild personality gave the college much-needed leadership. Frequently, he waived tuition and fees for another day.

---

56   John M. Filion, s.j., letter to William H. Hingston, S.J., 20 February 1929; George F. Bradley, S.J., letter to William H. Hingston, S.J., 21 February 1929, AJC, Box D-516; DJB, vol. 1, 26.

57   DJB, vol. 1, 145–146.

Such kindness and understanding of the plight of hard-pressed parents won the hearts of many. When he left Regina in 1933 to assume the rectorship of St. Paul's College in Winnipeg, Campion College was still solidly fulfilling its educational mandate. It was, however, still in danger of collapsing from its financial pressures.

During the late 1920s, the idea had been mooted of banding the several junior colleges in southern Saskatchewan together to form in Regina a degree-granting institution that would be affiliated with the University of Saskatchewan in Saskatoon. The head of Regina College at the time, the Reverend Ernest William Stapleford, was keen on the idea, and especially on having the three junior colleges in Regina itself—Campion College, Luther College, and Regina College—in such a union. On 15 November 1930, he wrote Holland with his proposal: "If Campion College and Regina College could join hands in this plan, I feel confident that it would be brought to a successful issue." The president of the University of Saskatchewan, Dr. Walter Murray (1908–1937), however, was implacably opposed, and nothing came of the idea.[58]

E. Leo Burns, S.J., was appointed Rector on 28 August 1933. At the time, he had been a professor of philosophy and religion at Loyola College, was approaching his thirty-ninth year, and upon arrival in Regina, was filled with energy and determination to keep Campion College open. It was not easy. Because it was hard to collect tuition fees, the college had serious debts. As Burns noted, "We are educating so many of their boys for nothing." Hope for improving the financial status of the college was dismal. The years of drought and financial ruin in Saskatchewan were taking their toll. He wrote to the Provincial Superior: "Regina is in the very centre of the dried-out area. The city depends upon trade with the farmers, and when these have nought to sell or money, you can imagine the results."[59]

58 *Local Provision for Higher Education in Saskatchewan*, by W. S. Leonard, Staff Member, Carnegie Foundation for the Advancement of Learning, and E. W. Wallace, Chancellor, University of Victoria College, Toronto, 1931; Ernest W. Stapleford, letter to John S. Holland, S.J., 13 November 1930, AJC, Box D-516. Cf. also James M. Pitsula, *An Act of Faith: The Early Years of Regina College* (Regina: University of Regina, Canadian Plains Research Center, 1988), for an account of the early efforts to establish a campus of the University of Saskatchewan in Regina.

59 DJB, vol. 1, 39–40; E. Leo Burns, S.J., letter to Henry J. Keane, S.J., 11 December 1934, AJC, Box D-516.

Undaunted, Burns set to work. In 1935, he established a Ladies Auxiliary at the college with the help of Mrs. Gracie (Walter) Hill. She became its first president. Over the next four decades, Hill, with many other women, would make an extraordinary contribution to the college's financial stability. It is evident that without their never-ending assistance in fundraising, the college might not have survived the 1930s.[60]

Along with the burden of finances, there was the long-standing matter of the college's uncertain academic affiliation. A substantial amount of Burns' attention, therefore, had to be directed towards Campion's affiliation with St. Boniface College at the University of Manitoba. By the summer of 1934, the University of Manitoba was taking steps to sever its affiliation with colleges outside Manitoba's boundaries. By early September, the Provincial Superior, William H. Hingston, S.J., had managed to convince the president of the university, Dr. Sidney Smith, not only to delay Campion's severing of affiliation but to extend it, first for only another year, then later for another two years. Hingston made the same request to Dr. William J. Spence, the university's registrar, that affiliation be extended until such time that "the University of Regiopolis College … should be in a position to affiliate Campion College." In 1936, however, the University of Manitoba finally terminated its degree-granting arrangements with all educational institutions outside the province. Meanwhile, at the University of Saskatchewan, President Murray, in response to Hingston's request, had granted an extension to Campion's affiliation on 6 September 1934.[61]

To anticipate the eventual loss of affiliation with St. Boniface College, Burns entered into negotiations with the University of

---

60   E. Leo Burns, S.J., letter to William H. Hingston, S.J., 7 October 1934; E. Leo Burns, S.J., letter to Henry J. Keane, S.J., 10 December 1934, AJC, Box D-516.

61   Joseph Béliveau, s.j., letter to E. Leo Burns, S.J., 11 October 1933; William H. Hingston, S.J., letter to Dr. Sidney Smith, 3 September 1934; Dr. Walter Murray, letter to William H. Hingston, S.J., 6 September 1934; William H. Hingston, S.J., letter to Dr. William J. Spence, 7 September 1934; Dr. William J. Spence, letter to William H. Hingston, S.J., 8 September 1934; Dr. William J. Spence, letter to E. Leo Burns, S.J., 8 September 1934; Dr. Sidney Smith, letter to William H. Hingston, S.J., 12 September 1934; William H. Hingston, S.J., letter to Dr. William J. Spence, 18 September 1934; William H. Hingston, S.J., letter to Dr. Sidney Smith, 18 September 1934; Dr. William J. Spence, letter to E. Leo Burns, S.J., 8 June 1935, ibid.

Ottawa. Yet because that university required a fluency in French for its students—the majority of Campion's students preferred to study German, not French—the arrangement did not fully work out. An agreement of affiliation with Ottawa was drawn up in 1936 that would be valid only until 1937; the university would give credit for courses taught at Campion College during that one year only. Burns then managed to reach an agreement with the Université de Montréal, which accepted German as a second language. On the whole, however, although that affiliation lasted until 1942, it was almost useless, since the majority of students graduating with a Bachelor of Arts degree from Campion College intended to pursue graduate work at the University of Saskatchewan. Yet that university did not recognize the degrees of the Université de Montréal.[62]

Roderick A. MacGilvray, S.J., succeeded Burns as Rector in 1939. Although he had no experience in administering a college, he was a man known for his common sense, good judgment, energy, and geniality. He was also known to be direct, even at times outspokenly blunt.[63]

On arriving in Regina, he was not optimistic at what he found. A few months after becoming Rector, his letter to Thomas J. Mullally, S.J., Provincial Superior at the time, was a scathing assessment of the situation at Campion College: "The Philosophers and Second Arts (this year a mere handfull [sic] in both classes combined) are bohunks of an elder-growth. They come, listen to a few words on philosophy and the odd science lecture and that is all. Personally I think that Philosophy has fallen to a pretty lowly level."[64] He also found the financial situation of the college equally unimpressive: "In the length and breadth of Saskatchewan there are few, if any, well-to-do Catholics or even well-disposed Protestants.... Hence, I can state that the possibility of getting $10.00 in the province is very slim. Besides, there is the fact that we are not exactly popular."[65]

---

62   Philippe Cornellier, O.M.I., letter to E. Leo Burns, S.J., 14 September 1936, ibid. Over the fifteen years following the first graduation in 1926, an average of six students a year graduated from Campion College.

63   DJB, vol. 1, 199.

64   Roderick A. MacGilvray, S.J., letter to Thomas J. Mullally, S.J., 24 September 1939, AJC, Box D-516.

65   Roderick A. MacGilvray, S.J., letter to Thomas J. Mullally, S.J., 9 November 1939, ibid.

Two months later, he seemed slightly more hopeful about financial matters: "We are a short stride ahead of the bailiff, but it is a stride at least." Yet he believed that until the relationship with the archbishop and the diocesan clergy improved, the college would continue to suffer. On 1 December 1939, he observed, "I do not think you can underestimate the latent hostility of the diocesan clergy—at least the ill-repute in which we are held.... Your Reverence knows the antipathy of the archbishop, Peter J. Monahan, and the clergy to us."[66]

The misunderstanding between the Jesuits and the diocesan clergy was of long standing. It had earlier arisen from the belief among the diocesan clergy that the Jesuits were not willing to participate in parish ministry, and hence were alienated from archdiocesan life. That was not so. As well as educating the Catholic youth of the archdiocese for two decades, the Jesuits had been and remained fully engaged in ministry in the parishes throughout the archdiocese and in the convents of Regina, often at great personal cost of time and energy. Yet the perception of their alienation had remained. MacGilvray was determined to turn that around.

At the same time, he recognized that, given the poor state of education at the college, the Jesuits themselves had to accept some responsibility for the bad relationship with the archdiocese. He caustically pointed out to the Provincial Superior that "there is absolutely nothing in the Arts course that I would send a brother of mine to get." One solution, he thought, was to improve the academic quality of the Jesuits who worked in the college: "It may be that we can get some badly needed replacements—Priests, Scholastics, Brothers. It is a desperate situation."[67]

Over the early winter months of 1940, he searched for solutions to improve the academic standards of the college. To that end, in March 1940 he revived the proposition with the Provincial Superior that had been squelched in 1931: federation with Regina College and Luther College: "We could strike some sort of cooperation that would amount to a 'modus vivendi' (with Regina College and with Luther

---

66 Roderick A. MacGilvray, S.J., letter to Thomas J. Mullally, S.J., 1 December 1939, ibid. "Your Reverence" was used by Jesuits when formally addressing a Provincial Superior.

67 Ibid.

College). That some sort of federation and cooperation (even in one department—say Science) would not only lift the college course out of the rut, but also do away with rather wasteful competition."[68]

Those arguments MacGilvray similarly presented to the archbishop, with whom he had been cultivating better relations. He reminded the archbishop of the earlier efforts of Stapleford during 1930 and 1931 to establish "a quasi-University of Regina", even if that had "led to the pronouncement of the Commission from the Carnegie Institute strongly advising against the extension of the field of Junior Colleges and duplication of the work already being done by the University [of Saskatchewan]." It was, in MacGilvray's opinion, time to readdress that issue. Fearful, however, of harmful Protestant influence on Catholic students, the archbishop was less than enthusiastic about the idea. Thus, the development of a federated system of colleges in Regina would have to wait for another twenty years and more.[69]

MacGilvray found, too, that the library greatly needed attention. In 1939 he asked Holland in Winnipeg whether he might have "Mr. Voisin for a little extra time here. He is an expert librarian and our library is in bad shape. He will doctor it." Then later, during the summer of 1942, MacGilvray was successful in persuading Féré to return to the college. There he would spend another ten years in the library completing what he had begun over twenty years earlier.[70]

When MacGilvray left the office of Rector in the summer of 1945, Campion was a changed place compared to what it had been six years earlier, at least financially and in its relations with the archdiocese. As well, Campion's affiliation with the Université de Montréal had been guaranteed in an agreement of August 1939. MacGilvray had sent Filion to Montreal to negotiate the agreement; it was, according to Filion, "very similar to that of Loyola" with the Université de Montréal.[71]

---

68   Roderick A. MacGilvray, S.J., letter to Thomas J. Mullally, S.J., 4 March 1940, ibid.

69   Roderick A. MacGilvray, S.J., letter to Thomas J. Mullally, S.J., 17 April 1940; Thomas J. Mullally, S.J., letter to Roderick A. MacGilvray, S.J., 19 April 1940; Roderick A. MacGilvray, S.J., letter to Joseph J. Monahan, S.J., 2 May 1940, ibid.

70   Roderick A. MacGilvray, S.J., letter to John S. Holland, S.J., 1 August 1939, ibid.; DJB, vol. 1, 110. Voisin was a Jesuit Scholastic teaching at St. Paul's High School who eventually left the Jesuits.

71   John M. Filion, s.j., letter to Thomas J. Mullally, S.J., 25 August 1939, AJC, Box D-516.

Campion College, meanwhile, maintained an inactive status as a junior college affiliated with the University of Saskatchewan; since 1942, it had been in all but name a high school only. It was not for lack of trying for better standards on MacGilvray's part that the classes in the arts and philosophy programmes had to be discontinued. Rather, it was because most school graduates were being called up for military service. He had tried to build up Campion's level of academic standards, yet enrolment kept falling. As often as he could, he preached throughout the archdiocese in favour of higher education; on 23 July 1939, for example, he preached at all three Masses in the cathedral "and stressed Campion Education". Still, the war years took their toll on enrolment in the college.[72]

During the term of office of MacGilvray's successor, Vincent Murphy, S.J. (1945–1948), little changed, with the exception of the physical size of the college. Due to a gradual increase in enrolment, the post-war years required new space in the college's building. In collaboration with prominent Catholic lay people, Murphy established a capital campaign to raise the funds for an extension. By the time he stepped down three years later, he had constructed a fine new west wing on the college building that included two dining areas—one for students and one for the Jesuit Community—classrooms, science laboratories, Jesuit living quarters, and a students' dormitory. The wing opened in September 1948. By then, though, Murphy had left Regina, due to exhaustion and general poor health.[73]

In 1948, after Francis J. Boyle, S.J., had been appointed Rector, Campion College resumed its earlier active status as a junior college of the University of Saskatchewan. Along with the usual courses in the arts and sciences, courses were offered in pre-medicine, pre-law, nursing, education, and pharmacy. Boyle also unsuccessfully petitioned the university for permission to add a full course of an engineering programme. Significantly, too, he drew up plans to construct an auditorium/gymnasium. Its construction, however, was left to his successor, Richard C. Johnston, S.J., and was opened in the autumn of 1957, three years after Boyle had moved to become Rector of Regiopolis

---

72   Roderick A. MacGilvray, S.J., letter to Thomas J. Mullally, S.J., 23 July 1939, ibid.

73   DJB, vol. 1, 23–24; 253–254.

College. He died there four months later. The new recreational and theatrical facilities were named in his memory.[74]

While in Regina, Boyle had been supportive of Féré's efforts to develop the library. Although he had continued on as librarian until his death early in 1952, Féré had not always been the easiest man to deal with, being rather strong-willed and opinionated. Rectors and others found him formidably protective of "his" library. That became more noticeable in his declining years, for although frail and frequently hospitalized, he maintained a firm grip on anything that pertained to the library. Shortly after becoming Rector in 1948, Boyle quickly found that out. He reported to John L. Swain, S.J., Provincial Superior, that "We are waging a battle royal with Father Féré to obtain the books that had been assigned to the students but which belonged to the Fathers' Library. But he has defeated all our efforts since he maintains that most of the books that were chosen are on the Index, and therefore forbidden to students. Father Féré also threatened to leave if we dare to cut down a tree."[75]

These personality issues notwithstanding, Boyle pointed out to Swain a couple weeks later, Féré's mind was "very keen; he gives excellent advice on all matters with the exception of trees and books." Certainly he knew how to develop a library, as Boyle acknowledged in June 1951: "The college libraries were increased during the year by approximately five hundred volumes." A valued member of the Province of Saskatchewan Library Board, Féré worked diligently up to a month before his death at age eighty-seven, while all the time insisting that he wanted to live to be 100, or failing that, at least for another month in order to finish cataloguing the library. Certainly in every way and as much as anyone else, Féré was responsible for establishing Campion College's excellent undergraduate library.[76]

---

74 Ibid., 156–157. The Boyle Memorial Gymnasium was formally dedicated on 2 November 1957. Three years earlier, in August 1954, Boyle had left Campion to become Rector of Regiopolis College. He died there suddenly from heart failure on 16 November 1954. Despite the several differing uses of the old Campion College building since the mid 1970s, the gymnasium/auditorium still bears Boyle's name.

75 Francis J. Boyle, S.J., letter to John L. Swain, S.J., 13 September 1948, AJC, Box D-516.

76 Francis J. Boyle, S.J., letters to John L. Swain, S.J., 26 September 1948; 14 June 1951, ibid. "Libraries" refers to the three libraries at Campion: that of the college, of the high school, and of the Jesuits. All three were under Féré's watchful eye.

On his death, the college again needed a librarian. Boyle found one in John J. Lepine, S.J. Though an historian by profession, he took on the responsibility of librarian in 1954. His task was not easy, at times; he set out to establish a new system for cataloguing books that took him several years to complete. It did not help his work that on 2 January 1960, a fire of unknown origin did severe damage to the college's library and the nearby chapel. Many books were destroyed; others were badly burned, while still others suffered water damage. Yet despite these various setbacks, Lepine proved to be a successful librarian: "[He] spends a lot of time and energy on the library and seems to be getting it organized. [The] main complaint seems to be the length of time it takes to obtain books. Some of the faculty have had to wait months after requesting books to use in connection with their classes." The hope was that with an increase in monies for the library, some of the concerns would be met: "Something like twenty five hundred dollars were spent last year ... [the] plan is to spend several times that amount this year."[77]

To improve his skills as a librarian, in 1960 Lepine set out to acquire a Master of Arts degree in library science during summer school at the University of California, Berkeley. He graduated in 1962. That gained him considerable confidence professionally. He was helpful and generous towards other librarians in the city, was active in several library associations in western Canada, and became president of the Regina Library Association in 1960. Over seventeen years, he grew to be an effective librarian, and until his retirement from the post in 1971, he succeeded remarkably in continuing Féré's dream of developing a first-rate undergraduate library.[78]

Richard C. Johnston, S.J., who succeeded Boyle in 1954, was a kindly man, but highly nervous and reluctant to make decisions. He worried about everything. To add to his usual daily worries, he had inherited a major building project, an addition of an auditorium/gymnasium, to which he was expected to devote himself completely.

---

77 DJB, vol. 2, 160–163; James J. Farrell, S.J., letter to Gordon F. George, S.J., 23 September 1959; Thomas G. Finucane, S.J., letter to Gordon F. George, S.J., 6 January 1962, AJC, Box D-516. In today's value, $2,500.00 would be nearly $20,000.00.

78 DJB, vol. 2, 161–162.

That was not an easy task, and gave him plenty of justifiable extra reasons for worrying. At heart, he was highly unfavourable towards the project. He believed that the money raised should have been directed towards academic purposes. In the end, however, because the building was too far advanced to change, he had no choice but to continue with it. As was his way, therefore, he threw himself wholeheartedly into enlisting the necessary financial support, and worked tirelessly with the fundraisers, especially the college's Ladies Auxiliary, to meet the financial targets. Gratefully, he reported to the Provincial Superior that "last Monday night [the Ladies Auxiliary] gave me a cheque for $4,100.00 towards the gym. They are one of the most active organizations I have ever met." Nonetheless, the strain gradually took its toll; he had taxed himself to such a degree, from worry and long hours of work, that his health broke down. He resigned after only three years in office, and left Regina permanently to recuperate.[79]

During the rectorship of Johnston's successor, James J. Farrell, S.J. (1957–1960), the high school continued to expand while the college remained stationary, even if undergraduate enrolment continued to increase somewhat. Given the growing need during the post-war years for higher education, Farrell began to search out which areas of undergraduate academic growth might be possible for the college. To that end, in 1958 he petitioned the University of Saskatchewan for engineering and commerce programmes. To his frustration, the first was denied again. The university unanimously refused permission on the grounds that "the granting of the request would mean a change in the essential character of our affiliated junior colleges." A commerce programme, however, for first-year students was granted to the college.[80]

In his letter of 17 April to Gordon F. George, S.J., the Provincial Superior, Farrell expressed his disappointment at Dr. J. Francis Leddy, vice president academic and dean of arts and science at Saskatoon,

---

79 Ibid., vol. 1, 156–157. Richard C. Johnson, S.J., letter to George E. Nunan, S.J., 3 April 1957, AJC, Box D-516. The amount raised by the Ladies Auxiliary would be more than $33,000.00 at today's value.

80 DJB, vol. 2, 102–105; James J. Farrell, S.J., letters to Gordon F. George, S.J., 17 February 1958; 25 March 1958, AJC, Box D-516.

and a long-time friend of the college. Despite having encouraged Farrell to write his request, Leddy "voted against it if the decision was unanimous." The vote had been unanimous.[81]

Rumours had been floating about for some years that the University of Saskatchewan was about to establish a second campus in the buildings of Regina College on College Avenue. In the late spring of 1959, the university formally announced that it was opening a campus in Regina. Later, Farrell wrote to the Provincial Superior on the matter: "You may recall that when you were at Campion last March we spoke about the possibilities of a University at Regina and our part in it. It seemed at least five years away but certain. Of a sudden there was an about-face on the part of the powers that be. At Convocation, President Thompson mentioned the possibilities of giving the full Arts course in Regina. This came as a surprise and jolt to many. It still seemed a good way off."[82]

Farrell lost no time in following up the possibility of the college becoming federated with the university. He met with Dr. William A. Riddell, principal of Regina College, then with Archbishop Michael C. O'Neill, Chief Justice Emmett Hall, chairman of Campion's advisory board, and later, on 24 August, with Leddy, concerning a future federated status for Campion. Each of them supported the idea of Campion making representation for some kind of federated or affiliated arrangement with the University of Saskatchewan.[83]

Farrell urged George to visit Regina to discuss the matter with him and with Archbishop O'Neill but, due to his busy schedule, George declined. Instead, and wanting to have a comprehensive understanding of what might be the role of Campion College in such a development, George appointed Gerald F. Lahey, S.J., to study Campion's future in a federation with the university similar to that which St. Thomas More College enjoyed in Saskatoon. Lahey had been appointed during the summer of 1959 as the special assistant to the Provincial Superior in matters of Jesuit education; he set out to examine thoroughly all

81   James J. Farrell, S.J., letters to Gordon F. George, S.J., 17 February 1958; 25 March 1958; 17 April 1958, AJC, Box D-516.

82   James J. Farrell, S.J., letters to Gordon F. George, S.J., 11 July 1959; 23 September 1959, ibid.

83   James J. Farrell, S.J., letters to Gordon F. George, S.J., 11 July 1959; 24 August 1959, ibid.

aspects of the situation in Regina and Saskatoon. He interviewed the archbishop, the university president, officials at Regina campus, several prominent lay people, and the Jesuits.[84]

On 15 October 1959, Lahey presented his report to the Provincial Superior. In a meticulous assessment, he wrote that the possibilities were many for the college in a future federated arrangement. What greatly impressed him, he concluded, was that there seemed to be plenty of interest and goodwill among most people in Regina and Saskatoon to justify further steps being taken. He strongly recommended that the matter of federation should be taken up seriously by the Jesuits.[85]

Based on this report and on his discussion with Farrell, the Provincial Superior became convinced that however the future might unfold, Campion College should look towards cooperating with the University of Saskatchewan. On 4 October he wrote to Farrell: "I can assure you that it is generally agreed, and this is my opinion too, that the Province [of Upper Canada] will be ready and willing to undertake whatever kind of expansion of Campion's university courses the University of Saskatchewan will permit. My present problem is what to ask Father General? There are so many questions which, apparently, only the passage of time will answer. Is Regina College moving to a new campus? When will they have the permission for the final year of Arts and Science?"[86]

In response to the positive reaction of the Provincial Superior, Farrell began the official negotiation to federate Campion College with the University of Saskatchewan. In a letter of 25 July 1960 to the president of the university, Dr. John W. T. Spinks (1959–1974), he stressed the interest the Jesuits and the college had in pursuing the possibility of a federation with the proposed campus in Regina. He formally requested that the college might receive the identical

84 Gordon F. George, S.J., letter to James J. Farrell, S.J., 25 August 1959; James J. Farrell, S.J., letters to Gordon F. George, S.J., 11 September 1959; 14 September 1959, ibid. St. Thomas More College had been founded in 1936 by the Basilian Fathers.

85 *A Report Presented to Very Reverend Father Provincial 15 October 1959*, by Gerald F. Lahey, S.J., ibid.

86 Gordon F George, S.J., letter to James J. Farrell, S.J., 4 October 1959, ibid.

federated status that St. Thomas More College had been given in Saskatoon. In his reply, Spinks expressed his interest in supporting Farrell's proposal should the university pursue the establishing of a Regina Campus in the future.[87]

In fact, although still not publicized, the university had every intention of extending itself to Regina. Within a year, during the summer of 1961, the Regina Campus of the University of Saskatchewan opened in the buildings of Regina College on College Avenue, with Riddell appointed as its first principal. An area of the newly established Wascana Centre, which in time would develop into a vast and beautiful urban park, lake, and nature preserve, had already been selected for a new campus site. In 1963, Premier Woodrow Lloyd laid the cornerstone of the first building there, and a year later, in September, the University of Saskatchewan welcomed its first students to its Regina Campus in the Wascana Centre.

Farrell's term as Rector finished on 15 August 1960. For some months prior to that date, he had been pressing George to have Angus J. Macdougall, S.J., appointed as his successor. During May, therefore, and at a time when the decision was being taken or had already been taken for a replacement to Farrell, George had promised him that "I will see what can be done to give you an academically qualified man to help this development [with Regina College]."[88] True to his word, and convinced that an academically oriented Jesuit was needed to guide the college during the 1960s, and most especially through any developments towards federation, George persuaded Macdougall to become Rector. Intelligent, optimistic, filled with boundless energy, skilled in languages, and gifted with common sense, in every way he seemed entirely to fit the office.[89]

Macdougall had accepted reluctantly. He was writing his doctoral thesis in classics at the University of Toronto, and had hoped to complete it shortly. Nonetheless, and after his arrival in August in Regina, he threw himself whole-heartedly into his work, and began to build

---

87   James J. Farrell, S.J., letter to Dr. John W. T. Spinks, 15 July 1960, ibid.

88   Gordon F. George, S.J., letter to James J. Farrell, S.J., 18 May 1960; James J. Farrell, S.J., letters to Gordon F. George, S.J., 16 May 1960; 7 June 1960, ibid.

89   DJB, vol. 2, 170–175.

important relations and goodwill. Almost immediately he took up the matter of federation. He could report to George by 31 August that, at the recent installation of the abbot of Munster, Jerome F. Weber, O.S.B. (1960–1990), "I also met Dr. Leddy.... He has written me too, and said in one paragraph: 'The next few years will be very important ones on the development and the progress of Campion, and I wish to assure you that I will be glad to be of assistance to you whenever the occasion arises.' I do think that he will be a great help to us."[90] If Macdougall knew about Leddy's earlier lack of support for Campion and had any misgivings about his promise of assistance, he did not express them to George.

Two months later, on 24 October, Macdougall met Spinks informally and they had a "brief chat". They arranged to meet in Saskatoon in "the near future to discuss University-Campion problems and relations." What he was hoping for was "... to see made possible a de facto growth to parallel Regina College's de facto growth from Junior College to full university arts and science status — Second year 1961-62; Third Year 1962-63 — pending the de facto federated college agreement.... We could, I think, grow de facto without too much trouble, as long as we could do some planning this fall."[91]

During those first few months in Regina, Macdougall continued to press the university for an official response to Farrell's letter about federating Campion with the new Regina Campus. Spinks had established a committee during that autumn to study the idea of federated colleges in Regina, including Farrell's request for federation. On 18 November, Campion's official application for federated college status came before the university's senate. As Macdougall later reported to George, because at the same time "request for federation were entered by Luther College here and Teachers' College, the Senate played it cautious and recommended setting up a special committee to study the matter more carefully." It was to present its findings at the senate's May 1962 meeting.

---

90 Angus J. Macdougall, S.J., letter to Gordon George, S.J., 31 August 1960, AJC, D-516.

91 Angus J. Macdougall, S.J., letter to Gordon George, S.J., 26 October 1960; 31 October 1960, ibid.

Clearly, however, the university was playing for time, concerned about federal grants "and a few other wrinkles". Macdougall continued to keep in close touch with his contacts, Leddy, Spinks, and Riddell. During the third week of February 1961, Macdougall was buoyed by "a most pleasant and profitable meeting" that he had had with Spinks, who expressed strong appreciation for federation in Regina, and who was "personally extremely favourable to our plans. Federation," Macdougall felt assured, "will be pushed with all expedition." It brought him considerable satisfaction, and optimistically he wrote that "I feel, then, much more cheerful about things and have surer hope of advancing Campion's university cause in timely fashion."[92]

To further Campion's application, in a letter to Spinks on 1 March 1961, Macdougall outlined in the greatest detail the kind of federation he envisioned. He proposed that the college would have full undergraduate status in the university; that it would have the right to the tuition fees of its own students "as provided in the regulations presently governing St. Thomas More College"; that it would have the privilege of holding its lectures in the university's classrooms; that it could construct its own building on the Regina Campus; and that all governmental educational grants would go to the college after its own building was finished. At heart, his was an imaginative and farsighted proposal. When the final document of federation was approved in 1964, it consisted essentially of Macdougall's proposals.[93]

Although over the previous months the university may have seemed cautious in taking up the idea of federation, Macdougall did receive a courteous, even sympathetic reaction from the university to his proposals. By January 1962, the fact of federation seemed promising. Meanwhile, the university had already begun building on the new campus: "The first building on the new campus of the university will be ready in the fall of 1964. It looks as if we would not be able to build till after that. However Father Macdougall is working on a firm commitment from the university both as to location and time.

---

92   Angus J. Macdougall, S.J., letters to Gordon F. George, S.J., 6 December 1960; 18 January 1961; 19 February 1961; N. K. Cram, letter to Angus J. Macdougall, S.J., 10 January 1961. ibid. Cram was registrar and later secretary of the University of Saskatchewan.

93   Angus J. Macdougall, S.J., letter to Dr. John W. T. Spinks, 1 March 1961, ibid.

He would like to see our buildings up at the same time as theirs. We have a building committee set up and are ready to get to work as soon as the green light is given."[94]

By the late summer of 1962, the pace towards federation on Regina Campus had increased. Under the guidance of Leddy and Riddell, Macdougall was able to report that, with Dr. Rex Schneider, president of Luther College, the colleges had been invited to sit on the university's planning committee meetings and also to arrange joint courses and examinations with the university. It was therefore important, Macdougall believed, that Campion be "hard on the heels of any initial university construction work in Regina." He was supported in that by three long-time friends of Campion College, Fred Hill and Robert Kramer, who promised financial backing, and Archbishop O'Neill, who guaranteed $500,000.00 in financial support.[95]

During the following winter months, Macdougall attended meetings, wrote letters, and held telephone conversations with university officials concerning the academic and financial arrangements of federation and matters pertaining to the building site of a new campus in Regina. On 22 December 1962, he reported to George: "Doctor Francis Leddy, Fred Hill, Fr. Nash and I had an interesting meeting the other day. We were reviewing our application for federation, especially the timing aspect. I am going to talk with [Chief Justice Edward M.] Culliton right after the holidays and then intend to get in touch with Dr. Spinks, the President. We are anxious to have the spring meeting of the University Senate to clear both the building site and the exact timing."[96]

A few weeks later, however, not a lot of Macdougall's hoped-for progress towards a federated agreement had been made: "He

---

94   E. Peter W. Nash, S.J., letter to Gordon F. George, S.J., 6 January 1962, ibid. Nash had become dean of Campion College during the summer of 1961.

95   Dr. J. Francis Leddy, letter to Dr. William F. Riddell, 21 September 1962; Dr. J. Francis Leddy, letter to Angus J. Macdougall, S.J., 21 September, 1962; Angus J. Macdougall, S.J., letter to Gordon F. George, S.J., 3 October 1962, ibid. Fred Hill and Bob Kramer were wealthy businessmen and prominent Catholics in the city. The archbishop's financial support would be, in today's value, worth nearly $4 million.

96   Angus J. Macdougall, S.J., letter to Gordon F. George, S.J., 22 December 1962, ibid. Because Culliton, a Catholic, was chancellor of the University of Saskatchewan, he was an important link for Macdougall with the university.

[Macdougall] is also diplomatic in his dealings with the university authorities and the departments of government. I think he sees now that we cannot push the university authorities and that the fulfilment of the promise of federation may be much slower than we had hoped."[97]

Macdougall was anxious to get the matter of a future building site settled. Ever since 1961, he had not been satisfied with the area on campus that had been proposed for the federated colleges, "and this we hope to change."[98] As well, in April 1962, Macdougall had begun to look for architects to design a new Campion College building. When in Vancouver that month, he contacted the renowned architect Peter Thornton; in late October, Thornton visited Regina. He met with Macdougall and the college's advisory board. There was general satisfaction with him, and the board, along with Macdougall's Jesuit Consultors, agreed that "he would be an excellent choice because of his experience and because he is such a persona grata at the University of Saskatoon [sic]." There was also, Macdougall acknowledged, a local Catholic architect "whom we could engage as associate architect." Thornton was chosen to be the architect of the new building.[99]

In early 1963, the move towards federation once again accelerated; by April, considerable progress had been made on every side. Macdougall had even been able to win over Riddell—who had been less than enthusiastic about federated colleges—to support federation: "When I encountered Riddell one day last week he very promptly assured me that he no longer had any reservations on our federation for 1965–1966, and would not in any way be a stumbling-block (which he has been in a way heretofore). As long as we can initiate the planning at this stage, we shall know that the future of our operation has been secured."[100]

On 12 September 1963, Spink's committee examining the implications of federation recommended that Campion College become

---

97   E. Peter W. Nash, S.J., letter to Gordon F. George, S.J., 6 January 1963, ibid.

98   Angus J. Macdougall, S.J., letter to Gordon F. George, S.J., 19 November 1961, ibid.

99   Angus J. Macdougall, S.J., letters to Gordon F. George, S.J., 26 April 1962; 27 October 1962, ibid. He did not indicate who the local Catholic architect was.

100 Angus J. Macdougall, S.J., letters to Gordon F. George, S.J., 14 April 1963; 20 April 1963; Angus J. Macdougall, S.J., letter to John W. Spinks, ibid.

federated, but with a proviso that it not become effective before July 1966. That recommendation was formally adopted by the university in December 1963, and the agreement was approved on 11 March 1964. Without significant changes, Macdougall's proposals of 1 March 1961 had become the basis of the federated college system in Regina.[101]

Certainly, there were many people involved from 1959 to 1963 at the university, at Campion College, and at Luther College in establishing the federated system, without whose contribution Campion's application for federation would never have been realized. Yet it has to be acknowledged that a good deal of acclaim must go to Macdougall for his vision and leadership, his tenacity and unfailing drive, his optimism and his unwillingness to accept defeat, in bringing about the federated system whereby Campion College would have a programme leading to the Bachelor of Arts degree. In fact, without Macdougall's skills in negotiations, his optimism and his handling of difficult situations and individuals; without his hours of dogged work; without the endless hours he sat through meetings discussing various federated scenarios; without his firm determination not to take "no" for an answer; and without his insights about university life and the role of a small college within a larger academic institution drawn from his experiences of the federated and affiliated colleges at the University of Toronto, it is safe to say that the present federated system at the University of Regina, which mirrors his original proposal, might well be a different arrangement, and not necessarily to the benefit of the colleges. History shows that there was then, and there has remained since, some strong opposition to the federated colleges in Regina.[102]

During his first year as Rector, Macdougall had quickly realized that he needed assistance in administering and in establishing strong academic credentials for the college if ever his proposals for federation

---

101 *Minutes of the Senate of the University of Saskatchewan*, 22 November 1963; E. Peter W. Nash, S.J., letter to Angus J. Macdougall, S.J., 10 December 1963, ibid.

102 In the past, in the historical accounts of Campion's lead-up to and establishment of federation, James J. Farrell, S.J., and Angus J. Macdougall, S.J., far too frequently have been given little recognition, indeed sometimes not mentioned at all. Cf. for one example, Pitsula, *As One who Serves*, op. cit., 251–256, in which Farrell gets one mention in an endnote while Macdougall gets one in the text and two in the endnotes. Indeed, Farrell took the first major step, while Macdougall then pursued Farrell's initiative over a three-year period, and thus became greatly responsible for negotiating, planning, and bringing about the federated system in Regina.

were to be implemented. In fact, within a month of assuming office, he acknowledged that there were few Jesuits at Campion with acceptable academic qualifications to offer the university. It was not a rosy picture he drew: "Having received the minimum requirements demanded by the University for professors, I am rather aghast at our rather poor showing. The MA in the subject is called for, and this we really do not have in psychology, economic[s], French and chemistry. This ... we shall correct so as to deal with the University authorities from a position of strength.... Perhaps we should, in the dearth of Jesuit priest science teachers, secure good lay-men for chemistry and physics-maths, in order to have continuity and avoid embarrassing changes."[103] He pressed George to appoint well-qualified Jesuits to Campion College.

In early 1961, in Macdougall's judgment, one possibility for the appointment of a Jesuit professor at the future Regina Campus arose; its department of philosophy would be newly established and in need of professors. Anticipating that, he requested both from the university and from the Provincial Superior that Campion be allowed to appoint a professor to that department whenever the Regina Campus would be established. He had in mind E. Peter W. Nash, S.J., for that position, and for the position of dean of the college.[104] Given Nash's good academic record and his outgoing personality, he was a first-rate choice. In the late summer of 1961, he became dean of the college and at the same time, by his acceptance of a post in philosophy, he would become, when the Regina Campus opened, the first Jesuit professor there. He quickly settled into the dean's office and, as Macdougall wrote within a month of Nash's arrival, had "thrown himself into the new job, and to my way of thinking, has achieved a great deal in a short period. He is already well acquainted with the various university officials and is hitting it off nicely with them."[105]

---

103   Angus J. Macdougall, S.J., letter to Gordon F. George, S.J., 18 September 1960, ibid.

104   DJB, vol. 2, 242–245. A professor of philosophy for several years at the Jesuit Seminary, 403 Wellington Street West, Toronto, Nash was appointed to teach philosophy in 1958 at Mount Saint Michael's, Spokane, in Washington State, a philosophate for young American Jesuits. He moved there along with twenty-nine young Canadian Jesuits studying philosophy.

105   Angus J. Macdougall, S.J., letter to Gordon F. George, S.J., 14 September 1961, AJC, Box D-516.

Over the next two years, Macdougall and Nash became a most impressive team. The first assisted in the structural formation of the federation; the second in overseeing the academic life within the college and within the proposed federation. Cordial, highly approachable, intelligent, good-humoured, and altogether civil, they worked closely with the university to develop Campion's federated status.

Macdougall, however, would not remain in Regina for long. On 31 July 1963, he became Provincial Superior of the Upper Canada Province, replacing Gordon F. George, S.J. In the late spring of 1963, John L. Swain, S.J., Vicar General of the Society of Jesus (1960–1965), appointed J. Aloysius Graham, S.J., a Jesuit and professor of chemistry at Loyola College, Montreal, to succeed Macdougall. For several reasons, however, Graham begged to be excused from the appointment. Swain then replied that Lawrence C. Braceland, S.J., who had been for nineteen years a professor of classics at the Jesuit Juniorate, Guelph, Ontario, was "apt" for the position of Rector. In the end, however, Swain appointed Nash as successor to Macdougall.[106]

Thus, in late June, George wrote Nash that his appointment would become effective "on July 31st with the reading in the refectory of the accompanying letter [of appointment]." At the same time, George also announced that there would be a new dean: "Although he will not be officially appointed until the supplementary status on August 15th, I think you should know in advance that it will be Father Gerald Lahey. This will help you in the worrisome task of [planning for the coming semester]. Both of these appointments should be kept secret. There should be no correspondence with Father Lahey until the Provincial gives the green light—as he [Lahey] does not yet know of the coming changes."[107]

---

106 DJB, vol. 1, 24–26; 331–332; Gordon F. George, S.J., letter to Angus J. Macdougall, S.J., 26 June 1963, AJC, Box D-516. A Canadian Jesuit, Swain had been appointed in 1960 Vicar General of the Society of Jesus when the Superior General, Jean-Baptiste Janssens, s.j. (1946–1964), had become incapacitated. Swain remained in that office until 22 May 1965 when a new Superior General, Pedro Arrupe, s.j., was elected. On 31 July 1963, Braceland became dean and professor of classics at St. Paul's College, University of Manitoba.

107 Gordon F. George, S.J., letter to E. Peter W. Nash, S.J., 20 July 1963, AJC, Box D-516. At the time, all appointments of Jesuit personnel in a Province ordinarily occurred on 31 July, the feast of Saint Ignatius Loyola, founder of the Society of Jesus, and would be announced in a "Status", the Latin term Jesuits used for the annual list of their new assignments. Such appointments were

Unaware of the other possible choices for Rector, Nash willingly accepted the assignment. He was not, however, as happy about Lahey's appointment. He did agree that "Lahey will be a fine asset in negotiations with Saskatoon and with the Regina campus. And I also get on with him well." Yet Nash was concerned that, given Lahey's previous experience in university work at Loyola College and at St. Paul's College, as well as his uncertain health—he had suffered a severe heart seizure in late 1961—Campion might seem to be "a real come-down.... I do not see how his being dean is going to be of any real help."[108]

Nash need not have worried. It was an astute appointment. Lahey had a wise, unflappable, candid demeanour, and an integrity that strongly influenced the institutions and people wherever he had served. Just as important, he was a humanist with a deep appreciation for the liberal arts and of their place both in a Jesuit college and in society as a whole. All that, coupled with Lahey's considerable experience in administration, went a long way in helping Nash take Campion to the next step towards federation from 1963 to 1968.[109]

Immediately upon assuming the office of Rector on 31 July, Nash plunged in. Having worked closely with Macdougall over two years, he was well informed about the college and about the state of the

---

strictly confidential until that date. On 31 July, the appointment of a new Rector customarily took effect at the beginning of the midday meal. The outgoing Rector would sit at table in his usual place until after the new appointment was read from the refectory's pulpit. Then he would exchange places with the incoming Rector, who had been placed beside him at the beginning of the meal. Other Jesuits sat at tables in whatever order they entered the refectory in separated and allocated areas for priests, Scholastics and Brothers. Superior Generals, Provincial Superiors, Rectors, Masters of Novices, and Masters of Tertians were the only ones who sat in a designated place at table. This Jesuit custom, long-standing since the sixteenth century, gradually disappeared during the late 1960s and early 1970s.

108 E. Peter W. Nash, S.J., letter to Angus J. Macdougall, S.J., 28 July 1963, ibid.

109 DJB, vol. 1, 177–178. Lahey had lived at St. Edmund's Hall, Cambridge University, England, from Michaelmas Term, 1928, until the end of Trinity Term, 1929. There he wrote and, in 1930, published through Oxford University Press the first critical analysis of the poetry of the renowned nineteenth-century Jesuit Gerard Manley Hopkins. Lahey's book remains among the very best biographies of the poet. In 1948, he was appointed dean of St. Paul's College, University of Manitoba, and was a member of the university's senate for eight years and a member of the examining board for fourteen years. During those years at St. Paul's, he regularly produced articles for publication, and often was invited to give talks and to participate in discussions on radio. From 1955 to 1959, he had served as Rector of Loyola College, Montreal, and then again as dean of St. Paul's College from 1960 to 1963.

federated agreement, as well as of the further negotiations necessary.[110] Affable, witty, cheery, and a good storyteller, Nash quickly found his seat as Rector among his colleagues on the Regina Campus. The move towards federation seemed to be progressing well, despite some snags.[111] Within six months after assuming office, Nash optimistically, and at length, summarized the state of federation to Macdougall in Toronto: "We have had another meeting of the sub-committee on federation to hammer out terms. Right now the terms on which we have agreed look pretty good. Oddly enough the Regina Campus is so allergic to anything that Saskatoon has done, might do or might suggest that it wants to give us more than is on the books for S[aint] T[homas] M[ore]. On paper S.T.M. is in an odd position: all its faculty members are members of the Faculty of Arts and Science. Where does this put the Principal of S.T.M.? The Regina people want us to be ourselves a college of Arts and Science with the Rector equal of the Dean of the University College of Arts and Science. Also they want us to continue teaching all the humanities and social science classes that we are teaching at present (English, French, Latin, Economics, History, Psychology and Sociology). Personally, I think we should make every effort to comply."[112]

As he pointed out to Macdougall, not without a certain note of triumph: "Well, the Regina Campus cannot say that we haven't done our best to cooperate with them." On that he was correct. Furthermore, in his judgment, it would be much easier to receive approval from the university for such classes within "the terms of federation rather than later on when any new course has to go through Council." As later practices would prove, Nash's assessment of this situation was also correct.[113]

110 E. Peter W. Nash, S.J., letter to Angus J. Macdougall, S.J., 20 September 1963, AJC, Box D-516. In his reply to Nash on 23 September, Macdougall showed that at heart he still scarcely trusted Riddell: "He will scuttle the ship yet!" Angus J. Macdougall, S.J, letter to E. Peter W. Nash, S.J., 23 September 1963, ibid.

111 E. Peter W. Nash, S.J., letter to Angus J. Macdougall, S.J., 3 November 1963; E. Peter W. Nash, S.J., letter to Chief Justice Edward M. Culliton, 12 November 1963; Dr. John W. T. Spinks, letter to E. Peter W. Nash, S.J., 17 December 1963, ibid.

112 E. Peter W. Nash, S.J., letter to Angus J. Macdougall, S.J., 2 February 1964, ibid.

113 Ibid.

In the meantime, as dean of the college, Lahey likewise began in earnest to establish himself in office. Among his first tasks was to continue developing Campion as a liberal arts college, but always with an eye for its place in the new federation with the university. To that end, he had to create a new role for the dean's office within the complex university structures. That meant endless hours of meetings with the deans and heads of departments of the university to determine precisely what federation would mean in practice; the statement of federation was in fact a brief document with few embellishments and explanations. At the same time, he had to do the practical work of being dean of a college. Despite whatever misgivings Nash may have had about Lahey in the summer of 1963, by December he could confidently write that Lahey was "doing a very thorough job as dean. I see now all the things that I should have been doing." Among these was a long-range plan that concerned the projected ratio of students to professors. Nash reported to Macdougall in June 1964 that "I had Principal Riddell in the office this morning. We are going over Fr. Lahey's projections re the student body and staff, and we came to a rough sort of working agreement. I'll look it over with Gerald first and then let you judge on same. It is roughly to the effect that in the first year or so we set a ceiling to the number of students we enrol so that we can then judge exactly how many professors we will have to get. Otherwise we could find ourselves badly caught. And so could the University."[114]

It had been evident for some time that there was a need to hire more professors. Lahey set out to recruit several well-qualified, mainly young lay professors for the college, and over the following three to five years, he hired several who would remain professors there for the next forty years and more. In 1964, Lahey himself had become a professor in the university's department of English, while a year earlier, in 1963, John J. Lepine, S.J., had become a professor in the department of history, the second Jesuit after Nash to be appointed to the university.

---

114   E. Peter W. Nash, S.J., letters to Angus J. Macdougall, S.J., 14 December 1963; 26 June 1964, ibid.

With Lahey's careful guidance of the academic life within the college and with the university, Nash was relieved of considerable burdens. Yet given his teaching load in philosophy, his duties as Rector, his ongoing negotiations over funding with the government of Saskatchewan's department of education, and especially his overseeing the planning and construction of the college building on the new university campus, Nash's task was not easy and at times the results not always satisfactory. Even if the basic structures of federation had been approved, many details had to be worked through to the satisfaction of many. Ever optimistic and eager, and seemingly filled with boundless energy, Nash worked tirelessly on the minutiae of the federation agreement, and in harmony with Riddell much progress was made by February 1964. At that time, Nash could report that "Dr. Riddell showed Dr. Spinks the final draught of the terms of federation on which the sub-committee on federation agreed and which are also satisfactory to the Regina Campus faculty. Spinks, whom I ran into at the opening and blessing of the new wing of S[aint] T[homas] M[ore] on Thursday, said he liked the terms and, in an amused tone, said: 'You know, I think they are growing up'!"[115]

Three months later, Nash sent a brief note to Macdougall that "Tonight Dr. Riddell will publicly announce at our Closing Exercises the approval of federation."[116]

In the midst of the negotiations for the terms of federation, Nash also had to oversee and finish that which Macdougall had had to leave unfinished: the planning, designing, and construction of the college's new building on campus. Peter Thornton had been chosen as architect: "Peter right now is working out the rough sketch of what we require. I hope he hurries up because I want to get our last bid in for a site before other interests start pre-empting all the choice ones."[117]

Thornton's task was to design a building that embraced the Jesuit ideal for teaching and other intellectual activities, for providing the spiritual needs of students, and for creating an atmosphere where

115　Ibid.

116　Ibid.

117　E. Peter W. Nash to Angus J. Macdougall, S.J., 9 February 1964, ibid.

culture and relaxation might thrive. To that end, a student centre, a library, a chapel, lecture and seminar rooms, an auditorium, a cafeteria, and faculty and staff offices were laid out within a five-storey building. The hours involved were at times long and tedious, and the architectural plans had to be approved by both the university and the Wascana Centre authorities. This called for a lot of energy and time and travelling by Nash and others. The situation was not made any easier by the fact that Thornton changed the plans more than once, most times in response to Nash's suggestions, and that he lived on the west coast, over 1,000 kilometres by air from Regina. Nash described one such hurried visit to see the architect: "On January 16th I dashed out to Vancouver to spend two days with Thornton and then dashed right back. They were worthwhile and we really got a lot of work done. We thoroughly thrashed out the programme of requirements. I really think he will come up with something within the $800,000 limit for a pretty adequate first stage...."[118]

Once federation had become a reality in July 1966, Nash became Campion's first principal. His previous title, "Rector", one in common usage in Jesuit colleges since the sixteenth century, was changed to "principal", the title to be used at the Regina Campus for the heads of the university and of the federated colleges. That title changed to "president" in 1974, when Regina Campus became the independent University of Regina.

The building on Albert Street became solely Campion High School. Those Jesuit professors teaching at the college continued to live there with the high school Jesuit Community until the new college building was opened. Meanwhile, the college's offices and classes were temporarily accommodated in the university's buildings.[119]

Although yet not fully completed, the college building was officially opened on 20 January 1968. At the inaugural ceremony, Nash

---

118 E. Peter W. Nash, S.J., letters to Angus J. Macdougall, S.J., 22 March 1965; 24 March 1965; 14 April 1965; 25 April 1965; 5 May 1965; E. Peter W. Nash, S.J., letter to Peter M. Thornton, 24 March 1965, ibid. On 5 May, Nash was able to report that the architectural plans had been approved at last.

119 When the Jesuits withdrew from Campion High School in 1971, it became the responsibility of the Catholic Separate School Board of Regina. In the late spring of 1975, the school moved to a new site, and there changed its name to Dr. Martin LeBoldus High School.

captured the moment when he spoke about the building itself and its future: "It [the new building] strives to satisfy harmoniously the spiritual, intellectual, cultural and social needs of the students. Through these facilities, open to all Catholic students and, in fact, to any student, Campion hopes to contribute towards a synthesis of faith and culture and be of real service to the university community."[120]

Certainly, the new college building was successful in almost every way, and allowed for plenty of space for student activities and public events. Its physical appearance, however, was less successful. Unfortunately, due to financial restraints, the exterior of the building was never finished as originally intended, with slabs of white stone matching those of the university's administrative building placed over the surface of the concrete exterior. Instead, the college was left with a grey exterior that on overcast and rainy days makes the concrete building appear dull, bulky, and unattractive amid the lighter-coloured buildings on campus.[121]

Never a man who found delegating authority easy, Nash maintained a firm grip on everything within the college and, although as principal he was responsible for the building and its condition, he sometimes gave the impression that the building and everything therein was his. Thomas A. O'Keefe, S.J., a Jesuit professor of philosophy at the college, observed to the Provincial Superior that "were Father Nash to have an accident, or even our engineer, no one here would know how to turn the heat on or off, much less how to proceed in our dealings with the University officials or (above all) with the bank." One Jesuit, when visiting the college for the first time, humorously observed that "Every brick has E. P. W. Nash engraved on it!" In the minds of some by the early 1970s, his comment seemed not too far off the mark.[122]

At times, too, Nash's relations with Lahey and others in the college could become quite strained because, seemingly, he wanted to do and control everything. Although Lahey acknowledged Nash's splendid

---

120 E. Peter W. Nash, S.J., *Welcome Address*, 20 January 1968, ibid.

121 By the first decade of the twenty-first century, the building's exterior was showing considerable decay due to excessive moisture and the wind weakening the concrete walls.

122 Thomas A. O'Keefe, S.J., letter to Edward F. Sheridan, S.J., 18 January 1970, ibid.

qualities of hard work and his "pleasing personality," he also pointed out to the Provincial Superior that Nash had to delegate more. "His nature," Lahey went on, "is to hold the stage, especially in social gatherings and priestly assemblies."[123]

Consequently, because of his overwork and never-ending fatigue, which he continued to complain about for several years in letters to the Provincial Superiors, many worried that Nash was straining his health. Others, too, and markedly some of the younger faculty members hired by Lahey after the mid 1960s, in time grew increasingly restless at the lack of communication and at the top-down paternalistic administration by Nash and Lahey alike. The latter 1960s and early 1970s was a time of considerable unrest throughout the universities of North America, as faculty members demanded, sometimes quite noisily and disruptively, more voice in the running of a university, and especially in those matters that affected them directly. Campion was no exception, although the unrest was less forceful than elsewhere. In 1968, during a period when Lahey was recuperating from various health issues, some faculty members decided to press Nash to allow for departments within the college. Nash acquiesced, but then had to face Lahey's displeasure—for Lahey also was ever disinclined to share authority—when he returned from his convalescing, only to find in place that which he had been opposing for some time: academic departments within the college.

For several years, Nash even took on the extra job of recruiting new students for Campion. Undoubtedly, there was a great need for such recruitment. There remained over the years a widespread misunderstanding among the Catholic population, especially in the smaller towns and rural areas, about the nature and purpose of Campion College. During the 1960s and 1970s, many Catholics thought that it was a high school only, and therefore never considered having their sons and daughters register in the college for university studies. It took a lot of work by the college's recruitment officers to convince Catholic parents otherwise.

---

123 Gerald F. Lahey, S.J., letter to Angus J. Macdougall, S.J., 18 January 1966, ibid.

Nash's resultant amount of travel visiting high schools throughout southern Saskatchewan may have been remarkable, but it was not always the wisest task for him personally, even if the enrolment in the college began to increase after 1965. It demanded a lot of his time and, as he related, sometimes the driving could become difficult, tiring, and hazardous during a prairie winter. "This is a very busy season for me. I was around the country, visiting the larger high schools, trying to sell the Regina Campus and Campion. I find driving getting more tiring, and had a lovely bloodshot eye after one session...." A year later it was much the same: "I got back only last night [29 February 1972] from a two-day jaunt into the southern boondocks of the Prov. of Sask., speaking at seven high-schools and covering 600 miles of total whiteness ... white fields, white highways and white sky, ... tough driving." Five days later, he noted that, after having visited the schools east of Regina in Balgonie and Qu'Appelle, he had hoped to visit Indian Head but was dissuaded from that when a blizzard warning was issued. He headed home instead, "despite a 40 mph cross-wind blowing snow that at times almost wiped out all visibility."[124]

Although the college's library had served well in the past, it was evident that in the new federated arrangement, it was necessary to develop its holdings further. The original plan was that the library would house about 80,000 volumes. In 1968 it was a long way from that. Thus, during the summer of 1968, when the Oblates in St. Norbert, Manitoba, were wanting to dispose of their theological library, the college's librarian, John J. LePine, S.J., went through that library to assess the books. He reported to Nash that he had found it good in most areas, especially in Scripture, while the periodical section was excellent. On 4 September, Nash could report to Macdougall that "I have just agreed to buy seventeen tons of books, an entire theological library, for $50,000.00.... The Oblates are being really generous in letting us have the library for $50,000.00. They also are quite content that we pay it off over a ten year period.... We are also trying to get the university to contribute something towards the purchase of shelving and cataloguing. After all, the University is most interested in this

---

124 E. Peter W. Nash, S.J., letters to Edward F. Sheridan, S.J., 21 March 1971; 1 March 1972, ibid.; *Campion College Journal*, History of Campion College File, 6 March 1972, ACC, file B65.

library: it gives the university a real talking point in the establishment of a religious studies program."

Yet, as Nash added, not without some note of triumph, Campion was not the only contender for the Oblates' library. St. Paul's College, University of Manitoba, and St. Joseph's Seminary in Edmonton had also been interested. "I really think we have made quite a scoop."[125]

The sudden death of Lahey from a heart seizure on 21 February 1969 shocked Campion and the university. Lahey's death was an especially serious blow to Nash. He had come greatly to rely on his confrère's presence in the dean's office. After six years, he was not only a reliable promoter of the college on campus but for Nash, Lahey was also a trustworthy confidant and administrative colleague. In Nash's mind, Lahey seemed almost irreplaceable.[126]

Fortunately, there was a replacement: Desmond P. Burke-Gaffney, S.J. On 31 July 1969, he was to step down as Rector of St. Paul's College, Winnipeg. Although in the end Nash seized the opportunity to resolve the vacancy in the dean's office, he had reservations about Burke-Gaffney becoming dean; Nash believed that he should finish his six years as Rector in Winnipeg. He himself, he assured the Provincial Superior, could handle the dean's office along with everything else. Macdougall thought otherwise. Burke-Gaffney became dean on 1 August 1969.[127]

By the end of the 1960s, the load from the college's debt weighed heavily at $830,891.79, with a monthly interest payment of $5,906.59. In 1966, the provincial government had assisted the college with a grant of $150,000.00, which went towards 10 percent of the total cost of the new college building. Nonetheless, the debt was a great deal of money, and by 1969 there seemed little hope of paying it off. For Nash, the only possible way was an "increase [of] enrolments and ... [the] sale of the high school property." His latter suggestion would prove far more contentious than he could have ever wanted. Yet as early as

---

125   E. Peter W. Nash, S.J., letter to Angus J. Macdougall, S.J., 4 September 1968, AJC, Box D-516.

126   DJB, vol. 1, 178.

127   Ibid., 36–38; E. Peter W. Nash, SJ., letters to Angus J. Macdougall, S.J., 28 May 1969; 23 August 1969, AJC, Box D-516.

the autumn of 1964, he had been mulling over that idea of using the revenue of the high school to finance the college's building.[128]

To counter any move on that front, for some time the members of the Jesuit Community at Campion High School had put up a solid wall of opposition to such a sale. The matter came to a head when, in 1968, Henry B. Bedard, S.J., was appointed Vice Rector of Campion High School by the Provincial Superior. The intention was that, in effect, Bedard would be the Superior over the high school Jesuits and head of the school. Macdougall hoped that in this way the Jesuits' growing opposition to Nash would subside. Nash had other ideas, however. Even if he, along with the Jesuits working at the college, had been living for two years on the university campus, separate from the high school Jesuit Community, as Rector, Nash insisted that there was only one person in charge over all the Jesuits in Regina and their ministries: himself. Of course, from a traditional Jesuit point of view, he was right.[129]

Not surprisingly, Macdougall's arrangement did not work out. Although Bedard was a kind, gentle, and cheerful man, not easily given to emotional outbursts or bouts of unreasonableness or stubbornness, within a year he was begging Macdougall to remove him as Vice Rector. He felt taxed beyond endurance. No longer could he bear, he said, the strain from "quarrelling over the title of Vice Rector", and what he saw as Nash's meddling in the high school's affairs and in the high school Jesuit Community.[130]

Nash had refused to give way to Bedard. He wrote to Macdougall that Bedard was "quite confused about his real status, and I think you can expect some static on the point."[131] Little did Nash know. A day earlier, and with some bitterness, Bedard had written to the Provincial Superior that Nash "[would] take over when he sees fit,

---

128 *Regina Leader Post*, 5 May 1966; Angus J. Macdougall, S.J., letter to E. Peter W. Nash, S.J., 11 November 1964; E. Peter W. Nash, S.J., letter to Angus J. Macdougall, S.J., 16 October 1969, ibid.; E. Peter W. Nash, SJ., *Campion College Journal*, 25 August 1969, CCA, file B65. At the present value of the Canadian dollar, these three sums would be in the region of over $5 million, $36,000.00, and $1.35 million respectively.

129 DJB, vol. 2, 6–8.

130 Henry B. Bedard, S.J., letter to Angus J. Macdougall, S.J., 1 February 1969, AJC, Box D-516.

131 E. Peter W. Nash, S.J., letter to Angus J. Macdougall, S.J., 2 February 1969, ibid.

the running of our school: finances at least.... [I] asked him to take over 'then': [he] said he hadn't the time! Last year, his interests in our High school matters was just 'nil'; even his interest in the [high school Jesuit] Community was 'nil'".[132]

Macdougall accepted Bedard's resignation in the early summer of 1969, and then tried another tactic: he appointed Alfred J. Colliard, S.J., not as Vice Rector but as Rector of the high school Jesuit Community and head of the high school. That became effective 31 July 1969, the same day that Macdougall himself was stepping down as Provincial Superior. His understanding, or at least his hope, was that Nash as Rector would handle only the affairs of the college Jesuit Community and of the college itself, and thus act as if there were in fact two separate Jesuit Communities and ministries with two separate Rectors. That did not work out. The problem was that there was canonically only one Jesuit Community, albeit in two parts—high school and college—under one Rector, Nash. To add to that problem, the high school depended on the corporate status of the college—The Catholic College of Regina—while the college depended on the finances of the high school. Nash wanted to keep it that way, at least until he could free the high school's finances for the college's use.

It would take several more years before an agreeable and permanent solution was found for such an ambiguous situation. Eventually, towards the middle to the latter part of the 1970s, a Jesuit system in Canada evolved whereby a Director of the Ministry was appointed to be in charge of the day-to-day running of a ministry, but still would remain accountable to the Superior (or Rector) as the one responsible for all the ministries and Jesuits in a local area. In Regina, it took another seven years before that system came into effect. Daniel J. Hannin, S.J., was appointed Superior of the college's Jesuit Community in 1978 while, as president of the college, Nash became solely the Director of the Ministry but remained responsible to the Superior.

Meanwhile, during the summer of 1969, the situation between Nash and the high school Jesuit Community had gotten more than a little tense. On the one side were Nash and the college Jesuit

---

132   Henry B. Bedard, S.J., letter to Angus J. Macdougall, S.J., 1 February 1969, ibid.

Community favouring the status quo, which in effect meant that the college would have access to the high school's assets; on the other side were those favouring the independence of the high school from the college, which, in the minds of these latter, meant two Jesuit Communities and corporations, administratively and financially separate from one another, with two independent Rectors. To plead their cause and to counter Nash's move to take over the high school's assets for the college, Nash's House Consultors of the high school's Jesuit Community wrote a joint letter on 16 October 1969—a rare event—to the new Provincial Superior, Edward F. Sheridan, S.J., complaining strongly about Nash's intentions and behaviour. "The operations of the two Jesuit communities in Regina," they wrote, "are separated rather than combined, and the high school's assets reside with the Campion High School Jesuit Community rather than with both Jesuit Communities." In short, and contrary to Nash's scheme, they were insisting that the college should continue with its original incorporation as "The Catholic College of Regina", while there would be a new and separate corporation established that included the high school and all its assets along with the Campion High School Jesuit Community. That procedure, they hoped, would successfully trump Nash's effort—he wanted to maintain the single corporation for both institutions and communities—to grab the assets of the high school, as the Jesuits in the high school saw it, in order to help cover the mounting debt of the college. Needless to say, Nash was opposed to what his high school House Consultors were proposing.[133]

Yet, to push their point even further with Sheridan, and with what in less than two years would turn out to be an extremely incongruous remark, they wrote that "the future of Campion College, given its serious financial difficulties, is hardly bright, and that the prospect of its visibility might well be based on broader and sounder considerations than the absorption of the High School's assets." Little did they foresee that the Jesuits would leave Campion High School in the summer of

---

133 "A new corporation structure", submitted to Edward F. Sheridan, S.J., by the House Consultors of Campion High School Jesuit Community: Alfred J. Colliard, S.J.; Patrick J. Boyle, S.J.; John Toth, S.J.; John C. Trainor, S.J.; Henry B. Bedard, S.J., 26 October 1969, ibid.

1971, and all the members of the Jesuit High School Community, with the exception of one person, would be dispersed elsewhere.[134]

Eventually, Nash won out. He would get the high school's assets for the college. It would take, however, another two years until after the Jesuits had left the high school before the sale of the property and transferral of investments would be realized, and that not without plenty of complications.

From one perspective, the solution for the disagreement between them and Nash would have been to have separated physically and financially the two Jesuit Communities at the time the college was moving to Regina Campus. For each of those, two Superiors (or Rectors), equal in status but separate in every way, should have been appointed, the one for the high school, the other for the college. Yet Nash would never have agreed to that solution.

In the end, however, and apart from Nash's desire to get the school's assets to pay down the college's debt, other factors were also playing against the Jesuits maintaining their high school in Regina. Not only was there a growing lack of support by Catholics to send their sons to the school—there were other options in Regina—but there was also an increasing shortage of Jesuit manpower as well as a growing lack of interest by younger Jesuits to work in the high school ministry. Thus, there was not much enthusiasm among many Jesuits in the Province of Upper Canada to keep Campion High School. By the late 1960s, in the minds of several Jesuits elsewhere than Regina, the high school's days were numbered.

The whole quarrelsome episode among the Jesuits came at a heavy cost, and not least to Nash himself. By late 1969, he was frequently complaining to Macdougall about his workload and constant fatigue and lack of time for his teaching. The pressures on him never seemed to abate. Not only had he spent a lot of energy over the unfortunate situation about his authority and about ownership of the assets, he also was worrying constantly about the college's debt load and the payment of interest on the loan. With that, too, was the shock of Lahey's death; the search for a replacement, along with the extra workload he

---

134 Ibid.

had for six months, February to August 1969, when he acted as dean until a replacement was hired; his responsibility within the college and university as principal and professor; his insistence on attending every event, whether in the city or in the college and university or among his friends; the endless travelling throughout southern Saskatchewan in recruiting students; his duties as a Consultor to the Provincial Superior, which meant a flight to Toronto every month for a two-day, sometimes longer, Consultors' meeting; and his obligations as Superior of some twenty or so Jesuits. Small wonder he was exhausted at times. Yet, he usually appeared buoyant and cheerful, with a good sense of humour, a good conversationalist and storyteller, and ever willing to give of his time, especially to students.[135]

The arrival of Burke-Gaffney as dean in August 1969 did help to ease some of Nash's workload. An experienced administrator, intelligent, and easy-going, Burke-Gaffney quickly settled into the position. Almost immediately, he and Nash took up the proposal, which had been floated for some time, to establish courses in religious studies. Along with the university's principal, Dr. John Archer, and the dean of arts and science, Dr. Edgar Vaughan, of the Regina Campus, they hoped to set up such a programme for credit. The enquiry into establishing a religious studies programme began in 1969, when Dr. Bernard Zagorin introduced a motion in the university that the College of Arts and Science should create such a programme.[136]

By 30 June 1970, Nash could write to Edward F. Sheridan, Provincial Superior, that they were moving faster than previously hoped on the introduction of that programme: "[Archer and Vaughan] both reacted very favourably to my suggestion that Father [Isidore] Gorski offer one course at least in Biblical Literature under the aegis of the Humanities Division. I won't get definite word for a month on this, but it looks hopeful. I think it is important to get our feet in now before the University sets up a formal department of religious studies (which won't be until 1973 according to latest forecasts)."[137]

---

135   DJB, vol. 2, 243–244.

136   Ibid., vol. 1, 38–39.

137   E. Peter W. Nash, S.J., letter to Edward F. Sheridan, S.J., 30 June 1970, AJC, Box D-516.

A course entitled "Sociology of religions", offered by Daniel J. Hannin, S.J., was considered another possible "foot inside the door" in establishing religious studies courses. In similar ways, other specific courses were included or set up to constitute a programme of instructions, and a religious studies programme was introduced on campus in 1974.[138]

Nash and Burke-Gaffney were wise to depend upon Isidore Gorski for introducing the programme in the college. He was a priest of the archdiocese of Regina who had been at Campion College for several years as professor of scriptural studies. Among the best of the teachers on campus and a first-rate academic counsellor and spiritual advisor, Gorski had a knack of remembering everyone by name. With his engaging personality, sense of humour, intelligence, and many contacts throughout the university, the archdiocese, and the city, he became an enormously important ambassador for the college, and was greatly helpful in furthering and developing the religious studies programme.

With his congenial disposition, Burke-Gaffney had soon gained the confidence and respect of his academic colleagues and students. His quiet persuasiveness, calm judgment, and objectivity made him a valued figure on campus, and he was quickly recognized on all sides as one who always remained fair and impartial. He was elected member of one of the more difficult committees on campus, the university's Appeal Committee, and for two successive terms, he chaired the Committee of Standards in English. Always a popular lecturer in English literature, as professor and counsellor he enjoyed a relaxed relationship with students and faculty members.

Fiery he could be, however, if the occasion demanded—he had a rather explosive temper, but would cool down quickly—and would put up with no nonsense. His relations with Nash were usually of the best, although Nash's controlling tendencies could irritate Burke-Gaffney. Instead of confrontations, however, he usually chose to work his way around Nash to achieve what he believed to be the best for the situation. Yet he would not hesitate to challenge Nash, especially

---

138   Edward J. Dowling, S.J., letter to E. Peter W. Nash, S.J., 2 July 1970, AJC, Box D-516; DJB, vol. 2, 120–122.

if he judged that Nash had overstepped his authority by interfering in the dean's office in matters relating to faculty members. Usually, Nash knew better than to annoy Burke-Gaffney.[139]

Nash and Campion, however, would not have Burke-Gaffney's presence for long. During the late summer of 1976, to the alarm of everyone, he began to have serious lapses of memory and bouts of disorientation. The cause was an inoperable brain tumour. To the overwhelming shock of all at Campion and on the university's campus, he died on 4 December that same year. Again, Campion was in mourning.[140]

Thoroughly shaken at Burke-Gaffney's sudden illness and death, Nash had to go searching for another dean. He found one in Thomas O'D. Hanley, S.J., who assumed office during the summer of 1977. Intelligent, congenial, but somewhat shy, yet always cheerful and ever a gentleman even under stressful circumstances, Hanley handled the dean's office very competently for seven years. It was sometimes not easy for him; he fretted about many things. Nonetheless, he quickly learned how to use all his many skills, intellectual and personal, both within the college and on the many university committees on which he sat *ex officio*. He became a most valued and respected figure on campus whose wise advice, good humour, and sense of fairness helped resolve many tense moments. As well as carrying out his several duties as dean, he lectured in the science faculty at the university, remained a fine scholar who published widely, and became highly regarded internationally in the scientific study of ice.[141]

In many ways, the early 1970s were difficult years to be an administrator on a university campus due to the frequent disruption to campus life by student unrest, protests, and sit-ins, often encouraged by disgruntled faculty members. By the mid 1970s, there was a growing unrest among the college's faculty members, who wanted more of a voice in the academic decisions of the college and particularly in

---

139 DJB, vol. 1, 37.

140 Ibid., 37–38.

141 Ibid., 131–132. Thomas O'D. Hanley, S.J., (1923–1987) remained in office until he resigned in 1984 because of ill health. Beset with heart problems, he died suddenly three years later while recuperating at the Jesuit Infirmary, Pickering, Ontario, following surgery on his heart valves.

the policies concerning the college's chaplaincy, which had been the source of deep divisions within the college due to conflicting views between some faculty members and the chaplains about how to serve pastorally both the college and the university. Although at first Nash was reluctant to change his style of governance—among other factors, he worried about his own authority—he eventually realized that such a change was essential.[142]

In early 1978, therefore, Nash agreed that a "Faculty Forum" would be established in the college consisting of all the faculty members, the president and the dean, the head librarian, and the chaplains. The dean chaired the meetings. At first it was envisioned to be a forum to advise the president on academic matters, and where the dean would inform faculty members of various activities and developments on campus. Eventually, its mandate expanded. It became an important council for the dean's own purposes, as well as a place where departmental and committee reports from the college and the university were presented; suggestions made for the annual budget; search committees established and recommendations for new faculty members offered; new academic programmes proposed; and on at least two occasions, in-depth reports drawn up on long-term planning for the college (1980–1981 and 1992–1993). By the new century, after nearly twenty-five years, through its monthly meetings during term time, the Faculty Forum had become an integral part of the college's academic life, and a key voice in the overall governance of the institution.

---

142 A few weeks before Nash left the office of President on 31 December 1978, he admitted to his successor, Joseph B. Gavin, S.J., that his biggest regret in leaving Campion College was that he had not resolved this worrisome conflict in the college. In the minds of several in the college, the chaplaincy was not fulfilling its mandate to serve the Catholic students in the college or on campus. The chaplaincy and chapel had been turned into a quasi parish—referred to as "the Community"—which, in effect, was greatly made up of outsiders who had little or no connection with the college or university. Several parish priests objected to Campion's attracting parishioners away from the parishes, while from within the college, certain faculty members—lay people, Jesuits, and priests—objected that so much of the chaplains' time and energy was being spent elsewhere but on serving the Catholic students on campus. Much pressure to resolve this matter also arose from the Provincial Superior, William F. Ryan, S.J. (1976–1984), the archbishop of Regina, Charles-A. Halpin (1973–1994), and from some prominent local parish priests. It would take another two years, by means of a special college committee, a year of "grace" with no appointed chaplain, new general policies in place concerning chaplains' duties, and a new Jesuit chaplain before harmonious relations were restored among the personnel of the college.

During the years following the establishment in 1971 of Luther University College as a federated companion college on campus, the two colleges formed a strong bond of friendship and cooperation.[143] Of particular note in that regard was their cooperation to establish with the university a religious studies programme. Dr. Roland Miller, professor and dean of Luther University College (1976–1993), and Gorski together were greatly responsible for developing that programme, and especially in avoiding obstacles on the way. Not everyone in the university was pleased that religion was to be given such prominence on campus. The success of this programme in religious studies was also watched over carefully and supported fully by Nash, and by his successor as president, Joseph B. Gavin, S.J. (1978–1986), by Dr. Morris Anderson, president of Luther University College (1964–1986), and by the then president of the university, Dr. Lloyd Barber (1976–1990), who strongly supported the colleges in their desire for such a programme. Of course, as in so many academic undertakings, many others contributed greatly to the establishment and success of this programme. Yet to Miller and Gorski must go abundant gratitude. With tact and good humour during difficult committee meetings, with their balanced views and strong Christian faith, with their firm conviction that such an academic programme was essential for a modern-day university, and with their excellent contribution to the programme as professors, they patiently helped to build it to the point that, over the subsequent years, it has become a successful and integral department in the faculty of arts at the University of Regina.[144]

By the mid 1970s, Campion College was a flourishing undergraduate university college at the University of Regina. The dream of federation envisioned by Farrell and Macdougall, and carried forward by Nash and Lahey, had been realized in ways that were not imagined

---

143 At about the time in 1959 that James J. Farrell, S.J., wrote to Dr. Spinks concerning future federation of colleges in Regina, the Luther College Board of Regents was also discussing a similar role for its college. In 1961, the board made formal application to the university, but the matter was deferred. Again in 1965, the board endorsed the idea of federation, and a petition was forwarded to the university. Federation was approved, and Luther University College opened its new building on campus in 1971. Although the aim of the college was principally to serve the Lutheran Church community in Saskatchewan, it soon attracted students from other denominations.

144 The religious studies programme became a department in 2001.

in the early 1960s. Financially sound due to the agreement with the government of Saskatchewan to fund through annual grants about 80 percent of the federated colleges' expenditures, with an enrolment of nearly 400 students and an admirable teaching faculty and staff, the college was well known on campus for its excellent teaching, its competent and welcoming staff, its friendly collegiate atmosphere, its facilities—particularly the cafeteria, the library, and the splendid chapel—and its personal academic and spiritual counselling.

Personal academic counselling by faculty members was among the more important responsibilities in the college; in the pre-computer registration era, each faculty member, along with other staff members, was fully engaged in guiding students in choosing their courses and programmes. Notable, too, was the role Mrs. Loretta Leibel, the college's registrar, played over many years in college life, and especially in academic counselling. As registrar, she came to know almost every student personally; her wise advice and kindly care endeared her to them, and many kept returning to visit her long after they had left the campus.

When Nash stepped down in December 1978, in almost every way he left a sound academic institution to his successor. When Gavin took over the office of president on 1 January 1979, his vision was to build on what was already there—"a Community of Learning"—and to strengthen further the academic, cultural, and spiritual life of the college. He immediately established the annual *Nash Lecture* (later changed to *The Nash Memorial Lecture*) in 1979, and strengthened the college's philosophy department as well as the religious studies programme, in which he himself became a professor.

In the long run, however, his major contribution lay in his understanding of the traditional Jesuit university college as a centre not only of humanistic learning, but also as a patron of the arts. Following his predecessor's love for painting and music, Gavin helped create a special cultural collegiate atmosphere by rehanging paintings for better effect throughout the public areas of the college and by establishing, in 1979, *Musica Sacra*, the tri-annual free concerts—now bi-annual—of sacred music performed in the chapel.[145] For nearly thirty-five years, this popular concert series has offered sacred music that otherwise would not have been performed regularly in the city, as well as displaying the extensive musical talent in the college, in the university, and in the city to a consistently loyal and appreciative audience. Under the direction of Professor Vernon McCarthy, the musical series thrived, and remains a significant musical contribution to the cultural life of Regina under the guidance of Professor Samira McCarthy.[146]

A two-manual chamber pipe-organ, on permanent loan from the University of Regina, was installed during early 1986 in the chapel for both liturgical and concert use. Eventually, during the presidency of Joseph G. Schner, S.J. (1986–2001), the organ was returned to the university to be replaced by a new concert pipe-organ that his brother, George P. Schner, S.J., had rebuilt. During several periods when he taught at or visited the college, George Schner, an accomplished organist, gave recitals on this organ.[147]

During the 1980s, a programme of film studies, which had begun in the late 1960s, came to play a significant role on campus, and in time has become a well-regarded department in the university. From the outset, Campion College was extensively involved in this programme. With the encouragement of Dr. Terence Marner, a distinguished professor of film studies in the university, John D. Matheson, S.J., was responsible over many years for the college's presence in the film studies on campus. Matheson's commitment to his students and their work, his own vast knowledge about and love of films as works of art, along with his theological and literary backgrounds were major contributions to the programme. He was also influential in establishing and maintaining the excellent film collection that for years has remained available for use through Campion's library.

---

145 Gavin also participated considerably in the musical life of Regina. He was one of the founders of the Saskatchewan Opera Guild, and for five years was a member of the board of governors of the Regina Symphony Orchestra, and an executive member of it for two years.

146 On 22 November 2013, for example, the University Chamber Singers presented *Music of the Tridentine Rite*, which consisted of a splendid performance of Giovanni Pierluigi da Palestrina's *Missa Papae Marcelli* along with appropriate Latin Gregorian Propers for a Mass.

147 DJB, vol. 2, 291–294.

For many years, the college's excellent library and its holdings—which Féré, followed by Lepine, had established—has been a notable feature of the college. Not only the attractive library space itself but its considerable collection of books and periodicals have given the library a prominence on campus far beyond its size. In the 1980s, plans were put in place to focus the library's collection principally in the humanities: English literature, history, religious studies, philosophy, film studies, psychology, and a *Jesuitica* collection. This latter emphasizes Jesuit history, spirituality, and writings about and by Jesuits. It is the largest collection in western Canada of published material on the Jesuits. The other several libraries on campus were left to develop their own areas of academic interest. Every student and professor in the university and federated colleges has access to all the libraries on campus.

Renovated in the early 1980s under the supervision of the librarian, Myfanwy Truscott, a fine atmosphere for reading and working was put in place. Along with the library's enhancement, the college's small but excellent archival collection was organized. Gavin hired graduate students in the history department to collate and catalogue the assortment of files and documents relating to the history of the college and the Jesuits, including also some related to the history of the city and the province. The collection is made available to scholars and other interested persons.

As with all university colleges, Campion College regularly offered occasional public lectures, Lenten and Advent lecture series, public seminars, and other events to the general public, sometimes alone, sometimes in cooperation with other academic units on campus or with groups from the church, both Catholic and Protestant, or the arts. Among such cooperative efforts was a major international conference held on 4 December 1983 at the university. It was sponsored jointly by the Fraser Institute of Vancouver, the University of Regina, Luther University College, and Campion College, with Gorski and Gavin being participants from the college. The theme was theology, third world development, and economic justice, all areas of substantial concern in the 1980s. The papers by the ten panellists and the discussions following were published in 1985.[148]

It was unfortunate, however, that the inclusion of a representative from the Fraser Institute and of a couple of panellists who represented more left- and right-leaning contemporary positions on social and economic matters was a source of controversy in the weeks leading up to the conference. In effect, a small group from both ends of the social and political spectrum tried hard—but unsuccessfully—to stop the conference altogether. Gavin came under some attack from both the more conservative and the more liberal Catholics in Regina, who were objecting to having certain members on the panel. During the early planning stages, Archbishop Halpin had given his support to the conference and raised no objections on seeing the list of panellists, and indeed welcomed the holding of the conference. He rightly pointed out that it was in such forums held on university campuses, including Catholic ones, that important issues of the day can be aired, argued, disagreed or agreed to for the benefit of many. In fact, he suggested that those who were objecting should attend in order to offer their positions in an open discussion. He was right: time after time during the day of the conference, opportunities arose to emphasize, discuss, or quote the Catholic Church's contemporary social teachings and thinking on any number of social, economic, religious, and political questions. Fortunately, and despite such efforts to boycott the conference, if not shut it down completely, it was an immense success, with a large, enthusiastic crowd of several hundred attending on a very cold Saturday.[149]

Gavin also made a special effort to reach out to the Anglican community on campus and in the city. Anglicans had no chaplain or chapel

---

148 *Theology, Third World Development and Economic Justice*, eds. Walter Block and Donald Shaw (Vancouver: Fraser Institute, 1985).

149 A Canadian Catholic bishop, well-known for his promotion of social justice and the social teaching of the Catholic Church, and for his support for the poor, was invited to be a panellist. A recognized and articulate voice in Canada on social justice issues, the bishop was one of the few who had the credibility to face on behalf of Catholics and others those who he strongly believed were harmfully unmindful of a need to support the poor, socially, politically, and economically. Regrettably, however, he refused to participate as a panellist, because a member of the Fraser Institute would also be present, even if, as was pointed out to him, the archbishop of Regina was fully supporting the conference.

on campus. Yet often they would attend the college's midday Masses. Although they were welcome to attend those, Gavin felt that in the end it might be more beneficial for them to offer their own chaplaincy services. He approached the then bishop of Qu'Appelle, Michael G. Peers (1977–1986), to offer him the college's facilities free of charge for Anglican use. With much appreciation and enthusiasm, the bishop accepted. As a result, an office was made available in the college for the newly appointed part-time Anglican chaplain, the chapel was used once a week for their Eucharistic service, and the auditorium, classrooms, and cafeteria were often requested for their public events. One such occasion was their annual meeting of representatives from the parishes and organizations of the diocese. Held on a weekend, the whole college—chapel, auditorium, classrooms, seminar rooms, and cafeteria—was given over to their use.[150]

Although for years there had been at Campion a wide selection of scholarships and bursaries for students, Gavin put considerable energy into adding new ones annually. By the mid 1980s, the college was able to distribute many scholarships and bursaries at its convocation.[151] During those years, too, student enrolment had gradually increased from a low of around 300 students in the late 1970s to over 700 students by 1986. That increase was greatly due to a renewed recruitment programme under the direction of Carol Ariano in the early 1980s, in cooperation with the University of Regina and with Luther University College. It was also due to the members of the Catholic Women's League (CWL). Over several years, they freely offered the college their assistance in recruiting Catholic students by providing Campion with free mail-outs of its information for Catholic parents, and in reminding parents at every opportunity, especially in smaller towns and rural areas, that Campion was a Catholic university college on the University of Regina campus. As well, Gavin was invited a number of times to speak at meetings of the CWL about the college, its various academic, social, religious, and cultural programmes, and the advantages of a small college on a large campus. To meet the

---

150 A similar free offer was extended to and accepted by Catholic organizations, such as local parishes, the Catholic Women's League and the Knights of Columbus.

151 By 2012, at Campion College there were over seventy scholarships given out annually.

resultant growing enrolment, parts of the college's physical facilities were reconstructed and improved, new faculty members were hired to keep in step with the increased numbers of students, and the college began, by 1985, to introduce computers to assist in the registration of students and in other administrative duties.

Although at times difficult to sustain due to a shortage of Jesuit manpower, the Jesuit presence in the college remained stable throughout Gavin's tenure in office; he maintained an annual core of long-term and short-term Jesuit professors and chaplains. Additionally, in 1985 he oversaw the introduction of a board of regents which, as in the majority of Canadian Jesuit educational institutions, was set up to assist the Jesuit Corporation of Campion College in its governance. The majority of the board's make-up has been laywomen and laymen; the Jesuits have representatives as well. In effect, the Jesuits have created a two-tiered system of governance of the college: the Jesuit corporation board and the board of regents, to which the Jesuits have given the ordinary governance of the college.

When Gavin stepped down in the late summer of 1986, the college was strong in student numbers, in the quality of teaching, in its Catholic identity, and in its Jesuit educational ideals. The college's relationship with the University of Regina and the other two federated colleges, Luther University College and Saskatchewan Indian Federated College (renamed First Nations University of Canada in 2003), especially remained excellent. In every way, the federated system continued to function easily and without serious friction.

Prominent among the appointment of Jesuits during Gavin's presidency was Joseph G. Schner, S.J., a distinguished psychologist, counsellor, and professor of psychology who went on to become dean (1984–1986) following Hanley's resignation, and then president (1986–2001). He served in both offices with noteworthy distinction. Good humoured, erudite, cultured, imperturbable, and having considerable administrative experience, as dean and as president Schner guided the college extremely well. His fifteen years as president were especially marked by continuing stability and good rapport with the university and with the provincial department of education.

At a time when the threat of cutbacks in government funding was ever a reality, Schner's governance—he was ably assisted by the deans, Isidore Gorski (1986–1995) and Dr. Kenneth McGovern (1995–2002), and the business manager, Mr. Fred Marcia (1978–2011)—went a long way in maintaining security in the college's finances. Inevitably, there were crises, but Schner's common sense and thorough understanding of the federated system—he had taken his doctorate at the University of Toronto—allowed the college to get through whatever arose. As well, his own love of academic life, his professional outlook, his experience as a scholar, teacher, and respected member of the university's department of psychology, and his love for the arts helped greatly to preserve high standards of academic and artistic life in the college. He balanced his responsibilities as president, his teaching, and his directing of various graduate and honours theses with a commitment to assist in local parishes on Sundays. As a result, he came to know a large number of people in the city.

He undertook the reconstruction of sections of the college building to make it more convenient and welcoming for students, and in practical terms more in tune with the requirements for space due to the increase in enrolment during the 1990s. Notable among those physical improvements has been the grand entrance-foyer, a masterpiece of architectural style and form. At heart, the entrance expresses a significant and long-standing objective of the college: to be friendly, welcoming, and all-embracing. The foyer has done this wonderfully well.

Other significant contributions were his establishment of the Pastoral Studies Programme. Arranged in partnership with the University of Regina's Centre of Continuing Education, the programme aims to train men and women to serve in lay ministries in churches, hospitals, schools, and other institutional settings. It offers a certificate in pastoral studies. Schner became the first director. He also set up the Hannin Lecture Series, which honoured a long-time faculty member, Daniel J. Hannin, S.J., who had taught sociology and had worked with native people in the city.[152]

---

152   DJB, vol. 2, 120–122.

By the end of Schner's presidency, the student numbers had leapt to 1200 and more. Many factors had brought about that growth. Not least of those were the continuation of a strong outreach by the college into the Catholic community in southern Saskatchewan, the excellent reputation of its professors as teachers and academic counsellors, and the extensive awards and scholarship programme available for students, all of which greatly enhanced the college's quality of education and its enrolment.

In several ways, too, the opening years of the 2000s were a period of transition and academic expansion, especially with the rise in student population and the subsequent need for more faculty appointments. Many of the professors who had been appointed professors by Nash during the mid to late 1960s were reaching retirement age, while new professorial appointments opened, notably in classics, theatre, and political science, along with the restoring of a position in the department of history. To fill these gaps, a new and younger generation of lay faculty members—ten in all—with impressive academic backgrounds would be appointed in the college between 2003 and 2009. Strikingly, too, a substantial amount of new research and publishing output would begin with these professors, and as a consequence would give the college greater prominence on campus. At the same time, however, the decline in Jesuit faculty members during this period was evident. In general, the pool of Canadian Jesuit academics was diminishing yearly; by the new century, the number of Jesuits involved full-time at Campion had dwindled noticeably.

When Schner retired from the office in 2001, he left a prosperous undergraduate college for his successor, David R. Eley, S.J., who served for eighteen months, until December 2002. His successor, Dr. Kenneth McGovern (January 2003–June 2005), the first lay president of the college, was brought back to the college from retirement. He knew the college and university well. Hired by Nash in 1966 as professor of philosophy, he carried impressive academic credentials, had served in the faculty union at the college and university and with the Canadian Association of University Teachers on the national academic scene, and had been dean of Campion College from 1995 to 2002. As a result, he had come to know almost everyone on campus and many people nationally. To a large extent, he was the right man for the time. Outgoing and articulate and in every way well prepared to be president, his commitment to Campion and to the Jesuit educational ideals were without parallel. With the assistance of the college's dean, Samira McCarthy (2002–2009)—a long-standing faculty member in the college's department of English literature and the first woman appointed full-time to the college's faculty in 1968—McGovern set out to direct the college.

Although the finances of the college were by no means the only responsibility of the president, they were nonetheless a major part of that, especially the annual provincial government grants. Ever since Campion had become a federated college, those grants were the principal source of funding for its annual budget. They were based not so much on the college's annual financial needs, but rather on the government's estimation of the cost of living and the overall financial state of the province.

Significant, therefore, was the annual meeting of the presidents of Campion College, Luther University College, and St. Thomas More College at the University of Saskatchewan with the minister of education, or the deputy minister, before the provincial budget was introduced in the legislature. The presidents usually met with each other, if possible, before their meeting with the minister of education to discuss their colleges' financial needs and to coordinate their presentation. Although the presidents could speak during those meetings with the minister about their financial needs, generally it was not a time for bargaining. Rather, the meeting was to inform the presidents what the percentage increase (or decrease) in the annual grant to the colleges would be. At the same time, however, the minister might be influenced by what was raised during the meeting, and thus reconsider before making a final decision about the annual grant. Over the years, this arrangement had been satisfactory for the colleges, even if at times the government's grants were never sufficient to cover a college's total annual expenditures.[153]

---

153 Capital funding for a college is discussed by the president with the ministry of education on a case-by-case basis. Annual grants to the fourth college—originally the Saskatchewan Indian Federated College, but since 2003 the First Nations University of Canada—are negotiated separately from the three other federated colleges with the federal and provincial governments.

Of equal financial importance, therefore, were the college's annual tuition fees. Based on a well-balanced agreement worked out with the university since the 1960s, the colleges' tuition was shared with the university according to the number of students registered in the college. In general, it was to account for the various academic and other services the colleges enjoyed as federated institutions within the university. This fee-sharing agreement functioned well, for the most part, at least until the 1990s.

By the early 2000s, however, because the federated colleges were educating what they considered a disproportionate number of the university's students, rising financial pressures necessitated a new fee-sharing agreement with the university. Negotiations began during Schner's presidency and continued with McGovern. The agreement between the colleges and the university was brokered by the government—the Desrossier Commission—and helped ease the financial stresses on the colleges. A skilful negotiator, McGovern played a key role in bringing this about.

During nearly three years in office, McGovern led the college through some difficult times. His consistently sound leadership, his level-headed approach to issues, and his calm personality helped to maintain confidence among the faculty and staff that the college was in good hands. Among his legacy was the establishing of the Nash Chair in Religion, which began in September 2005. It is a six- to twelve-month appointment held by a scholar tied academically to the Jesuit tradition of education.

McGovern stepped down during the summer of 2005 to return to his interrupted retirement. Benjamin Fiore, S.J., was appointed president. A Jesuit of the New York Province, he came to the college from Canisius College, Buffalo, New York, where he had been a professor in religious studies for several years. As well, he was not unfamiliar with the college, since he had taught at Campion during the summer of 1984, and spent time there as the Hannin Visiting Professor from 1990 to 1991.

Fiore scarcely had time to settle in before he was faced with a crisis. The University of Regina was not happy with the new fee-sharing agreement. The federated colleges were prospering while the university faced increasing financial difficulties. Many in the university saw, or imagined, the colleges to be a financial threat. To a large degree, that was not new. Ever since the establishment of the federated system, resistance to the colleges existed within the university. Indeed, opposition to denominational colleges on campus was particularly present from the beginning in the 1960s, however carefully disguised it might have been at times. Equally notable was that more than a few in the university held the mistaken belief that if the colleges did not exist, their allotted governmental annual grants would have been given to the university. Yet it did not work that way. The government granted funds to the federated colleges independently of the two universities in the province. What monies went to the colleges would not necessarily have gone to the universities.

Other factors were at play as well. Since the 1990s, support for the colleges among the university's administrators had been gradually declining. That arose from an increasing and deep-rooted lack of understanding, even of sympathy for the college system itself. As the long-serving university administrators and professors, who had been generally supportive of the federated system on campus, gradually gave way to new faculty members and to new and ever-changing university administrators, the problems for the colleges deepened. Many at the university held strongly negative views about the purpose and need of federated colleges, and did not hesitate to express their opinions at every opportunity. Others were ambiguous in their support at the best of times.

The situation reached a crisis stage at the end of 2005. A public dispute developed between the university and the two colleges over the proportioning of tuition fees among the three institutions. Despite the objections of the colleges, and against the long-standing procedures and the spirit of the federated agreement, the university's administrators took unilateral action by ordering the colleges to cut back the number of classes and class sizes. That would so diminish the ability of the colleges to fulfil their educational mandate that their existence on campus could be in jeopardy. In some quarters, there was even talk of doing away altogether with the original federated agreement, which had been so carefully thought through by Macdougall and his university colleagues, and had been carried into being by Nash, Lahey, and their contemporaries.

Undaunted, Fiore showed excellent leadership in dealing with the university's administrators and rallying public reaction at the university's unfair move against the colleges. Ever calm and clear-headed, yet at times sharp-tongued and relentless in his refusal to concede defeat under attack, he maintained the colleges' position firmly. Eventually, in 2007, the university backed down, thanks to the vision and common sense of the university's new acting president and its board of governors, and to the colleges' coherent presentation of their needs and purposes.

It took three years of negotiations, from 2006 to 2009, on academic and financial fronts to put a settlement in place. While Fiore met with his counterparts on campus, the deans of Campion College and Luther University College met with succeeding university academic vice presidents to create a document based on the original federated agreement; they also clarified the relationships between the colleges and the University of Regina that had evolved over the previous many decades. The college's principal financial officer, Fred Marcia, along with the financial officer of Luther University College, drafted a new fee-sharing agreement with the university. In the end, harmony and general good relations were restored, and Campion College was able to continue with what it did best: teach, counsel, and offer its students an attractive alternate place for learning on a large secular campus.

As president, Fiore contributed greatly to the academic well-being of the college. He was also greatly assisted in his presidential duties by McCarthy in the dean's office. Not only was she a very competent dean, firm and at times outspokenly frank, she was also cheerful, good-humoured, and fair. For decades, she had been thoroughly grounded in the federated system, in campus life, and in the principles of Jesuit education and spirituality, and had come to know a vast number of people on campus, many of whom supported the college. In general, too, as dean in the day-to-day running of the academic life of the college, she helped Fiore preserve equilibrium during some worrisome years.

Of his many involvements, Fiore's participation in the choral musical life of Regina has given a different and special public profile to the college. His establishing in 2007 of a Catholic Studies minor programme at the college has also been significant. It emphasizes that, at heart, Campion is a Catholic college serving the Catholic population of southern Saskatchewan as reflected in its original mandate of 1917. That, and the presence of new Jesuit professors and chaplains—in many ways due also to the persistent efforts of McCarthy to attract them to the college—either full-time or for shorter periods, has helped to show that Campion remains a Catholic and Jesuit college.

Ironically enough, though, the last few years have seen a worrying decline in the college's student population, due in part to the decrease in students' interest in the liberal arts, in part to the university's emphasis on the professional faculties, and in part to the computerization of students' application and course registration. To some degree, the computer age has been detrimental to Campion, which has since the 1960s relied on and rightly prided itself on its personal attention and academic counselling for students. That reputation for excellent counselling seems no longer relevant to many students, or at least not of much interest. The ease of registration and the choosing of courses on one's personal computers have led many to discount the importance of human contact and career counselling. Of course, because Campion College continues to offer personal academic counselling, many students avail themselves of it. The hope is that the computer will not take entirely from students the value of the personal academic counselling that is offered at the college by its staff and faculty members.

When McCarthy retired in 2009 both as dean and as a professor of English literature, R. Frank Obrigewitsch, S.J., the assistant dean, succeeded her as dean.[154] Ably assisted in his office by Suzanne Hunter, who has been in the college since 1979, over his years as dean he has overseen the academic life of the college in an atmosphere of

---

154 McCarthy still teaches the occasional course in English literature. Her special interest has been in the poetry of the nineteenth-century English Jesuit Gerard Manley Hopkins. McCarthy's understanding of the Spiritual Exercises of St. Ignatius Loyola, and of Jesuit spirituality in general, has given her the ability to bring a fuller and often neglected spiritual level of understanding to Hopkins' poetry. This has been important especially in her teaching and in discussions with her colleagues.

excellent teaching, publishing, and student academic counselling. His easy-going personality, his good humour and friendly style of governance, his years in administration and in teaching English literature, and his thorough understanding of Jesuit academic life have given the college's professors excellent leadership and encouragement. As of 2013, twenty-three full-time and several part-time college faculty members—among whom are four young Jesuits—offer courses in the faculties of arts, science, and fine arts to over 700 students enrolled in the college and to many more university students: courses include Arabic studies, astronomy, English literature, history, humanities, classical studies, media studies, pastoral studies, Catholic studies, political science, psychology, religious studies, philosophy, and theatre studies.[155]

In July 2013, John D. Meehan, S.J., became president of Campion College. An historian by profession, gregarious and multi-lingual, with a number of publications to his credit, he has brought to the college a wealth of scholarship, talent, and vision. Already familiar with the college—he had been a professor of history there—it is above all his international experience that may well be his greatest service to Campion and to the University of Regina. Not only has he studied in Canada and abroad extensively, but his special academic interests, his publications, and his contacts in Japan and China are important resources for the University of Regina in its special relations with Xiamen University of Technology in China.[156]

Installed as president on 30 November 2013, Meehan began his term in an atmosphere of optimism and enthusiasm. During his installation address he observed that, as Canada's only Jesuit liberal arts college, "Campion has a mission, a mission it shares with Jesuit works around the globe. It is called to form the whole person—intellectually, socially, culturally and spiritually—in a world that often compartmentalizes these aspects of life." At the same time, he continued, "in

---

155 Despite the fact that Campion had included French as part of the curriculum for many years, the college no longer offers courses in French language and literature.

156 Along with several articles in learned journals, Meehan has published two major works: *The Dominion and the Rising Sun: Canada Encounters Japan, 1929–1941* (Vancouver: University of British Columbia Press, 2004); and *Chasing the Dragon in Shanghai: Canada's Early Relations with China, 1858–1952* (Vancouver: University of British Columbia Press, 2011).

a culture that can reduce students to clients or consumers, Campion seeks to care for the whole person, in the Jesuit tradition of *cura personalis*." Indeed, amid "a growing divide between rich and poor," Campion embodies the Jesuit mission of a faith that does justice...." In a world of division and alienation, "Campion is to be an agent of reconciliation with God, with others and with creation" because "Our Campion community is dedicated to the pursuit of truth, excellence and beauty, wherever we find these in the human experience. We seek depth in a world of often superficial sound-bytes and tweets, of constant activity and noise.... At Campion, we invite our students to a greater depth of analysis and understanding, a greater sense of awe and wonder at the world. This is why we seek to embrace the wonderful diversity we see in the students who come to our college." As with Edmund Campion himself, the college's patron, the students of the college "become men and women for others, people who exemplify the spirit of generosity so prized by Ignatius of Loyola; the spirit of service ... [which is] expressed in the motto of our university, 'As one who serves.'"

Thus Campion College approaches its first 100 years of existence with a vigour and determination to fulfil the dream of its founder, Archbishop Mathieu: to be the Catholic College of Regina. He chose the Jesuits to make real that dream. Their educational ideals, inspired by their *Ratio Studiorum*, which MacMahon implanted in the college in 1918 and which so many Jesuits, diocesan priests, lay professors, and students have maintained and built on ever since remain very much in evidence today.

WINNIPEG: ST. PAUL'S COLLEGE, 1926–2013

"Cor Pauli cor Christi"
—Motto of St. Paul's College

Unlike Campion College, which, although founded by the archbishop of Regina, became a Jesuit college within a year, St. Paul's College in Winnipeg, founded by Archbishop Alfred A. Sinnott in 1926, became a Jesuit college seven years later. The archbishop had been eager to meet the demands of English-speaking Catholics in Winnipeg for their own college. That was not an easy undertaking, however, given the shortage of priests and educated laymen who were qualified to teach. To resolve this issue, he decided to call upon Religious men to help him found a college. That, too, was not easy to achieve.[157]

In 1921, the archbishop requested the Reverend Thomas W. Morton to visit England to persuade the English Benedictines to establish a college in Winnipeg. They were not interested. By 1926, he had appealed to the Jesuits, to the Basilian Fathers, and finally to the Oblate Fathers for their assistance. The Jesuits and Basilians were reluctant to give a positive response to his request. The Oblates accepted on 10 August 1926 to take responsibility for the college. Thus, under the direction of the first Rector, Alphonse Simons, O.M.I., and with the assistance of diocesan priests and laymen, they opened the newly established St. Paul's College on 15 September 1926 in the former YMCA building on Selkirk Avenue on the north side of the city.[158]

The college's facilities, however, were inadequate. The building was old and greatly in need of repair. Within a short time, the Oblate Fathers found the situation unmanageable: the financial stress was severe, the building was overcrowded, and the location of the college made it awkward to get to. In addition, because of the Great War, anti-German antagonism was prevalent in Canada during the 1920s. Since the Oblates at St. Paul's College were of German descent, the lingering hostility to Germans by the diocesan clergy and the Catholic population was a major hindrance to the future of the college. In fact, the prejudice against Germans was so deep-rooted that Archbishop Sinnott felt obligated to maintain some secular priests at St. Paul's in order to "neutralize", as he termed it, the German presence, and so make the college more "attractive to the [Winnipeg] south-enders."[159]

By March 1931, the Oblates had decided to hand the college back to the archbishop. They had, they pointed out, neither the funds nor the staff to maintain a college. Under pressure from his diocesan

---

157 Friesen and Lebrun, 113–116.

158 For a history of the college, cf. Nicholas Laping, "History of St. Paul's College" (Winnipeg: University of Manitoba, unpublished M.Ed. dissertation, 1971), and Friesen and Lebrun for wide-ranging recollections and brief historical accounts of St. Paul's.

159 Laping, 19–25.

priests, who had been highly critical of the Oblates, the archbishop judged it better not to staff the college with Religious priests. Instead he appointed seven of his diocesan priests to the college, along with two laymen. Nevertheless, he continued to face severe financial shortfall and staffing problems; as well, he created a shortage of priests in the parishes. Moreover, the diocesan priests had not been well trained to be teachers, especially for university-level students; the resulting poor quality of education and complaints from parents were further burdens for the archbishop.

To meet the problem of space, in August 1931 the archbishop purchased what formerly had been the Manitoba College Building. Situated centrally in Winnipeg at the junction of Ellice Avenue and Vaughan Street, it had been built in 1882, but was already showing serious decay. What soon became apparent and of immediate concern was that this building also proved to be insufficient for the more than 200 high school and twelve university students who had registered that September, and for the fifteen faculty members.[160]

To alleviate the crowding, Archbishop Sinnott prevailed upon a prominent Catholic, Mrs. Margaret Shea, the wife of Patrick Shea, a wealthy entrepreneur and brewery owner, to fund the construction of an extension that included a gymnasium and classrooms. When it opened in 1932, it was named the Paul Shea Hall after their son who had died as a young man. For her financing of the extension and for supporting other archdiocesan projects, the Holy See appointed Margaret a Dame of the Order of Saint Gregory the Great.[161]

That extension allowed for an increase in students and faculty members that autumn: some 250 high school and fifty-two university students, and twenty-two professors. That was also the first year that a full Bachelor of Arts programme was offered at the college. An order-in-council of the lieutenant governor of Manitoba was passed on 22 October 1932 that fully qualified St. Paul's as a liberal arts college of the University of Manitoba.[162]

---

160   Ibid., 24–41; 35–36; AJC, Box E-622.

161   AJC, Box E-622.

162   Laping, 30–32; AJC, Box E-622.

Earlier, during the late 1920s, worried about the antagonism towards the Oblate Fathers and about their threats to leave the college, as well as about the ever-present problems of staffing the college and the mounting debt load, the archbishop had appealed several times to the Jesuits to reconsider his offer to assume responsibility for St. Paul's. The Provincial Superior, William H. Hingston, S.J., however, remained firmly uninterested. His attention lay elsewhere: attempting to fulfil his dream of establishing a national Catholic university at Regiopolis College in Kingston. As well, there were other hindering factors for Hingston. He was well aware that among the English-speaking Jesuits there was no support whatsoever for his opening another college west of Ontario, or in their assuming the mounting $140,000.00 debt on an established one. From every point of view, St. Paul's financial situation seemed insolvent and the college unfeasible. The prospect of having to assume and pay off a large debt during the opening years of the worst national economic depression in living memory even gave pause to the ever optimistic Hingston and to his Consultors.[163]

Nonetheless, Archbishop Sinnott persisted. Recognizing that he might never get a positive response from the Jesuit Provincial Superior, and yet increasingly unable to finance and staff the college with his own priests, he went directly to Rome, to the Jesuit Superior General, Wlodimir Ledóchowski, to plead his case. That paid off. Pressure was placed on Hingston by Rome to reconsider his refusal, and after a great deal of hesitation, the Jesuits accepted responsibility for St. Paul's College on 19 August 1933. John S. Holland, S.J., after only three years as Rector in Regina, was appointed on 24 August to be the first Jesuit Rector.[164]

Holland was joined in Winnipeg by Erle G. Bartlett, S.J., who became dean of studies; Christopher J. Keating, S.J., a professor of philosophy; Francis J. McDonald, S.J., the prefect of discipline; and Brother Charles Hill, S.J., building and maintenance manager. Eight secular clergymen and two laymen, who already had been staff members, remained. It was more than a little fortuitous that Holland had

---

163 William H. Hingston, S.J., letter to Wlodimir Ledóchowski, s.j., 26 March 1930; Archbishop Arthur A. Sinnott, letter to William H. Hingston, S.J., 26 August 1933, AJC, Box E-622; Laping, 41. The sum of $140,000.00 would be over $2 million today.

164 DJB, vol. 1, 145–146; AJC, Box E-622.

endured three years filled with penury and want at Campion College. Whatever he was facing at St. Paul's College during the late summer of 1933, the situation could not have been any worse than it had been in Regina. Or it did not seem so to the imperturbable Holland. Yet his challenge of taking responsibility for a penniless college during a severe economic depression was daunting. As well, in truth St. Paul's was principally a high school with an unimpressive college made up of forty first- and second-year students and underqualified professors. There was also not enough financial assistance to keep the mounting debts in check, and yet Holland had to find the money for the salaries of the diocesan priests and laymen on staff. His first year was an ever-increasing nightmare of problems.[165]

To make matters worse, by the summer of 1934, Bartlett was compelled to leave the college due to serious health problems, while Keating was appointed Rector of Regiopolis College, Kingston. Holland was left with one Jesuit professor, McDonald, who also served as prefect of discipline. Holland urgently appealed to the Provincial Superior for help. In particular, he requested that Charles J. Kelly, S.J., be appointed from Campion College to assist with the financial problems of St. Paul's. Affable and especially competent in financial matters, Kelly had served as Minister and prefect of discipline in Regina since 1931. While he was Rector there, Holland had come to rely greatly upon Kelly's ability during very hard times to keep the Jesuit Community and the college from bankruptcy. He hoped that Kelly might accomplish the same in Winnipeg.[166]

It was a shrewd move to bring Kelly to St. Paul's in the late summer of 1934. For the next several years, he managed the college's finances with much success by building up a network of lay friends to support St. Paul's financially. Accordingly, enrolment increased while financial pressures began to ease. Yet Holland still had to increase the number of Jesuits in the college courses to make the Bachelor of Arts

---

165   John S. Holland, S.J., letter to William H. Hingston, S.J., 1 October 1933, AJC, Box E-622; DJB, Vol. 1, 6–7; 162–163; 221–222; 224–225; Laping, 45.MacDonald had been Rector from 1924 to 1929 at Saint Stanislaus Novitiate, Guelph, Ontario. Hill later left the Society of Jesus.

166   Archbishop Alfred A. Sinnott, letter to John S. Holland, S.J., 26 August 1933, AJC, Box E-622; DJB, vol. 1, 7; 145–146; 162; 166–167; 224; Friesen and Lebrun, 5; 22; 124. McDonald would remain for the next nine years at St. Paul's as prefect of discipline.

programme sustainable. To that end, by the summer of 1934, he successively had convinced Hingston to appoint Austin L. Bradley, S.J., to teach English literature, political science, and economics; Eugene F. Chabot, S.J., to teach psychology and to succeed Bartlett as prefect of studies; James J. McGarry, S.J., to teach philosophy; and Arthur G. Cotter, S.J., to teach Latin, Greek, and religion.[167]

A year later, in August, James F. Carlin, S.J., arrived from Campion College, where he had been teaching French, German, religion, and mathematics since 1928, to become prefect of studies. Plagued with poor health, he died that December. With McGarry's departure to take his year of Tertianship in St. Bueno's College, North Wales, again Holland had to beg for assistance from the Provincial Superior, this time from Henry J. Keane, S.J. (1934–1938), who had replaced Hingston. Once again Holland was successful, and over the next four years, several Jesuits were appointed to the college: the distinguished English literary scholar Gerald F. Lahey, S.J., arrived in 1936; C. Eric Smith, S.J., among the most brilliant of linguists, in 1937; Thomas G. Malone, S.J., a professor of French literature, in 1938; and Edwin G. MacCormac, S.J., professor of philosophy, in 1939. The presence of those Jesuits, along with the lay professor George L. Amyot, who taught physics, chemistry, and mathematics, greatly strengthened the college's Bachelor of Arts programme for the next many years, and went a long way in lessening Holland's burdens. By December 1938, he could write quite confidently to the Provincial Superior, Thomas J. Mullally, S.J., that with the full support of the archbishop and the Catholic population, the college was doing well.[168]

From the beginning of the college, and for the next several decades, similar to most Jesuit colleges, along with the academic programme St. Paul's emphasized the necessity of non-curricular activities for students. Debates, dramatic presentations, music, sports, the Sodality of the Blessed Virgin Mary, the St. John Berchman's Society, the Newman Club, student parliaments, the student newspaper, all were part of college life. At the same time, the college's Catholic connections were

---

167 DJB, vol. 1, 26–27; 47–48.

168 John S. Holland, S.J., letter to Thomas J. Mullally, 1 December 1938, AJC, Box E-622; DJB, vol. 1, 43–45; 160–161; 166–167; 177–178; 195; 207; 324–325.

continuously in the forefront. With rare exceptions, the students were Catholics. Since the founding of St. Mary's College in Montreal in 1848, the Jesuits had accepted the responsibility that their mandate was to educate male Catholics. By the twentieth century, those of other faiths—Protestant, Jewish, and Orthodox—might be admitted for varying reasons to Jesuit colleges. A general rule of thumb prevailed: up to approximately 10 percent of the student body at the university level might not be Catholic. They were excused from attending religious services or taking the obligatory courses of Catholic theology.[169]

Although it carried no university credit, Catholic theology was mandatory for all Catholic students during each year. They were also expected to attend the annual retreat, usually on a weekend in February. Those Catholics who boarded—about one third of the student body—and the non-boarders were obligated to attend morning Mass in the college chapel at 8:15, while all Catholic students were also required to be present at Benediction each Friday afternoon, and to show up monthly in the chapel on the "First Friday" to hear one of the Jesuits deliver a somewhat dry at best—or boring at worst—exhortation on the Sacred Heart of Jesus, a topic that, however devotional for the time, was not especially uppermost in the minds of most male undergraduates on a Friday afternoon. Those obligatory religious exercises generally began to disappear in the mid to late 1950s.[170]

The chapel itself was a rather large, low-ceilinged barren room on the second floor. Until 1951, the chapel had but a single aesthetical relief: a beautiful round stained glass window over the high altar that for reasons long since forgotten was removed, and now hangs in Bryce Hall at the University of Winnipeg. A rather gloomy atmosphere prevailed throughout, especially during the winter mornings when no daylight penetrated the chapel. Augmenting that gloom were the dark wooden panels everywhere around the altars, along with the heavy maroon damask drapes hanging behind the high altar and the two side flanking chapels that the Jesuits used to celebrate their

---

169 Although St. Paul's remained predominantly Catholic following the Second Vatican Council (1962–1965), with the changes the council brought about, those of all faiths, or of none, were eventually admitted to the college.

170 Friesen and Lebrun, 4; 6; 21.

Latin Masses every morning. Masses began at six o'clock at every altar, and continued every half hour until seven-thirty. Boarders and Jesuit Scholastics were assigned to serve those daily Masses, and had to know from memory the Latin responses that were to be recited in a voice sufficiently loud for the priest to hear, but not so loud as to disturb other priests simultaneously celebrating their private Masses.[171]

During the early months of 1935, the Jesuits of St. Paul's were seriously apprehensive about the size of the college's mounting debt to sundry suppliers and tradesmen and, given the severe depression at the time, wondered how they could meet the payments. Of a total college staff of more than twenty, only nine were Jesuits. Accordingly, there had to be a steady income to meet the relatively large weekly payroll. Yet there was no such income, and the debts accumulated. Undaunted by the seemingly impossible task ahead, and following his policy when in Regina, Holland never turned away a student who was unable to pay tuition fees.[172]

Well known for his frugality, Archbishop Sinnott felt no responsibility to come to the Jesuits' financial rescue. Indeed, he was adamant: they had assumed the debt in the contract drawn up at the time they took over the college, and were obligated to pay it down. The difficulty, at least for the Jesuits, was that the contract between them and the archbishop was not at all clear, and in fact had never been approved by the Congregation of Seminaries and Universities in Rome. Frustrated at the archbishop's refusal to resolve the matter, Holland observed that it had to be changed or, "if we are to be made responsible for the debt, we shall have to give the college and debts back to the archbishop." In the end, the Jesuits did not leave St. Paul's, although the relationship between the archbishop and Holland remained awkward for years afterwards.[173]

---

171 Ibid.

172 DJB, vol. 1, 145–146.

173 Ibid., 167; John S. Holland, S.J., letter to William H. Hingston, S.J., n.d. 1935, AJC, Box C-622. Years later, during the 1970s and 1980s until his death in 1987, Holland would recall those years of the 1930s and the awkwardness he felt in Archbishop Sinnott's presence. Never a vindictive man, Holland often chuckled at the various situations he had to endure when the archbishop would appear unannounced ("come calling", in Holland's words) at St. Paul's to relax with Holland or with the Jesuit Community.

It was not that the archbishop was a difficult man. He was not. It was just that he had had many financial worries in his archdiocese due to the accumulation of debts during the previous decade and more. His chief concern had been that he might not be able to pay his Dutch creditors. Most of the debt arose from the transferral to the archdiocese from the Oblate Fathers the huge debt on St. Mary's church of almost $500,000.00, along with the church itself, which would become the cathedral in 1918. The protracted negotiations with the Oblates, and their subsequent lawsuit against him in Rome over their being forced, as they viewed it, to leave St. Mary's parish, had made him increasingly averse to taking on the financial burdens of any Religious group in his archdiocese or, in some instances, even relying on them.[174]

Unquestionably, the archbishop had a strong personality and was used to getting his own way, while Holland was amiable by nature and conciliatory, and greatly disliked any kind of confrontation. The misunderstanding over the contract and the debt dragged on until 1946, at which time a new contract was drawn up which, it was hoped, would allow for more autonomy from the archbishop. The Jesuits still had the debt to pay off, even if by then it was dwindling through Kelly's careful financial administration and the generosity of benefactors. That new contract, however, was never signed.[175]

From 1933 to 1939, the enrolment of high school students increased significantly, while that of the college remained generally in the mid to high thirties and, from 1940 to 1942, in the mid forties. Part of the reason for the consistently low enrolment in the college was that it did not offer a full programme of courses for the third- and fourth-year students. Many of those had to move to the University of Manitoba if they wished to profit from a greater variety of courses.

---

174 During his thirty-five years in Winnipeg, Archbishop Sinnott established in the archdiocese one college (St. Paul's), ninety parish churches, seven hospitals, and three orphanages. The debt of $500,000.00 would be somewhere in the equivalent range of $5 million to $6 million in today's value.

175 The matter of the unsigned contract returned in the 1970s when discussions began about the transferral of St. Paul's College to the archdiocese of Winnipeg, "Memorandum Concerning the 'Beneplacitum' for St. Paul's", ibid., n.d.

Yet even if St. Paul's student population remained predominantly in the high school, by 1938 it was clear that a further extension, this time to the Paul Shea Hall, was needed for classrooms and dormitory space for both the high school and college. A fundraising drive throughout the archdiocese was launched in April 1939 to raise the $43,000.00 estimated to build the extension. The campaign for funds was part of a wider effort to raise $250,000.00 for various needs of the archdiocese. With the assistance of the archbishop and many lay volunteers, the campaign was successful, and the extension at St. Paul's was opened for university classes by September 1939.[176]

When Holland stepped down as Rector in 1941, he handed to his successor, Raymond G. Sutton, S.J., a relatively prosperous college. The days of penury had all but passed, and student enrolment, despite the war years, remained moderately high. Sutton was a good administrator, fair and just. Despite his workload in the college, he was in great demand throughout the archdiocese to conduct retreats and to assist and preach in parishes. It was during his time, in August 1942, that he brought Dr. Adam Giesinger, whom he had known in Saskatchewan, to teach mathematics, physics, chemistry, and calculus. Giesinger would remain on the faculty for the next thirty-five years, an outstanding professor with a sympathetic interest in each student he encountered.[177]

Sutton did not have good health, and during the four years he was Rector, he suffered from several ailments. As a result, during the summer of 1945, the Provincial Superior, John L. Swain, S.J., assigned him to lighter responsibilities at Campion College. He appointed Joseph P. Monaghan, S.J., to succeed Sutton. Kindly, completely dedicated, gracious, but compulsive and at times volatile, Monaghan had been Rector (1929–1933) and Master of Novices (1929–1944) at the Jesuit Novitiate in Guelph, Ontario. He knew, however, almost nothing

---

176 John S. Holland, S.J., letters to Thomas J. Mullally, S.J., 12 November 1938; John S. Holland, S.J., letters to Thomas J. Mullally, S.J., 25 April 1939; 21 June 1939; 6 October 1939; 14 November 1939, ibid. The estimated value in today's dollar would be for $43,000.00, around $700,000.00, and for $250,000.00, over $4 million.

177 DJB, vol. 1, 330–331; Friesen and Lebrun, 8; 124.

about universities, and scarcely had the temperament to cope with the complexities of campus life.[178]

When Monaghan arrived in Winnipeg, the college was expanding in numbers, and continued thus especially after 1945 with the return of the veterans from overseas who sought to take advantage of the federal government's financial support to pursue university degrees. Consequently, the enrolment of university students in the college grew from 104 in 1945 to 133 in 1946 and to 145 by 1947. That necessitated an increase in faculty members. Two laymen were hired in 1946: Armand LaFlèche to lecture in French, and Roy Dowling to teach physics and mathematics. In 1948 another layman, Paul Forstner, began a long and distinguished career at St. Paul's, lecturing in political science.

Significant, too, was the appointment of two Jesuits to the college's faculty: Vincent J. Jensen, S.J., arrived in 1948 to teach history, and the next year, John C. Hanley, S.J., joined the faculty to teach theology and oratory, and to work in the Newman Centre. Over the years, they would make outstanding contributions to St. Paul's and become the Jesuit "heart" of the college, not only because they were exceptional teachers, but also because they were there for so many years, came to know almost every student in the college, and involved themselves in a wide range of activities on campus, in the archdiocese, and in the city. Through their extensive activities inside and away from the college, their endless energy and their widespread knowledge about almost every topic, they seemed to exemplify the long-held belief that a Jesuit was capable of doing just about anything.[179]

In the minds of many over the next decades, Jensen especially became a towering figure, a kind of "Mr. St. Paul's" who could set his mind and hands to almost anything. During his forty years at St. Paul's, he was a professor of history, prefect of discipline (1951–1954), dean of studies (1954–1960), assistant dean of graduate studies (1960–1967), and Rector (1971–1976). What made Jensen particularly remarkable, however, was his talent for teaching, his encyclopaedic knowledge,

---

178   DJB, vol. 1, 240–242; 331.

179   DJB, vol. 1, 130–131; vol. 2, 141–144; Friesen and Lebrun, 26; 34–36; 45–47; 58–60; 124–125; 302–303.

and his tireless availability to assist and encourage students. He could not abide, however, poor grammar and lack of punctuation, inexact historical references and unverified footnotes, or careless research work and the late submission of assignments. On the other hand, he never turned away a student. He could refuse no one in need of assistance. His kindness was never forgotten, and students for years spoke of him as one who would do almost anything for them to help advance their academic standing.[180]

In the late summer of 1948, the college section separated academically from the high school with the appointment of Lahey as dean of studies of the college.[181] During the summer of 1936, he had been assigned to the college to teach English literature. In time, he came to know the college well. He would serve as dean until 31 July 1954, when he was appointed Rector of Loyola College, Montreal. During those eight years as dean, Lahey became a highly regarded member of the University of Manitoba's senate for eight years and of the university's examining board for fourteen years. As well, he was an excellent professor of English literature, was director of the Newman Club at the university, and regularly produced articles for publication and for radio broadcasts.[182]

During 1945, and in anticipation of what was already foreseen as an influx of university students within fifteen or more years, preliminary plans were drawn up for St. Paul's College to erect new buildings on its site, which was a few blocks from the campus of the University of Manitoba. The university and its affiliated colleges each had separate campuses, with the university divided between a campus in central Winnipeg and one with an agricultural college in the Fort Garry region of the city. In the end, the site at Ellice and Vaughan was inadequate for any expansion of facilities to meet future needs. Nothing came of those plans.

---

180 DJB, vol. 2, 142–143.

181 The two institutions were not incorporated separately until 27 April 1966, although after 1964, the administration and finances of the two were distinct, each with its own Rector and administrators, AJC, Box E-622.

182 Ibid., 177; Friesen and Lebrun, 7; 13; 125.

Four years later, in 1949, the university considered consolidating its departments and facilities at its Fort Garry campus. It opened discussions with the Manitoba government, St. Paul's College and St. John's College (Anglican) concerning a future university campus with affiliated colleges as an intimate part of it. On 7 September 1949, Albert H. S. Gillson produced a paper outlining a vision of an affiliated college university system for Manitoba on a new university campus having all the university departments and faculties together, and the colleges clustered around that. The paper created considerable interest and became the incentive for carrying into effect such a university plan by the mid to late 1950s.[183]

By July 1951, Monaghan was completing the usual six-year term in office. He had provided steady direction for the college, yet was an "old style" Rector, reminiscent of his earlier days as Master of Novices and Rector at the Jesuit Novitiate. He treated everyone with kindness as best he could, certainly, but he lacked a sense of humour and had a rigidity of mind and a formidable temper that could alarm even the most seasoned Jesuit and faculty member. As well, he had an irritating habit of brushing aside what he saw as obstinate opposition with a "tut, tut, tut" and a wave of his hand. Few ever ventured to oppose his ideas. In no way was Monaghan a man of vision or of new ideas for the advancement of university education during the post-war years. It was essential, therefore, that a Jesuit having good personnel skills, imagination, and a determination to carry ideas through should replace him.[184]

Fortunately for St. Paul's, Cecil C. Ryan, S.J., willingly accepted to be Monaghan's successor on 31 July 1951. Articulate, well-read, a lover of all sports, and a gifted speaker with a pleasing personality, Ryan easily adapted to college life. It did not take him long to become a close friend of the archbishop of Winnipeg, Philip Pocock, who was encouraging in his support that St. Paul's College should join any plan to move the University of Manitoba to the Fort Garry region.[185]

---

183 "Thoughts on University Education in the Province of Manitoba, 7 September 1949", AJC, Box E-622.

184 DJB, vol. 1, 242.

185 Ibid., 312; Cecil C. Ryan, S.J., letter to George E. Nunan, S.J., 20 August 1954, AJC, Box E-622.

Among Ryan's first undertakings was to strengthen the Jesuit presence at St. Paul's. In the summer of 1952, T. Gerald Sheridan, S.J., was appointed as professor of economics and sociology, an area that had been poorly served in the college. He brought with him a great love for teaching, a thorough knowledge of his fields, and high academic standards. He was an especially kind, generous man, devoted to his students and to his work. Before long he was greatly in demand by students as a spiritual counsellor and academic advisor. During the twelve years he spent at St. Paul's, all his skills and attention were at the disposal of others. Tragically, in 1964 he died suddenly of a cerebral haemorrhage just shy of his forty-seventh birthday.[186]

Two years after Sheridan had arrived at the college, two other Jesuits were appointed as professors. During the summer of 1954, Charles B. Kane, S.J., was appointed to teach Latin, classics, and English literature, while Patrick M. M. Plunkett, S.J., replaced Lahey as professor of English literature. Both would remain at the college for the next several years, and both would distinguish themselves as professors and Jesuit priests.[187]

Kane was a reserved but excellent, demanding teacher, fair with a sharp (if at times caustic) wit and an eye for the absurd. Students quickly saw through his reserve, however, and for years he was a wise counsellor and spiritual director for hundreds of them. He would remain at St. Paul's until poor health forced him to retire in 1984. Yet, he did not leave the college altogether, but remained in the Jesuit Community that was attached to the college's building. From there he would not only continue his interest in the college, but would assist in parishes and in the matrimonial tribunal of the archdiocese of Winnipeg.[188]

Plunkett, in contrast, was an aesthete, a somewhat eccentric man of discriminating tastes who often appeared around the college and in the classroom wearing a long black cape no matter the temperature. He spoke and wrote English beautifully. Indeed, his love of the English

---

186 DJB, vol. 1, 317–318.

187 Ibid., 281–283; vol. 2, 152–153; Friesen and Lebrun, 25; 36–37.

188 DJB, vol. 2, 153.

language and of its literature became legendary; poorly spoken or written English pained him acutely. He seemed never able to grasp why so many students did not care for English as he did. At the same time, he felt deeply about the French language and literature as well as Italian, both of which he spoke elegantly, and about Latin and Greek, which he also spoke. Poetry, however, was his greatest love, and he would recite passages from memory from all the great poets from the sixteenth century into the twentieth. Even to those students who cared little for his erudite ways or poetry, Plunkett could never be ignored. He inspired generations of them. They would listen spellbound as he sat slightly hunched forward in his chair with his cape wrapped about him, reciting poems or teaching the intricacies of English literature in his well-modulated accent. To listen to him, as one of his former Jesuit students observed, "was a liberal education"; to read his poetry, some of which he published, "proved a delight full of insights and witty surprises". He was at heart a distinguished sensitive Jesuit who drew from a profound sense of the spiritual within himself and others, and from "le Beau Dieu", as he expressed the origin of his spiritual experiences time and time again.[189]

Over the long period that Plunkett remained at St. Paul's, some twenty-one years altogether, he seemed almost oblivious to the influence he had on his colleagues, students, and fellow Jesuits. That was part of his charm, no doubt: his complete lack of egocentricity. When, in 1967, the college's student council awarded him a gold cup for his "outstanding contribution to student life", he found it hard to accept, not from any lack of appreciation for their thoughtfulness, but rather from his genuine humility that others were far more deserving. Yet his influence was far reaching, from his lectures in classrooms, his carefully crafted homilies in the chapel, his hours spent in the confessional, and his care of the poor, to his support of the fine arts in the college and on campus. "He knew who he was, and so never lost his gift of communicating to others 'the beautiful and the good.'"[190]

St. Paul's College was, as with other Jesuit colleges of the day, an all-male institution; the teaching staff was all men as well. By the 1950s,

---

189   Ibid., vol. 1, 282; Friesen and Lebrun, 39–41; 46–47; 102–106.

190   DJB, vol. 1, 282–283.

the young women of St. Mary's Academy, which was affiliated with the University of Manitoba as a department of St. Paul's, on occasion were allowed to attend a course at St. Paul's that was not offered at St. Mary's. In 1954, efforts were made to allow an interchange of faculty members between the two institutions. The Sisters of the Holy Names of Jesus and Mary ("The Holy Names"), who conducted the academy, were in agreement with such a joint endeavour. That was not to be, according to Jean-Baptiste Janssens, the Superior General of the Jesuits. He would not allow the Sisters to teach at St. Paul's. That concession would have to wait until after the college moved to the university's Fort Garry campus when, in 1964, a Holy Names Sister, Judith A. Kenway, S.N.J.M., was the first woman appointed full-time to the faculty. The college became fully co-educational, however, in 1958, the first Jesuit institution of higher education in Canada to become thus.[191]

In 1954, the then president of the University of Manitoba, Dr. Hugh H. Saunderson, formally invited St. Paul's College to relocate to the Fort Garry campus. Ryan and the Jesuits responded favourably, and with the support of the archbishop and a newly founded college advisory board announced on 20 October 1955 that the Jesuits were moving the college to the southern end of Winnipeg.[192] A fundraising campaign, undertaken to raise $350,000.00 for a new college building, was successful. The Canada Council granted the college $100,000.00 towards the building's costs, architect Peter Thornton of Vancouver was engaged, and the first sod was turned on 7 May 1957.[193]

Five months later, on 5 October, Ryan officially signed documents to mark the leasing of land for ninety-nine years from the University for $1.00. The following summer, a beautiful building wrapped in Manitoba Tyndale stone was ready to receive faculty and approximately 300 students. Six lecture halls, physics and chemistry laboratories, a university Catholic centre, a student cafeteria, a student club

---

191 Cecil C. Ryan, S.J., letter to George E. Nunan, S.J., 13 July 1954; Cecil C. Ryan, S.J., letter to Gordon F. George, S.J., 12 March 1958; Gordon F. George, S.J., letter to Cecil C. Ryan, S.J., 22 March 1958, AJC, Box E-622; Friesen and Lebrun, 126; DJB, vol. 2, xvi; Laping, 50.

192 Cecil C. Ryan, S.J., letter to Friends and Contributors, 20 October 1955, AJC, Box E-622; DJC, vol. 1, 312; Friesen and Lebrun, 126.

193 Cecil C. Ryan, S.J., letters to George E. Nunan, S.J., 20 August 1954; 22 August 1954; 20 September 1954; 13 October 1954; 25 February 1955; 2 April 1956; 20 September 1956; 13 October 1956; 12 March 1957; 27 April 1957, AJC, Box E-622.

room, offices for ten staff members, an administration wing—which also had private rooms for Jesuits—and a magnificent and detached college chapel made up the new complex. The interior of the college was designed in brick, wood panelled walls, lino tiles, brick and wood slats, all of which gave it a warm, welcoming atmosphere.[194]

The new college buildings were officially opened on 1 October 1956 in a special convocation of the University of Manitoba. The next day, Archbishop Pocock blessed and dedicated the college to Christ the King. The buildings were ready for the first students, a pleasant change from the dingy, crowded buildings at Ellice and Vaughan. The fact that students could complete all their courses on one campus was met with widespread approval.[195]

Despite so much expressed satisfaction with the new buildings, and however beautiful in every way they were, there was some minor disappointment with them. Soon it was apparent that the architect had not fully understood life on the prairies, or at least when it came to designing windows. Many of those, especially in the offices, were small and monastic-like, allowing little light from the blue sky and the available winter sunshine to penetrate inside. Indeed, Thornton had the notion that the college was similar to a Benedictine monastery; he had had that model in mind when he originally conceived his plans. The end result was that the offices were almost devoid of natural light. That error was not repeated in the college's later additions.[196]

In the overall plans of the college, the chapel remains the jewel, a masterpiece of simplicity, elegance, and "sacredness" of space which, before the Second Vatican Council, stretched the imagination and evoked extensive discussion both for its creativeness and its daring structure. Everything about it forms a perfect harmony of width and length, of colour and design, of light and shadow. The interior, with its purity of architectural form and magnificently plain, unadorned walls of the nave that soar upwards towards the skylights, is a true

---

194 Friesen and Lebrun, 126; 130–134.

195 AJC, Box E-622; Laping, 47.

196 Thornton similarly proposed for Campion College, which he was designing during the mid 1960s, a monastic-style building with small windows. It was only after much persuasion that he was convinced that a Jesuit college is not a monastery.

gem. The absence of pillars accentuates the sense of purity and draws the eyes along the walls towards the front, and to the centrepiece of the whole: the high altar. The copper-covered main doors, designed by the Winnipeg goldsmith Ludwig Nickel; the beautiful stained glass designed by John Meechan of Toronto, depicting the fourteen Stations of the Cross on the north wall; the glass curtains at the front and back; the polished brick floor; the blond pews; the embroidered picture of "La Madonna della Strada" patterned after the original in the Jesuit church, il Gesú, in Rome, holding the Christ figure who, in his turn, is holding St. Paul's College, together create one of the most extraordinarily beautiful collegiate chapels anywhere.[197]

Yet if the interior astounds people on first sight with its ethereal beauty, the chapel's exterior, with its greenish-blue tile and accented tesserae surface, and the gorgeous mosaic of Christ the King in Glory covering almost the entire wall above the western entrance can still bring near gasps of wonderment and pleasure at its splendour and sense of timelessness. The mosaic's placement so fully dominates the site that on first view from University Crescent and Dysart Drive, it is never to be forgotten. Designed in a Byzantine "primitive" style by the Toronto artist Lionel Thomas, the figure of the risen Christ, crowned in gold and robed in the most brilliant of colours, "is mild and peaceful, yet all embracing, as befits an educational institution."[198]

A short distance in front of the west door stands the bell tower, which soars on graceful columns to a point some 30 metres in height. Because of its extreme height on the campus, two beacons had to be installed at the top of the tower to warn low-flying airplanes. Whatever may be argued for or against the tower's position, which from some angles partially blocks the view of the mosaic, it is elegant and flowing.

After his arrival in the college as chaplain in the summer of 1959, Joseph V. Driscoll, S.J., set out to raise money for bells to be installed

---

197 For excellent and detailed analyses of the chapel and its decorative art, vessels, and other furnishings, cf. Patrick M. M. Plunkett, S.J., "Religious Artwork in St. Paul's College", and Dr. Lawrence A. Desmond, "The Transition Years, 1952–1972," in Friesen and Lebrun, 95–100; 131–142. In more recent years, long red ribbons were hung from the light fixtures in the nave, while various styled banners were hung on the wall behind the high altar depending on the liturgical season. Unfortunately, these added nothing of artistic merit to the chapel, and indeed for many, cheapened if not despoiled altogether the overall appearance of the interior.

198 *The Manitoban*, 21 September 1958, 7; Friesen and Lebrun, 134–135.

in the tower. This gregarious storyteller and interesting conversation-alist was an excellent and determined fundraiser. Seven years later he had collected sufficient money to purchase four bells. Cast in the Netherlands by the firm of Schulmerich Eijbouts Ltd., the bells range from 140 to 690 kilograms and from 62 to 104 centimetres in diameter. George Cardinal Flahiff, C.S.B., archbishop of Winnipeg (1960–1983), blessed the bells on 19 October 1966, and they were installed on the following day. On 1 January, as Canada began to celebrate its centen-nial year, the bells pealed for the first time. To salute the nation on its 100th anniversary, CBC radio carried the sound nationally from coast to coast to coast and overseas. Later that year, a fundraising dinner was held to finish paying for the bells which, on special occasions, continue to peal or toll across campus. Every day, they strike on the quarter hour along with the Angelus at 12:00 p.m. and at 6:00 p.m. Some forty years after they first rang out, on 7 April 2010 the bell tower was dedicated in fitting memory to Driscoll, and blessed anew by the archbishop of Winnipeg, V. James Weisgerber (2000–2013).[199]

By midsummer of 1958, Ryan had completed his six-year term as Rector. He had given sound leadership in the college, had built strong ties within the Catholic community in the city, and, most im-portantly, had successfully moved the college into a new building on the university's campus. His was a remarkable achievement in a few short years. That summer he left a college with a promising future to his successor, Hugh P. Kierans, S.J.[200]

Kierans arrived at St. Paul's after having been dean and professor of English literature for seven years at the Jesuit Juniorate in Guelph, Ontario. He had taken a Master of Arts degree in English literature at the University of Toronto, and for a year had been a post-graduate student in literature at Cambridge University, where he came un-der the influence of Frank R. ("F. R.") Leavis at Downing College. Intelligent and with an enquiring mind that pursued questions with determination, Kierans returned to Canada in 1951 to take up his position as dean and professor to the young Jesuit Juniors. His impact and inspiration on their intellectual development were profound and

199 DJB, vol. 2, 78–83; Friesen and Lebrun, 46; 111–110.

200 DJB, vol. 1, 312.

lasting. He arrived, therefore, at St. Paul's in July 1958 with serious academic credentials.

An immediate outcome of St. Paul's move to Fort Garry was that the autumn registration had increased by 70 percent, to 268 students, over the previous year. That was partially due to the college having become co-educational, and greatly due to the fact that St. Paul's and the campus provided sufficient courses for a four-year degree, which meant that students did not have to go elsewhere to complete their courses, as hitherto. Over the next three years, student numbers nearly doubled, to around 450, and during the 1960s continued to increase annually by about 13 percent or more. Such a steady increase in students necessitated the construction of extensions on the original building; by 1960, Kierans set out to plan for additional classrooms, offices, and science laboratories. Between 1960 and 1964, extensions were added, increasing capacity for up to 700 students with a wing for lectures (1960), a science wing (1962), and a student cafeteria (1964). A residence attached to the college for the Jesuits was also built in 1964.[201]

Although during the 1950s there was still not a great deal of pressure for professors in Canadian universities to have doctorates—it was generally sufficient to have a Master of Arts or a Master of Science— the increase in enrolment and rising academic norms by the 1960s began to require that men and women with doctorates be appointed to university faculties. To that end, Kierans was especially keen on improving the academic standards of the college. In 1960, among the eight Jesuits and seven lay professors in the college, two laymen and one Jesuit had received doctorates, while the remaining twelve had one or two Master of Arts degrees. The number of professors rose during the remainder of the 1960s, as did the number of doctorates. By the end of the 1960s, there were thirty-eight professors and eleven doctorates at St. Paul's. Yet that was still a disproportionately low number of higher degrees at a time when universities were increasingly demanding doctorates of their professors. At the same time, Kierans' effort to provide a highly qualified faculty before long moved beyond

---

201 Hugh P. Kierans, S.J., letter to Gordon F. George, S.J., 21 August 1961, AJC, Box E-622; Friesen and Lebrun, 154–165; Laping, 48.

what the college could afford: by 1964 the accumulated debt of St. Paul's had surpassed $40,000.00, an unmanageable sum for the time.[202]

Nonetheless, throughout the 1960s, a shortage of professors at the college was noticeable; at times, some were called upon to work in more than one department to cover the variety of courses being offered. During the academic year 1964–1965, there were only thirty-one professors to teach in fifteen departments. That was not untypical, and in any academic term Vincent J. Jensen, S.J., might offer courses in history and political science (he was an historian), Philip J. Leah, S.J., courses in mathematics and philosophy (he was a mathematician), Dr. Paul Forstner, courses in political science and German (he was a political scientist), Charles C. Kane, S.J., courses in English literature and classics (he had degrees in both disciplines), and Dr. Robert Bennett, courses in classics and French (he was a classicist). As with most Jesuit colleges of the day, the general custom at St. Paul's was that the professors had to be academic generalists, well-versed in more than one area of the humanities, and as far as possible, willing to step in whenever the dean requested. Almost no emphasis was placed on research and publication, at least not until into the mid to late 1970s. In fact, professors had been hired as teachers, not researchers or writers. The annual assessment of professors therefore rested on their teaching ability and upon their availability to take on courses outside their specified discipline.[203]

There were other factors at play, of course, that prevented the college from hiring more professors. Not least of those were finances. For years, while it had remained relatively small, St. Paul's College had relied upon a pool of Canadian Jesuits—all academic generalists—who would be appointed by the Provincial Superior to teach in the college. Up until the mid 1960s, the St. Paul's Jesuit Community might receive

---

202   Hugh P. Kierans, S.J., letters to Gordon George, S.J., 7 May 1963; 9 July 1963; 24 July 1963; Desmond P. Burke-Gaffney, S.J., letter to Angus J. Macdougall, S.J., 17 November 1964, ACJ, Box C-622; Friesen and Lebrun, 156–157; 188–189. The sum of $40,000.00 calculated in today's value would be worth slightly less than $300,000.00.

203   Friesen and Lebrun, 188–189; Laping, 52. It should be noted that in large Canadian universities, such as the University of Manitoba, by the mid to later 1960s, many academic generalists were taking retirement. In their stead, the universities were hiring professors with doctorates who would work in a single department, and who also were expected to publish.

some small financial recompense for the services of those Jesuits. Yet, for the most part, the arrangement was that of "contributed services": the Jesuit Community carried the weight of the college's expenses by either freely offering the teaching services of the Jesuits or by giving back to the college a large proportion of their salaries.

That arrangement, in effect everywhere in Canadian Jesuit colleges for decades, began to change after the 1950s. A Jesuit Community, such as that at St. Paul's, usually was composed of several members who did not teach in the college. Accordingly, Jesuit Communities began to insist on salaries—however meagre—and in turn to determine themselves what amount of the "contributed services" would be donated per year to the college. At a time when there was little money in the college to pay salaries, the "contributed services" arrangement functioned as well as any other system might have done. Yet by the 1960s, the colleges were already receiving government grants and could increasingly offer salaries to Jesuits, even at a reduced amount from those of their lay colleagues. The result was, however, that even with the system of "contributed services" in play, such reduced salaries to Jesuits began to add to the yearly expenses of a college, which sometimes prevented it from hiring new lay professors to whom just salaries and benefits had to be paid.[204]

To that were added other expenses. By the early 1960s, there were fewer Jesuits either available or willing to work in higher education. That created the need for a college to hire more and more lay professors to meet the growing enrolment and course offerings. To these, attractively fair salaries, pension plans, and other benefits had to be offered. As with the majority, if not all, of the small Canadian colleges of the day, at St. Paul's the pension and benefits plans in force since the 1950s were insufficient and non-competitive.[205]

To remedy that situation, shortly after assuming office, Kierans arranged for a study of pensions and other financial arrangements in

---

204 Until 1964, when a new Jesuit residence opened at St. Paul's College, those Jesuits who worked in the college—with the exception of a couple of Jesuits who had already been living at the college—lived in the Jesuit Community at Ellice and Vaughan in central Winnipeg with several Jesuits who were involved in other ministries.

205 Friesen and Lebrun, 157.

view of establishing a more equitable and attractive system at the college. Dr. Adam Giesinger was appointed to come up with a reasonable proposal based on what he could learn from other academic institutions and that would be acceptable to all. His proposal was agreed to during 1961, and all full-time lay professors were enrolled in the new pension and benefits scheme. That arrangement lasted until 1970, when the college's faculty was required by a new agreement with the university to enter the university's plan, which was underwritten by Great West Life. Exceptions could be granted to individuals who preferred to remain in the college's plan, but they were still to be insured under the same conditions as were those in the university's plan with Great West Life.[206]

During the 1960s, the Jesuits at St. Paul's remained outside the arrangement for pensions, principally because they were the "owners" of the college, and therefore were the "management". They were not receiving full salaries; the understanding was that what monies they did not receive would remain in the college as "contributed services". Only later, during the 1970s and into the 1980s, did they receive salaries commensurate with their status, although for years the Jesuit Community at St. Paul's continued to fund, through its annual budgetary surplus, many projects and financial shortfalls in the college. The Jesuits remained outside any benefits plans, the faculty association or faculty union, again because of their position as "owners" of the college.

There is no doubt that the 1960s were not an easy time to be an administrator in a university or university college. Increasingly, as his years in office passed, it became clear that Kierans was not a particularly good administrator or at least that he was an administrator of an older model, a top-down authoritarian, at times a paternalistic figure unwilling to share governance. What he and others in the college did not seem to recognize was that that approach to governing was already being questioned in many places, and that the years during which he was Rector were displaying the significant changes and complaints and disturbances that would sweep Canadian campuses by the latter

---

206 Ibid.

half of the 1960s. A good part of that centred upon governance within an institution, upon how administrators carried out their responsibilities, and upon the demands by faculty members and students to share in governing and decision making, especially in matters that affected them directly. At most times, and this was true at St. Paul's as well, what the professors and students wanted in the 1960s was a voice in defining the educational goals of the institution and in the use of the institution's resources to fulfil those goals. At other times, professorial demands centred on issues specific to themselves—salaries, pensions, travel/study grants, sabbaticals, course loads, and the like—to the relevance of courses offered, to the introduction of more pertinent courses, to students, and to library resources.

Although some at St. Paul's College might have thought that Kierans' controlling way of governing was endemic to Jesuit administrators alone, that was not necessarily so. Most Canadian colleges and universities into the 1960s were administered in much the same manner. A single figure on campus, or at most a small group of people usually appointed by the Rector or president, tightly and at times secretly governed without any cognizance of the opinions proffered by professors and students.

From another perspective, however, as with other Jesuit college Rectors in Canada, Kierans had little choice in the matter of governance. Traditionally, the Jesuit board of directors took almost no active role in governing; it left that to the Rector and to the dean. The Jesuit corporate board would meet once a year, as required by law, to approve the annual budget and the end-of-year financial statement, and to elect their new corporate Jesuit officers. On other rare occasions, the board would meet to appoint a Rector. Otherwise, it remained in the background, inactive. That was how the Jesuits themselves wanted and expected the college to be governed.

Kierans had set out in 1958 to govern with a Rector's Council consisting of the dean, Gerald F. Lahey, S.J.; Vincent J. Jensen, S.J.; Gerald P. McGinnis, S.J., Comptroller; and Dr. Adam Giesenger, professor. At first, because it was a departure from the traditional manner of governing St. Paul's with a single figure, the Rector, his governing by a council was met with general approval. The problem was that those on the Rector's Council were all hand-picked by Kierans; they met rarely and kept no minutes. By 1962, the councillors themselves were split into factions over the Rector's proposals, actions, and intentions for the college, a split that somewhat mirrored the professorial factions existing in the college. Kierans gradually moved further and further away from being the Rector, often did not show up in the college, and at times seemed bored and uninterested. He gave up even on his council, and sought advice for the most part from a single fellow Jesuit who was planning to leave St. Paul's as soon as he could find an academic position elsewhere.

To add to Kierans' difficulties was the newly formed Faculty Association, which had been established during 1960 and 1961. Although at times the association could be contentious within itself, it did provide a single voice for the faculty, notably one that demanded that the Rector meet with the faculty regularly to share in his plans and ideas and decisions. Kierans never felt comfortable with that, and usually such meetings ended in greater frustrations for faculty members because of his lack of openness and interest, and because of his refusal to answer questions or even to show up for a meeting.

As dean, Lahey tended to be sympathetic to the faculty's position, something that displeased Kierans' considerably. Added to that was the general recognition in the college that Lahey was also none too enthusiastic about Kierans' top-down domination and governance, a style of governing that had necessitated Lahey's own removal from Loyola College, Montreal, in 1959. Lahey found Kierans not only secretive and, by 1962, more and more difficult to consult, but also was frequently irked at Kierans' meddling in the dean's office or making unilateral decisions about academic matters. In 1963, Lahey stepped down as dean and left the college to accept the position of dean at Campion College. His departure was brought about, it has been argued, either because the Rector saw to that with the Provincial Superior—he was one of the Provincial's Consultors—or because of ill health—Lahey had had a severe heart seizure in 1961—due to the stresses of his office.[207]

---

207 DJB, vol. 1, 178.

Kierans, on the other hand, continued to be progressively more distant by 1963, and would regularly not keep appointments. His distrust of those around him, with rare exception, seemed to grow deeper as the years passed. By the time he left office in May 1964, he had alienated almost everyone in the college. In so many ways, his was an unfortunate situation, partially brought about by his unwillingness to share his governing authority, and partially arising from his own frustration in having had to give up that which he did best: teaching, guiding students, and other kinds of intellectual activities. Indeed, at heart he was an intellectual, a Jesuit teacher who loved the challenge of academic life, of directing a seminar, of tutoring students. Once he became Rector, he gave all that up. Only later, and when it was too late at St. Paul's College, did he come to recognize the effects that this had had on his personal and intellectual life. It would take several years after he left St. Paul's before he returned to university life as a professor.

To replace Lahey during the summer of 1963, Kierans was able to convince Lawrence C. Braceland, S.J., to accept the dean's position. For nineteen years he had been a professor of classics at the Jesuit Juniorate in Guelph, and in 1958 had succeeded Kierans as dean there. He came to St. Paul's College with an impressive record of teaching and administering. A kindly, patient man, and a true humanist, Braceland loved the classroom, loved the sparring in debate and intellectual conversation, and was never more enthusiastic than in his support of students being proficient in the spoken and written word. His seven years at St. Paul's as dean, and his fifteen years as a professor of classics there, may have been difficult, even tumultuous at times, but Braceland seemed to remain personally unaffected. His calm nature, optimistic outlook, and faith in the goodness of others carried him through. When he retired from St. Paul's in 1978, he may have had to leave the classroom, but he never left academic life. Being thoroughly proficient in Latin and Greek, French and English, he took up the translation of mediaeval manuscripts for the centre of Cistercian studies at Kalamazoo, Michigan. He accepted to edit and translate into English four volumes of the writings of Gilbert of Hoyland, a mediaeval Cistercian monk, and when he had completed that monumental work, he accepted to edit and translate into English the scriptural commentaries of another Cistercian monk, Serlo of Winton.[208]

Desmond P. Burke-Gaffney, S.J., replaced Kierans as Rector in 23 May 1964. Urbane, courteous, intelligent, and charming, he had studied English literature at Fordham University in New York City, from where he received a doctorate in 1959. For the next four years he taught English literature to Jesuit Juniors at Guelph. A perfectionist as well as a thorough academic, at times he was shocked at how young Jesuits could be so uninterested in his teaching and in their academic work. There was never any question of his being unapproachable, but he had an explosive temper that he was not hesitant in showing to any young, uncooperative Jesuit student. After four years, he was more than eager to move on, which he did: to his alma mater, the University of Manitoba, and to its English literature department. He accepted the post of assistant professor there in 1963. A year later, he was appointed Rector of St. Paul's College.[209]

Burke-Gaffney's appointment was met with relief and enthusiasm at St. Paul's. Not only did he come with the highest of academic qualifications, but much attention was focused on the fact that he was a Winnipegger by birth. He would therefore understand the ways of western Canada, unlike his Montreal and Westmount predecessor. A new and golden age was about to unfold. Or so many hoped and assumed.[210]

Yet that did not happen. Almost at once it became apparent that many of the difficulties that seemed to have arisen from the governance of Kierans were in fact endemic to St. Paul's itself: to its administrative structures, its faculty's conservative mentality, its uncertain financial arrangements, and its position as a college in the University of Manitoba. The next five years would sketch out all that in bold letters, with Burke-Gaffney progressively more ensconced in the middle of everything. They were, as it turned out, difficult years of transition for the college in its relationship with the university.

---

208 DJB, vol. 1, 24–26.

209 Ibid., 36–38.

210 Ibid., 37; Friesen and Lebrun, 147.

Notwithstanding Burke-Gaffney's initial positive impressions he gave within the college, and his sympathetic efforts to listen to as many voices as possible, he was of the same old school of Jesuit administrators as Kierans; he likewise remained attached to his own counsel and scarcely saw the need to seek it from elsewhere, whether from his Jesuit colleagues or from others. Certainly he was not inclined to turn to faculty members for advice. At first, though, he seemed amenable to suggestions and proposals for change that might lead to sorting out differences and even resolving disputes. He restored meetings with the Faculty Association, which Kierans had shut down, he convoked a general faculty meeting for early December 1964, and he continued to hold such meetings during the following years.

As well, on behalf of the Jesuits' corporation of the college, Burke-Gaffney oversaw the establishing in 1966 of a board of management composed of lay people and Jesuits. It was to advise the corporation and the college, especially on the matters of appointments of faculty and staff, and the hiring and removal of administrators, including the Rector. In the end, however, all of that did not turn out to be sufficient.[211]

It was during Burke-Gaffney's term as Rector, from 1964 to 1969, that significant changes began to be realized on campus that radically restructured St. Paul's College and its relationship to the university and that in time forced him to resign from his post. During his early days as Rector, he had noted a distinct shift in the university's attitude towards the colleges, and saw that the university would be "happier" were the colleges to give up their autonomy. By 1970, that was what had taken place: St. Paul's had lost almost all of its former independence in appointments and course offerings, and had changed from an autonomous affiliated college to one that was dependent on the university and its departments. St. Paul's became similar to a department in the university. Based on the various recommendations of the Funt Report of May 1967, which had been established to seek a resolution to the administrative and academic structures and problems on campus, the "new arrangement" that Burke-Gaffney signed

---

211 Ibid.

in early April 1968, and the final agreement that his successor, John E. Page, S.J. (1969–1971), signed on 11 June 1970, provided full funding from the University of Manitoba for the college. Conversely, though, it meant that the academic programmes at St. Paul's College became fully integrated with those of the university. Registration of students, class scheduling, the hiring of staff and faculty members, and maintenance all came under the university's responsibility. Although theoretically the colleges could still make recommendations to the university concerning faculty appointments, they effectively lost their right to recommend faculty members for promotion and tenure.[212]

Not surprisingly, the Funt Report and the final agreement with the university were by no means unanimously received at St. Paul's. The Jesuits there, for whom the 1960s seemed to have turned out to be the most difficult of years, were especially opposed to the agreement. They blamed Burke-Gaffney and Page. Indeed, some of them were harsh on the two former Rectors because of what they had signed, even suggesting for years afterwards that they had "sold out" the college to the departments and administrators of the university.

To those Jesuits, it was all part of a wider world gone wrong. From the sweeping changes in the Catholic Church following the Second Vatican Council (1962–1965), in liturgy (changes from the Latin to the vernacular; new forms of the Mass; and so forth), and in administrative practices, governance, and radical changes in Jesuit Community living (new ways of consultation by Superiors; the holding of Community meetings; no longer the wearing of the cassock or the biretta; and on and on) to the development of the University of Manitoba's policies and standards along with the protracted negotiations for a new agreement between St. Paul's College and the university; from the evolving priorities of the Upper Canada Province away from its traditional ministries to new and sometimes untried ones; and to the lack of interest shown by many younger Jesuits not only towards St. Paul's College but to academic ministry altogether, all of that deeply worried, then hurt, the Jesuits at St. Paul's. They felt betrayed, left out;

---

212 Desmond P. Burke-Gaffney, S.J., letters to Angus J. Macdougall, S.J., 3 July 1966; 1 April 1968; John E. Page, S.J., letter to Edward F. Sheridan, S.J., 24 January 1971, ibid.; Friesen and Lebrun, 199ff.

their world was disappearing. They became bewildered, embittered, defensive, then apathetic, not just at what they had gone through during the time of Burke-Gaffney and Page, but at the profound and scarcely understandable transformations they were witnessing within the Jesuits themselves. They often complained that "this is not the Jesuit Order I entered."

Because of the complexities of the negotiations and discussions leading up to the new agreement, and because of Burke-Gaffney's seemingly unwillingness to inform the faculty regularly of what was unfolding, most professors in the college also felt quite left out of the proceedings during the years prior to the final agreement, and time and again were frustrated, even fearful, at what they suspected would be decisions taken that would greatly affect their academic lives. Of course, to a large extent they were right to be concerned; their livelihoods depended on what would or would not be agreed to with the university. Even Braceland, not given to alarmist talk, complained at times about how little he knew as dean of what was developing.[213]

That St. Paul's ever had had any other choice but to go along with the university's determination to change the original arrangement it had with the colleges since the late 1950s is a moot point today. It was not considered a moot point, however, during the last years of the 1960s and during the next decade. In fact, it was an extremely contentious point. Many at St. Paul's, including almost all the Jesuits and certain lay faculty members, too, refused to acknowledge that Burke-Gaffney and Page may never have had much room to manoeuvre during the negotiations with the university.

Burke-Gaffney, especially, became profoundly unhappy as a result of those charges by his fellow Jesuits. He found it hard to carry on. A year before his six-year term as Rector was completed, he resigned. In a private conversation with some Jesuit colleagues at the end of June 1969, while they were visiting Winnipeg a few weeks before he left office, Burke-Gaffney observed sadly, "I pray nothing like this ever happens to you."[214]

---

213 Friesen and Lebrun, 147; 176.

214 Desmond P. Burke-Gaffney, S.J., letter to Angus J. Macdougall, S.J., 2 October 1967, AJC, Box E-622; Laping, 54–58.

Like Kierans before him, it may well have been that Burke-Gaffney ought to have remained a professor rather than accept an administrative position. Or at least for some, it was argued thus. Yet that question scarcely bears scrutiny, as his subsequent seven years as dean and professor of English literature at Campion College in Regina attest. Those were among the happiest in his academic life, a time when he proved himself to be a first-rate administrator. His untimely death in Regina on 4 December 1976 from a brain tumour seemed all the more poignant when it so suddenly ended his renewed intellectual career.[215]

As mentioned, John E. Page, S.J., became Rector following Burke-Gaffney's resignation. Page had taken his doctorate in urban studies from the University of Pennsylvania, and had been teaching in that area at the University of Manitoba since 1965. After only two years in the office, however, he resigned for personal reasons. Once again, St. Paul's was looking for a Rector.

Always willing to help, Jensen agreed to take the Rector's position on 30 June 1971; Giesinger had already replaced Braceland as dean the year earlier. In the minds of most at St. Paul's, the two made an excellent team. Both had been in the college for years, knew just about everyone on campus, and were highly respected academics.

Among his first responsibilities as Rector was to complete and finance a new library wing. The library had grown somewhat haphazardly from the days of Arthur J. Cotter, S.J., who in 1937 had started a Catholic lending library at St. Paul's. He was convinced that such a library, which had been a big success in the United States, would be greatly beneficial to Catholics in Winnipeg who, in the midst of the Great Depression, lacked the means to purchase books. With a band of generous volunteers who had completed a catalogue for the collection, by 1942 Cotter had collected over 2,000 titles. By 1949, the library had more than 5,000 books, and by the mid 1950s over 20,000 books were available for lending and for the college's use. The collection principally centred on Catholic theology, philosophy, moral theology, literature, biography, and hagiography. In 1958, with the move to the Fort Garry Campus, Cotter's lending library and those

---

215 DJB, vol. 1, 37–38.

books reserved for the college's use became the nucleus of the St. Paul's College library at Fort Garry.[216]

With the assistance of Margaret ("Peggy") Gardiner, who was hired at the time of the move, Cotter organized the library in its new surroundings. He remained at St. Paul's for only one year; in 1959, he left for St. Mary's University, Halifax, to oversee the financing and building of a new library there. Harold J. Drake, S.J., became St. Paul's librarian.[217]

Although at first Drake had no formal training in library science, he had a love of books and a talent for organization. To improve his work, he spent several summers at the Catholic University of America in Washington, D.C., studying towards a degree in library science, which he received with distinction in 1966. Over the next years he came to know well the library, its holdings, and how it could best contribute to students and faculty members and to the other libraries on campus. Drake worked long hours, silently, carefully, and good-humouredly; he was a quiet, unassuming man, although he permitted no breaching of the rules of silence, and could become distinctly displeased with anyone who did. For over thirty-three years he served as librarian. When he retired in 1992, he was the last Jesuit to hold an administrative post at the college. Deservedly, the library has borne his name since 1982.[218]

By the late 1960s, a severe lack of space for students to study in the library, along with an increasingly limited amount of storage room for books, had become critical. Drake had been requesting for some years—to no avail—that a library wing be constructed to ease the overcrowding. After years of discussion and proposals, the extension was begun in the summer of 1970.[219]

---

216 Ibid., 69–71.

217 Ibid., vol. 2, 75–78. On the new library wing, cf. Friesen and Lebrun, 27–29; 159–171; 177–178.

218 DJB, vol. 2, 76–77. Drake's workday was from 8:00 hrs until 22:00 hrs. During the late 1970s and into the mid 1980s, he was an active member of the Manitoba Library Association, and served as its Treasurer from 1981 to 1983. It seemed that the only time he permitted himself to be away from his library duties was for his annual retreat and for a visit with his family, or for the yearly organized tours to Europe as chaplain or leader.

219 Friesen and Lebrun, 167–177.

Jensen wisely accepted Drake's advice about what was needed in the library's expansion, and thus managed that project well. Jensen saw to it that the library would include modern offices for a faculty now numbering forty-five, a sunken lounge between the stacks and the carrels, classrooms for students who had been increasing yearly in numbers, and a theatre-in-the-rough (it was not completed until 1975). Into this new wing, during the summer of 1972, almost 40,000 items of the library were transferred.[220]

Jensen seemed to have an instinct for handling small details, about the new library wing and about other matters around the college; he knew how to get things done. The more difficult task concerned the Jesuit presence at St. Paul's. In that matter, his instincts were less assured. He faced two serious problems.[221]

On the one side, the Jesuits at St. Paul's College were all within a few years of retirement. Jensen recognized the need to replace them if the Jesuits were to remain there. His hope was that if he were to get younger Jesuits onto the faculty at St. Paul's, he might be able to salvage something from the agreement, and thus maintain an ongoing Jesuit presence. To support him in that endeavour, the newly appointed Provincial Superior, Terence G. Walsh, S.J. (1972–1978), wrote to congratulate him for his desire in getting Jesuits who could establish "some kind of foothold at the University of Manitoba." He mentioned the names of Jesuits who might be available for St. Paul's.[222]

In spite of this support, Jensen knew few Jesuits with doctorates. Nor did he know the younger Jesuits who were in graduate studies or who had graduated recently. Nor was he realistic about how to attract them to St. Paul's. He rarely, if ever, got in touch with those who were proposed to him as a possible appointees, including, over the next years, several Jesuits whose names were given to him both by Walsh and by Gerald W. Tait, S.J., the assistant to the Provincial Superior for studies for the English-speaking Jesuits. Jensen expected, as did many

---

220   Vincent J. Jensen, S.J., letters to Terence G. Walsh, S.J., 12 July 1972; 7 March 1975; 9 September 1975; Terence G. Walsh, S.J., letter to Vincent J. Jensen, S.J., 16 September 1975, AJC, Box E-621A.

221   DJB, vol. 2, 144.

222   Terence G. Walsh, S.J., letter to Vincent J. Jensen, S.J., 24 April 1972, AJC, Box E-621A.

Jesuit college administrators of the day, that the Provincial Superior would not only propose names, but would appoint Jesuits directly to the college, usually with the expectation that something would be found for them to do.[223]

Yet it did not work that way. The new agreement with the university had blocked that kind of approach to appointments. What was more, younger Jesuits were unwilling to accept appointments on that basis of uncertainty, especially were that to mean that their academic specialty might be disregarded, as was feared. They wanted appointments according to their field of study that would include the possibility of a tenure-track position.

After two to three years, nothing had happened. In an effort to seek advice and consultation about the future of St. Paul's and about the Jesuits' presence there, with Tait's support Jensen summoned a meeting on 25 May 1974 in Winnipeg, at the St. Paul's Jesuit Community's expense, of eleven young Jesuits who were either finishing doctoral studies or who had recently completed them. To his surprise, twelve showed up.[224]

Initially, they were interested in any possible departmental openings at St. Paul's and the university. Soon, though, it became apparent that the whole weekend exercise was futile. Jensen could offer nothing concrete, because he had nothing to offer. Everything seemed to rest on his famed ability to "pull strings" in the university, along with the vague notion that were a Jesuit to come to St. Paul's, "something" would be found for him to do. That was scarcely of interest to any of the group. Many of those attending began to speak frankly about St. Paul's lack of understanding and of communicating with younger Jesuits, and especially about life in the St. Paul's Jesuit Community itself. The Jesuits' style of living there, in the eyes of almost all those attending, was not only old-fashioned and stultifying, but uninviting, and dominated by one or two members of the

223 Vincent J. Jensen, S.J., letter to Terence G. Walsh, S.J., 5 December 1972; Vincent J. Jensen, S.J., letter to Gerald W. Tait, S.J., 22 October 1973; Gerald W. Tait, S.J., letter to Vincent J. Jensen, S.J., 30 November 1973; Jacques Monet, s.j., letter to Vincent J. Jensen, S.J., 25 February 1974; Gerald W. Tait, S.J., letters to Vincent J. Jensen, S.J., 18 March 1974; 9 April 1974; 4 November 1974; 17 December 1974; 7 May 1975, ibid.

224 Gerald W. Tait, S.J., letter to Vincent J. Jensen, S.J., 9 April 1974, ibid.

Community determined not to let a breath of the Second Vatican Council or any changes in Jesuit communal living into the place. That certainly was not what young Jesuits wanted or would accept.

A further problem for Jensen also became apparent to the Jesuits at the meeting: the hiring of faculty members no longer solely depended on St. Paul's, a fact that had not been made clear to them before they came to the meeting. After 1970, hiring had become principally the prerogative of the university's departments, although they might take into consideration the college's proposed candidates to fill the posts allotted to it. Even if some Jesuits were available, therefore, there was no guarantee whatsoever that there would be a departmental opening in their academic specialties, or that the university would even choose St. Paul's proposed candidate for the posts.

Nothing ever came of that Jesuit meeting of 1974. There was almost no follow-up with the younger Jesuits. Not surprisingly, following 1970 and during the next decade or so, no Jesuit was ever appointed to a full-time teaching position in the college or university.

It should be noted, too, that it was stated at the time, and noted subsequently over and over again, that one of the reasons why young Jesuits were never appointed to St. Paul's during those years was that there was a "decline" in their numbers. That assessment was not entirely correct. It was true, of course, that there had been a decrease in the overall number of Jesuits in the Upper Canada Province and in the number of candidates pronouncing first vows during the 1970s and 1980s. At the same time, the number of those studying in graduate schools and graduating with a Ph.D. remained high in proportion to the number in the Province itself, perhaps higher than ever in the Province's history. The reasons for the dearth of younger Jesuits at St. Paul's lay elsewhere, and for the most part were squarely at the door of the Jesuits at St. Paul's College.[225]

---

225 To take only one example among many: the present author, who graduated with a Ph.D. from McGill University in 1972, was never once approached by anyone at St. Paul's College about a posting there, and that despite the fact that several other places—Regis College, Toronto; Loyola College, Montreal; Università Gregoriana, Rome; and Campion College, Regina—all offered positions of teaching and administration. Each of these was accepted either as full-time or part-time appointments between 1971 and 1978.

A request was made in April 1975 to the Provincial Superior from the college assembly that "a Chair of Theology [be] established and endowed in this College by the Upper Canada Province of the Society of Jesus …", and that the Province "annually inform the Dean of the College of the names of all available Jesuit academics who might be considered for teaching positions in the college." Certainly, that action by the faculty assembly was resourceful and went well beyond any that the Jesuits at the college had taken. Yet it was unrealistic. It reflected the long-standing attitude besetting the Jesuits there: to wait for the Provincial Superior to inform the college when Jesuits were available, rather than the college administrators themselves searching out with both the Provincial Superior and the Jesuits who might be available and in what academic discipline. Besides, it was not the custom for the Province to endow chairs or other like positions in the colleges, even if it had the money to do so. It did not endow the chair.[226]

After four years as Rector, Jensen had grown ever more discouraged, anxious, and unable to act. Despite Tait's many pleas for him to contact the Jesuits who might be available for St. Paul's, nothing was done. In Jensen's mind, increasingly, all the problems he faced in getting Jesuits to the college went back to the 1970 agreement, to which he could not reconcile himself. In short order, it seemed to have undone all his dreams and achievements of his previous twenty-three years at the college. He had opposed the agreement, and vigorously so. Perhaps that was the reason he seemed incapable of appreciating the advantages and the opportunities that it brought to the college.[227]

Nor could Jensen dispel the "siege mentality" in the Jesuit Community (he was also the Superior of the Jesuits at St. Paul's). By 1975, he grew introverted, dispirited, and more and more dependent on alcohol. His health began to fail; he appeared old long before his time. Students and faculty members alike worried about what was happening to him. Gradually, his attention was turning towards other things, notably towards the college's gardens and grounds, which he

---

226 Dr. Lawrence A. Desmond, letter to Terence G. Walsh, S.J., 21 April 1975, AJC, Box E-621A.

227 Vincent J. Jensen, S.J., letter to Gerald W. Tait, S.J., 22 October 1973; Gerald W. Tait, S.J., letters to Vincent J. Jensen, S.J., 30 November 1973; 18 March 1974; 9 April 1974; 4 November 1974; 17 December 1974; 7 May 1975, ibid.

was so proud to have tended ever since the college first had opened on campus. Tired out, early in 1976 he asked to be relieved a year before his term of office was concluded.[228]

The disappointments during his time as Rector did not diminish by any means the esteem and affection in which Jensen was held by all on campus. He had become a legend, an icon of what a professor should be, to the students who were the children and grandchildren of those he had long ago helped and inspired. Until he took retirement in 1986 at age seventy, he continued to teach a full load in the department of history; after that, he taught one course per year until he died two years later.

Yet sadly, Jensen died a weary, disappointed man. His long-held dream to build an autonomous university college on the campus of the University of Manitoba, a dream that he and others had nourished during the late 1950s and sustained into the mid 1960s, was never fulfilled. Indeed, the changes in the relations between the university and the college at the end of the 1960s, his own frustrations and sense of failure as Rector in not being able to reverse the changes that had swept and were sweeping across campus, and the inexplicable—for him—decline of a Jesuit presence at St. Paul's helped turn his dream into disappointment.[229]

Still, those around him scarcely considered his time at St. Paul's in that light whatsoever, but rather looked upon him and his influence at St. Paul's with gratitude and affection. For his noteworthy contribution to education in Manitoba, he was invested in the Manitoba Order of the Buffalo Hunt. On three occasions, too, he was awarded honorary doctorates: at St. John's College, University of Manitoba, in Sacred Theology; at the University of Winnipeg in Laws; and at Regis College, University of Toronto, in Divinity.[230]

Harold ("Skip") E. Kane, S.J., was among the names that kept appearing as a possible appointee at St. Paul's. He had been studying history at the University of London for several years during the early

---

228 DJB, vol. 2, 144.

229 Ibid., 144.

230 Ibid.; Friesen and Lebrun, 201; 392–303; Laping, 54–58.

to mid 1970s, was a fine scholar, and seemed to have all the other qualities for becoming a professor of history in the college. In the end, he never was appointed a full-time history professor, but instead succeeded Jensen during the summer of 1976 as Rector. In short order, he recognized the predicament for the college: the government of Manitoba's cutbacks to education necessitated the university's cutting its budget for hiring; the correlating of Jesuits and their academic qualifications to the needs of departments was not at all certain.[231]

During the summer of 1974, Walsh had established a three-member *Consilium Academicum* consisting of R. Eric O'Connor, S.J., Gerald W. Tait, S.J., and Jacques Monet, s.j. It was to assist and advise the Provincial Superior in matters of Jesuit academic formation. Among the council's several tasks were the appointments of Jesuits to academic positions, or at least to assist in such appointments wherever or whenever possible.

During the early autumn of 1977, the *Consilium Academicum*— since 1976, Bela I. Somfai, s.j., had replaced Tait—pressed Kane to move quickly on looking for Jesuits as possible academic appointees at St. Paul's. Still, not much happened. On behalf of the council, Monet wrote Kane on 2 November 1977, urging him not to throw away "a magnificent opportunity" to rebuild Catholic academic presence in Manitoba "which had been allowed to deteriorate over the past decades." There were, he insisted, positions available in the university. Twelve days later, he again wrote to Kane that he must get in touch with Jesuits to fill "the positions open at the university".[232]

On 2 January 1978, after getting no response from Winnipeg, Walsh took a different approach. He expressed to the council his desire that the three members concern themselves for the "next six months with St. Paul's and strengthening the presence of the Jesuits there." Walsh also noted that "two full-scale attempts" had been made to "restaff [sic] St. Paul's during recent years", but with no success. Kane, he further commented, had been out of the Upper Canada

---

231 Harold E. Kane, S.J., letter to Pedro Arrupe, 22 April 1977, AJC, Box E-622.

232 Jacques Monet, s.j., letters to Harold E. Kane, S.J., 2 November 1977; 14 November 1977; Bela I. Somfai, s.j., letter to Jacques Monet, s.j., 21 November 1977; Jacques Monet, s.j., letter to Bela I. Somfai, s.j., 29 November 1977, ibid.

Province "for years", and had not "attended any academic meeting, even one held in Winnipeg." Yet Walsh did see fit to praise Kane and Arthur Mauro, a prominent layman on the college's board, because they were "the first for decades who were willing and anxious to find out what might be done regarding appointments." To further his arguments, Walsh drew up a list of eleven Jesuits who had either finished doctorates or were about to, who might become professors, chaplains, Rectors, deans. Nonetheless, not one Jesuit was ever appointed to St. Paul's from that list.[233]

Following Walsh's request for the *Consilium Academicum* to concern itself especially with St. Paul's, it shortly suggested to Kane that it would travel to Winnipeg for a meeting with him, and that it would "bend every effort to help". On Friday, 3 March 1978, the three members of the *Consilium Academicum* visited Kane. "Uninhibited exchanges" followed about the state of academics in the Province of Upper Canada and about the poor image St. Paul's College had in the Province. It did not take long for the three to recognize how unrealistic Kane was concerning the state of Jesuit manpower and the Jesuits' procedures in assigning Jesuits to colleges. The meeting was none too successful.[234]

Walsh was aware that, under Kane's direction, the college had been drawing up a five-year plan. That was partly in response to a firm rebuke from the university that the colleges had not lived up to the 1970 agreement by their failing to put together concrete programmes or creating a clearly perceptible ethos and recognizable identities for each of the colleges. Thus, during early May 1978, the college assembly and the board of management, under the direction of the Rector, produced a plan that, it was hoped, would serve the college over the next decades with new Jesuits, and that by 1983, five to seven Jesuits would be hired as professors in religious studies, the humanities, and the social sciences, and in the library and chaplaincy. It also was hoped

---

233   Terence G. Walsh, S.J., letters to the *Consilium Academicum*, 2 January 1978; 20 January 1978; "Memorandum Regarding St. Paul's College Project", 3 January 1978, ibid.

234   Jacques Monet, s.j., letter to Harold E. Kane, S.J., 16 January 1978; Jacques Monet, s.j., letter to Terence G. Walsh, S.J., 17 January 1978; Terence G. Walsh, S.J., letters to Jacques Monet, s.j., 20 January 1978; 21 March 1978, ibid.

that within the colleges, the spirit of the agreement of 1970 would be observed. Meanwhile, Kane requested from the university that he be granted the same authority in appointing faculty members at St. Paul's as the deans of the university had.[235]

As on so many other occasions, nothing followed. The plan for five to seven Jesuits being hired was naive, if not completely unrealistic. In any case, months passed without Kane making any contact with young Jesuits concerning upcoming academic positions at the university. By November, the new Provincial Superior, William F. Ryan, S.J., following the advice of his Consultors, urged Kane to discuss with Braceland how to produce an updated report on the college, including its various options and a "decision-making process and time-line to be followed." Braceland would have been just the right person to assist the Rector. Having accepted mandatory retirement that previous summer, he had the time, knew the college and the university well, and was congenial and obliging. If the college does not "take this last chance", Ryan pointed out to the *Consilium Academicum*, then circumstances will "all too soon dictate a lose-all situation." In the meantime, however, the *Consilium Academicum* was advising Ryan that, in its judgment, it was time for the Jesuits to leave St. Paul's "as elegantly as possible."[236]

Both the Provincial Superior and the *Consilium Academicum* were not optimistic that the "last chance" would be taken by St. Paul's. Yet to try something entirely different by assisting in opening up new possibilities for the college, in January 1979 Ryan appointed three prominent Jesuits of the Upper Canada Province to St. Paul's as the "directing group" to establish during the following summer a "Catholic Intellectual Centre", or as it was also called, "St. Paul's Centre for Christian Formation". Its aim was to aid the Rector in strengthening and developing at the college the intellectual and Catholic dimensions of the college's ministry by sponsoring programmes/courses in spirituality, scriptural studies, and theological reflection. The trio were

---

235 Harold E. Kane, S.J., letter to Terence G. Walsh, S.J., with enclosure of the "Five Year Plan", 11 May 1978, ibid.; Friesen and Lebrun, 206–207.

236 William F. Ryan, S.J., letter to Jacques Monet, s.j., 28 November 1978; Jacques Monet, s.j., letter to William F. Ryan, S.J., 22 December 1978, AJC, Box E-622.

Terence G. Walsh, former professor of philosophy and past Provincial Superior, who was the director; John E. LeSarge, former Rector of the Guelph Jesuit Community and Master of Novices there, was the co-director; and Michael F. Kolarcik, who later would take a degree in the Old Testament from the prestigious Jesuit Biblical Institute in Rome, was the third member of the "directing group".[237]

Rarely, if ever, had the Province of Upper Canada witnessed such a dynamic trio appointed at the same time to any of its institutions of higher learning. Ryan was convinced that with cooperation from St. Paul's, the opportunities were there for such a new adventure, and that the three would each bring a special talent to revitalize the college and give it a new purpose and direction on campus. The pro-gramme of courses to be offered was not to carry credit, but was to be held in the college under the auspices of the Rector and the Jesuit Community of St. Paul's College, and directed especially towards the university's personnel.

It did not take long before everything was going wrong. Within a month, on 2 October, Walsh informed the Provincial Superior that he was not optimistic about the centre's future. There was, he pointed out, no role for the three of them, due to three factors: "The resources [in Winnipeg] are greater than I had imagined; the general mental-ity is both more conservative and secular than I had realized; and the role of the Rector in this particular set up requires that he be not merely the support, but also the initiator and leader of any significant program or development."

Already, as Walsh also noted, LeSarge had difficulty keeping busy. Besides, he added, the centre was not really needed due to plenty of other groups in the city; there was no need of duplication by the Jesuits. Within another six weeks, Walsh again was insisting that the centre was a failure, and that the Rector was unable to give necessary leadership for the survival of St. Paul's as a Jesuit institution. The three have not managed, he went on, "any substantial contribution, and will not be missed." If their leaving helps give "a more realistic

---

237   William F. Ryan, S.J., letter to Harold E. Kane, S.J., 7 March 1979; Terence G. Walsh, S.J., letter to William F. Ryan, S.J., 24 April 1979, ibid.; Friesen and Lebrun, 207.

look at the situation at St. Paul's, all the better." Fifteen days later, he added that he believed "the best and perhaps only way of effectively promoting Christian Intellectual Presence is via committed Christian professional academics."[238]

It was indeed the "last chance". By January 1980, the centre was all but dead. Ryan's hope—or was he calling the bluff of St. Paul's?—that something might develop there to give new meaning to a Jesuit presence on campus had faded by early spring. The three assigned there by Ryan left the college to assume other positions in the Upper Canada Province.

Fortunately, during that same spring other initiatives were being taken at St. Paul's. A meeting was called by a group of interested lay friends of John C. Hanley, S.J., who had died nearly ten years previously, to discuss how they might honour his memory in a specific academic way. The initial meeting was held on 7 May, with others following until a decision was made final about what came to be known as the Hanley Memorial Lecture Series. The first annual lecture of the series was delivered in 1980. The series has been and remains among the most distinguished anywhere, with world-renowned speakers invited to deliver the lecture. Over the years, other outstanding speakers have been invited to the college in different capacities. Since 1990, another series, Religion in the Modern World, has helped greatly in placing a focus on St. Paul's as a Catholic college on campus that is open to discussing all the issues in the Church and modern society.[239]

Since the 1960s, there had been a chaplaincy at St. Paul's, sometimes doubling as the Newman Centre on campus, sometimes separated from that. It offered spiritual counselling, Eucharistic and other liturgies, spiritual retreats, and companionship. Usually on a Sunday, it offered a Mass, at times more than one, with one Mass for students and another for the other Catholics on campus. Soon the chapel began to be used by Catholics in the area as a quasi parish. That was not surprising. The liturgies were enthusiastically contemporary, the

---

238 Terence G. Walsh, S.J., letters to William F. Ryan, S.J., 2 October 1978; 29 November 1979; 5 December 1979, AJC, Box E-622.

239 Harold E. Kane, S.J., letter to William F. Ryan, S.J., 3 January 1980, ibid.; Friesen and Lebrun, 26; 34–35; 46; 223–224; DJB, vol. 1, 130–131.

singing was of the best, and many found the atmosphere a pleasant relief from studies or from the long Winnipeg winters.[240]

There was a move to create a parish in the chapel during the mid 1970s, with the chaplains involved as parish directors. That was not met with a lot of enthusiasm by the Provincial Superior, the Rectors, and the archbishops of Winnipeg. In particular, Kane was firmly opposed to the establishing of a parish at St. Paul's. A few months after he became Rector, he caused more than a little friction with the chaplains by firing a Sister on the team of chaplain coordinators, by refusing to sign tax receipts, and by rejecting a fiscal subsidy to the chaplains' ministry. His successor, Joseph V. Driscoll, S.J., who had been a chaplain there in the 1960s, was more understanding and sympathetic to chaplains and their work, although he was not too favourable at first towards the chapel becoming a fully established parish. In the years following the 1980s, and to the present, the chaplaincy continues to fulfil its primary purpose: to serve daily the Catholic student body on campus, faculty members, and other Catholics during term time.[241]

When Kane stepped down from office in 1981, a year short of his six-year term, the college had reached a critical stage for the Jesuits of English-speaking Canada: how best to withdraw from the college and leave it in the hands of others. There was by then no doubt in the minds of the Jesuits elsewhere than at St. Paul's that withdraw they must, and that an "elegant" solution had to be found for that process within a reasonably short space of time. It was not that Kane had left the place in a chaotic state; he had not. St. Paul's was slowly adapting to the new reality of its relationship with the university; many of its faculty members were highly qualified as professors, writers, and administrators; and students, as always, were finding the college a pleasant, welcoming place to be. Rather, it was more that Kane seemed

---

240   Deryk H. Hanshall, S.J., letter to Edward F. Sheridan, S.J., 8 February 1872; Edward F. Sheridan, S.J., letter to Gerald H. Gallagher, S.J., 23 February 1972; John D. Lynch, S.J., letter to Edward F. Sheridan, S.J., 1 March 1972; Edward F. Sheridan, S.J., letter to John D. Lynch, S.J., 15 April 1972; Terence G. Walsh, S.J., letter to Vincent J. Jensen, S.J., 24 April 1972; Terence G. Walsh, S.J., letter to Robert Gaudet, S.J., 16 August 1972, AJC, Box E-621A; DJB, vol. 1, 122–123; vol. 2, 301–306; 122–125.

241   Vincent J. Jensen, S.J., letter to Terence G. Walsh, S.J., 2 June 1975; Terence G. Walsh, S.J., letter to Vincent J. Jensen, S.J., 5 June 1975; Terence J. Fay, S.J., letter to Terence G. Walsh, S.J., 4 January 1977; Terence G. Walsh, S.J., letter to Terence J. Fay, S.J., 11 January 1977, AJC, Box E-622.

never to have grasped what Jesuit presence really had to mean there, and that if the college were to remain in Jesuit hands, as Rector he had to lead it into new ways of thinking, planning, and executing those plans, which would move the college away from the old notion of Jesuit presence, represented in the Jesuit professors and administrators there, to a new one, with Jesuits actively engaged in several different kinds of intellectual ministries centred in the college. The model had to be changed, but Kane was not the one to do that.

As early as 1973, Walsh had appointed three Jesuits to sit on the board of management: William M. Addley, Jacques Monet, and Jean-Marc Laporte. They were to assist the board in maintaining a Catholic, Jesuit presence at the college but also, as time went on, to bring that board towards becoming a board of directors with full governing authority within the college. They helped accomplish that by 1983. Afterwards, each of them remained on the new board for varying lengths of time.

During the winter before Kane was to leave office, the question for the Jesuits was this: who would or could or would even want to succeed him? Ryan, his Consultors, the *Consilium Academicum*, and the three Jesuits on the board of management were all agreed that someone should be found who could take the college forward during a brief period that would allow it a seamless transition to a non-Jesuit board of governors and a lay Rector. That individual was to be Joseph V. Driscoll, S.J.

At first, he seemed a most unlikely candidate for Rector of a university college. He did not have a graduate degree, had never shown much interest in studies or university life, and had spent most of his life in varying kinds of pastoral or high school ministries. He had been parish priest at the Jesuit parish, St. John Brebeuf, in Winnipeg, and Rector during the 1960s at St. Paul's High School in Winnipeg. In 1980, he was appointed Superior of the small Jesuit Community at the college. A year later, he agreed with the Provincial Superior to become Rector of the college for a three-year term. Already in his mid sixties, he still seemed indefatigable.[242]

---

242 DJB, vol. 2, 78–83.

Known for his kindness and good nature, Driscoll was a man filled with common sense. During his time as Rector, and recognizing the need to develop new approaches to Jesuit Community life, he opened up the Jesuits' residence by inviting numerous visitors from the university and elsewhere in the city for dinner, for social events, or for lunch. In consequence, his hospitality became renowned. He seemed to blossom, became energized anew, and was notable as a thoroughly gracious host to his fellow Jesuits and visitors alike. In a way, too, his opening of the residence to visitors set the stage for an eventual and entirely different use for it. In 1990, the Jesuits departed the building. It was leased to the university for office space, and renamed the Sinnott Building in honour of the college's founder.

In the college, Driscoll's task was considerably more difficult; to many he scarcely seemed fitted for such a post. Yet after his appointment and to the amazement of his naysayers—many of whom were appalled that he had been named Rector in the first place—he set to work with energy and determination to carry through his mandate. In general, he surprised almost everyone. He was careful not to go it alone, something he had tended to do during his earlier years as an administrator and a Superior; he frequently sought advice, especially from his Jesuit colleagues throughout the academic community in Canada. Clearly, at times he felt somewhat isolated and insecure in his post, something he found particularly trying given his companionable nature and his previous accomplishments. Yet he was determined to do his best in the college as Rector, to give the kind of leadership necessary so that by the time he stepped down in 1984, the college would have gained a renewed voice within the university's community, and its finances would be straightened out and placed on a more solid footing within the university itself, no mean feat, given the complexities of such a large university campus. He did all that, as well as overseeing the establishment of the eighteen-member board of directors in 1983, and a year later, the appointment of the first non-Jesuit Rector, Dr. David J. Lawless (1984–1990).[243]

---

243   Ibid., 82; Friesen and Lebrun, 209.

Although Driscoll would stay on until 1988 in the Jesuit Community as Superior and in the college as pastor of the newly organized parish centred in the college chapel, he was the last of the Jesuit Rectors of St. Paul's College. At his stepping down, the college, still firmly Catholic, would receive new direction and purpose from lay leaders. Yet an era had ended. Since 1933, the Jesuits had supplied faculty and administrators for St. Paul's College. That was to be no more, except on the board of directors where, over the following decades, some Jesuits would serve during a director's term of office.

In other ways, too, the presence of the Jesuits did not die out entirely on campus. In 1988, the Jesuit Centre for Faith Development and Values was established at St. Paul's with David G. Creamer, S.J., as its director; in 1998, the Jesuit Centre for Catholic Studies was also founded; and in 2000, construction began on the Arthur V. Mauro Centre for Peace and Justice. As well, individual Jesuits became professors at the University of Manitoba. Creamer has taught in the faculty of education and in the department of religious studies since 1990, and has been a member of the Jesuit Centre for Catholic Studies and an adjunct professor of the Arthur V. Mauro Centre for Peace and Justice. John F. Perry likewise was engaged as a professor at the University of Manitoba in religious studies, as a member of the Jesuit Centre for Catholic Studies, and as an adjunct professor of the Arthur V. Mauro Centre for Peace and Justice. Jeffrey S. Burwell, too, teaches in Catholic Studies and education at the University of Manitoba, as well as directing the Jesuit Centre for Catholic Studies at St. Paul's.

Many since the 1980s have understandably expressed regret that St. Paul's College is no longer under Jesuit direction. Yet, if there has been an essential norm for the Society of Jesus since its founding in 1540 that Jesuits are to be available to go anywhere in the world to work for "the greater glory of God", then, too, there has been a corollary norm that likewise has been fundamental to Jesuits' ministries: to depart from a ministry if it is deemed that others can do that ministry. Certainly, by their leaving St. Paul's College, the English-speaking Canadian Jesuits have reflected that latter norm completely.

VANCOUVER: A NEW MODEL
FOR CANADIAN JESUITS

When Timothy Casey (1912–1931) was appointed archbishop of Vancouver in 1912, the Catholic population of the city and surrounding area was a minority of the general population. Almost all the immigrants who had settled in Vancouver during the first two decades of the twentieth century were from Great Britain, and therefore were predominantly Protestant. Those Catholics who lived in the archdiocese were widely dispersed throughout the more isolated areas. Because of the small number of secular clergymen, Archbishop Casey sought out Religious priests, Brothers, and Sisters to staff many of the archdiocesan parishes and schools. His hope was also to found a college in order that Catholics would not have to attend the University of British Columbia, which at the time was considered secular and, consequently, a danger to their faith.

During November 1922, the archbishop first approached John D. Knox, S.J., chaplain to the Sisters of the Sacred Heart in Vancouver, requesting that he convey a message to the Jesuit Provincial Superior, John M. Filion: "Will you please inform your Father Provincial that I invite you to establish a parish, and when possible a Classical College in this archdiocese." Both should be established in the Point Grey area of the city.[244]

Initially, Filion was reluctant to satisfy either request, although two years later, he agreed to open a parish in the Point Grey area. In response to his enquiry on the matter later in 1923, the Jesuit Superior General, Wlodimir Ledóchowski, pointed out to Filion that they could accept to open a parish, but the establishing of a Jesuit classical college in Vancouver was out of the question due to a lack of manpower and funds. More importantly, though, since Archbishop Casey had promised the Irish Christian Brothers first choice in opening a college, they had a prior claim, even if they had no immediate plans for founding one. They had set up a school for boys in 1922, but since then had made no effort to open a college. Yet they did not want to

---

244   Archbishop Timothy Casey, letter to John D. Knox, S.J., n.d. November 1922, AJC, Box D-519. Cf. DJB, vol. 1, 170–171, for a brief biography of Knox.

give up their option for establishing one. The Jesuits, therefore, according to the Superior General, were not to involve themselves in that matter. In the end, it no longer mattered: under pressure from the Christian Brothers, the archdiocese revoked the invitation to the Jesuits to open a college.[245]

In 1932, after Archbishop William M. Duke (1931–1964) had succeeded Archbishop Casey, he asked the Jesuits to reconsider the offer to open a classical college. Again they demurred. Disappointed, Archbishop Duke tried again in 1934. He pressed the Provincial Superior, William H. Hingston, to establish a college. Yet he remained firmly opposed. The archbishop was not pleased at being rejected for a second time. He decided to search for another Religious Congregation to open a college, but he could find none that were interested. Still he remained resolute that during his episcopacy he would found a Catholic college in Vancouver. Over twenty years later, he did establish one: St. Mark's College on the campus of the University of British Columbia. In 1932, the Basilian Fathers had organized a Newman Club at the university that had become an active Catholic centre on campus. During the late 1930s, the archbishop invited them to set up a college. Although they accepted his invitation, it would take until 1956 before they were able to found St. Mark's, an affiliated residential theological college at the university that opened in 1958. In the meantime, the Jesuits remained in their parish in Vancouver.[246]

Over several years, especially from the mid 1970s onwards, several English-speaking Jesuits regretted that they had no academic presence in Vancouver. It was a fast-growing multi-cultural, multi-racial city, the third largest in the country, and with its deep-sea port—the busiest on the Continent's west coast—it had become an important gateway to the Pacific. With its two large universities, Vancouver also had become a significant intellectual centre.

The first Canadian Jesuit to take up full-time graduate studies in Vancouver was John W. McCarthy, S.J., in 1996, when he began graduate studies in forest-ecology at the University of British Columbia.

---

245 John M. Filion, s.j., letter to Wlodimir Ledóchowski, s.j., 13 December 1923; Wlodimir Ledóchowski, s.j., letter to John M. Filion, s.j., 31 December 1923, AJC, Box D-519.

246 The Jesuits eventually withdrew from their parish in 1984.

Although he maintained his connections at the university and in Vancouver after graduating in 2004, he did not return for five years. The newly appointed archbishop of Vancouver, J. Michael Miller, C.S.B. (2009–), was interested in Jesuits being at the university's campus. In response, the then Provincial Superior, James F. Webb (2008–2012), who had recognized the importance of having Jesuit academics in the city, in 2009 appointed McCarthy as chaplain at St. Mark's College, where he continued his research and writing in ecology. As well, that year Gregory M. Kennedy, S.J., was assigned for a two-year period as part-time coordinator of service-learning at Corpus Christi College, a newly founded Catholic liberal arts junior college on the university's campus. A year later, Kennedy also became a lecturer in philosophy for one year before leaving for further studies, while McCarthy became a sessional lecturer before receiving an assignment elsewhere in May 2012. To continue the Jesuit presence in Vancouver, by the late summer of 2013, Elton L. Fernandes, Robert J. Allore, John D. O'Brien, Adam Hincks, and Michael J. Stogre had been assigned to teach, research, and involve themselves with the chaplaincy on campus; with the newly established parish, St. Mark's, which includes the university's campus; and other ministries, such as the Spiritual Exercises.

Such a new and dynamic presence of younger Jesuits connected to a large western university campus is highly significant. Not only is Vancouver an important and influential city because of its geographical location on the edge of the Pacific, but the University of British Columbia is among the largest and most highly rated universities in the country. In the long run, therefore, and as the Jesuits' presence in Vancouver illustrates, it may well be that the Canadian Jesuits' future in higher education will be to include, alongside the Jesuit educational model of having their own academic institutions, a new model of a cluster of Jesuits working, yet not in their own institution, in different capacities as professors, chaplains, writers, and academic and spiritual counsellors on or nearby a secular university campus.

Considering this new model for their educational ministry in Canada in no way implies that the older model of having their own colleges and universities is unimportant for the Canadian Jesuits.

Indeed, the older model of the Jesuit educational institution, such as Campion College, will endure. It remains an essential means of fulfilling the ministry of higher education for the Canadian Jesuits of the future.

At the same time, history shows that over the centuries, but notably in Canada since 1842, the Jesuits' *Ratio Studiorum* has proven to be a flexible document, and that the Jesuits have adapted it and themselves continuously for the sole purpose of carrying out to the fullest the mission given them. A strong argument, therefore, can be made, as Vancouver shows, that without the burden of owning or administering a university or a federated college, Jesuits can be noticeably adaptable in expending their energies and resources on what they do best: teach, research, publish, preach, counsel, and be present to students and professors. However the future evolves, the presence of Jesuits at a university in Vancouver certainly points to a new way forward in their ministry of higher education in Canada.

POSTSCRIPT

This book has related the history of those English-speaking and, in some instances, bilingual institutions of higher education in which the Canadian English-speaking Jesuits were involved since 1842: first in their Mission; then, after 1907, in the Province of Canada; after 1924 in the Vice Province of Upper Canada; and, from 1939 to the present, in the Province of Upper Canada (since 2006, titled "Jesuits in English Canada"). Their commitment in those educational institutions could be for a short time, such as in Sandwich, Guelph, Charlottetown, Kingston, and Edmonton, or it could be of longer duration, such as in St. Boniface, Halifax, Montreal, Winnipeg, and Regina. What also becomes apparent on studying those various institutions is how they also served as centres for other Jesuit ministries, such as parishes, schools, and institutions involving social ministries.

However interesting it might have been to relate, this book has not dwelt on individual Jesuits who sometimes worked separately from Jesuit colleges and universities in Canadian or in foreign universities, such as—and to name only a few—Bernard J. F. Lonergan, who taught and published many of his major works at the Gregorian University in Rome; Jacques Monet, who was a professor of history and chair of the history department at the University of Ottawa during the 1970s, and president of the University of Sudbury during the early 1990s; David R. Eley, who in the 1970s was a professor and chair of the department of communication arts at the University of Ottawa, and at Saint Paul University, Ottawa, as well as a professor of communications at the Gregorian University; Roderick A. F. MacKenzie, who lectured for years at the Jesuits' Biblical Institute, Rome, and was Rector there from 1963 to 1969; David M. Stanley, who lectured from 1961 to 1964 in biblical studies at the University of Iowa, and also as a sessional lecturer over several decades at the Gregorian University; Lloyd Baugh, who has been a professor of theology and film studies for over thirty years and dean of the faculty of social sciences at the Gregorian University; and Gerald W. Tait, who taught Christology, ecclesiology, and hermeneutics beginning in 1980 at the University of Sudbury, was in 1984 and 1985 chair of Laurentian University's department of religious studies, and from 1985 to 1987 was professor of theology and chaplain at Lakehead University. Those several individuals who have been thus involved—for the most part internationally—exemplify the wide-ranging contribution English-speaking Jesuits have made elsewhere for decades. That extensive individual involvement deserves a separate study.

This book has also not referred to the joint Canadian English-speaking Jesuit publishing project *Tradition and Innovation: Essays by Jesuits from a Canadian Perspective* (Regina: Campion College Press, 1981), or, except for references in this volume, to the other joint publication in two volumes: *Dictionary of Jesuit Biography: Ministry in English Canada, 1842–1987* (Toronto: Canadian Institute of Jesuit Studies, 1991) and *Dictionary of Jesuit Biography: Ministry in English Canada, 1988–2006* (Toronto: Canadian Institute of Jesuit Studies, 2007). Those three publications, which occupied a large number of Canadian Jesuits, reflect their many other individual publications, books and articles alike, that have been so much a part of the Jesuits' intellectual life in this country. Such publications bear out the extent of their academic contribution for over 170 years to higher education in Canada.

Of the ten Canadian institutions of higher education in which English-speaking Jesuits have been involved since the founding of St. Mary's College in 1848, only one, Campion College, remains a Jesuit responsibility today. The other nine have either closed or been handed over to local diocesan or lay boards to administer. There have been many reasons for that, not least because of other priorities, such as the need to staff their institutions elsewhere or to found new centres. Yet even when leaving a college or university, the English-speaking Canadian Jesuits were fulfilling fundamental Jesuit ideals handed down since the time of their founder, Ignatius Loyola, that they leave a ministry if it were judged that others could continue it, and thus allow themselves the readiness to go elsewhere where there was a need, *Ad maiorem Dei gloriam inque hominum salutem.*

INDEX